At the Pillars of Hercules

Clive James's best-known writings are the three volumes of his autobiography: *Unreliable Memoirs*, *Falling Towards England* and *May Week Was in June*; he has also published criticism, novels—including most recently *The Silver Castle*—and poetry.

CLIVE JAMES

At the Pillars of Hercules

PICADOR

First published 1979 by Faber and Faber Ltd

This edition published with a new Introduction 1998 by Picador
an imprint of Macmillan Publishers Ltd
25 Eccleston Place, London SW1W 9NF
and Basingstoke

Associated companies throughout the world

In association with Jonathan Cape Ltd

ISBN 0 330 37214 9

9 8 7 6 5 4 3 2 1

A CIP catalogue record for this book is available from
the British Library.

Printed and bound in Great Britain by
Mackays of Chatham plc, Chatham, Kent

TO IAN HAMILTON

Introduction to the Picador Edition

A good screenplay writer writes fragments as if in the knowledge that eventually it is the fragment that will live. But he can't tell which fragment it will be, so he puts everything he has into them all. In *The Manchurian Candidate* George Axelrod gives Angela Lansbury a moment to ice the nerves, when she tells Laurence Harvey, 'I never knew it would be you.' She means that when she joined the plot they didn't tell her that the post-hypnotically programmed assassin would be her son. They didn't tell her that he would be the sleeper.

I never knew that my early critical bits and pieces would be the sleepers. One hesitates to imply that they are bound for immortality, or even that they have lasted in any integral sense: but there always seems to be a new generation of students—real students, the ones who don't need an exam to keep them reading—who seek out my first collections of criticism in second-hand bookshops and bring them to be autographed at book-signings. They hang around afterwards. I recognize them: they are the way I once was. Just from the way their clothes look slept in you can tell that they write in margins and fill endpapers with notes. Having hustled a second glass of the cheap white wine, they want to quarrel with some phrase that I long ago forgot I ever wrote. They've got it there, underlined, with three exclamation marks to indicate disbelief. They want to argue the point. They all have different points they want to argue, but on one thing they agree: they don't think I wasted my time writing this stuff. They think I wasted my time writing anything else.

It's the most frustrating brand of flattery, but there might be something to it. Some of us are the most ourselves—perhaps the nearest to being ourselves we will ever get—when talking about someone else. Certainly a magnificent detachment was an ideal I could never cultivate in my self-imposed role as the Metropolitan Critic. That was the title I gave my first collection in 1974: in 1995 (acting in response, as we say in my television production office, to several letters that flooded in) I reissued it with footnotes designed to mitigate its follies. This second collection likewise was left behind with my first publisher and went out of print for a length of time that should have ensured its irretrievable burial. But if there was a market for the reissue of the first volume, then the second might have the same chance of resurrection, especially since it contains, on the face of it, fewer excesses crying out for an appended disclaimer. The danger here might be that I was getting duller as I cleaned up my act.

Yet I can't remember putting any conscious limit on my determination to let enthusiasm rip. My aim was still, as it still is, to emulate Montale's desired quality for writing about art: *seriatà scherzevole*—a playful seriousness. It was just that by this stage I had accumulated enough experience of verbal aerobatics to pull out of the stunt before my smoking trajectory intersected with the ground.

In all other respects, the opportunity offered me by the London literary editors—overqualified, confident and mischievous to a man, especially the women—was too good to miss. Anything I felt like throwing into the review, they would print. Over the top was exactly the way they wanted me to go. As long as they understood it themselves, no reference could be too obscure or allusion too fleeting. In those days the reader, if he encountered something on the page that he could not immediately understand, was still trusted to renew his subscription. Kenneth Tynan accused me of having invented Gianfranco Contini but he knew that he was joking, just as he knew that showing off is a part of the theatricality and that theatricality is a part of this kind of writing. All you have to remember is that you're not the whole show. I sometimes think, looking back, that solipsism made my admiration for others seem the more selfless—with the concomitant benefit that I could do a hatchet job without being thought of as having laid claim to a monopoly of objective truth.

Some wishful thinking there, perhaps. A piece like the one on Lord Longford was designed to sting. I thought he was dangerously wrong. (Adding insult to injury, I also thought, during my long campaign of mockery against him, that by pointing out the essential hubris behind his vaunted quest for humility I was helping to save his life: I still believe that if he had secured Myra Hindley's release he would have been lynched along with her.) But the urge to excoriate was always tempered by the likelihood that you might bump into your victim in some salon, if not saloon. The Modish London Literary World (a term from Dr Leavis's demonology that I took delight in misappropriating whenever possible) still had finite boundaries, in which I was as pleased to feel at home as only the interloper can be. Of the writers still alive at the time I wrote these pieces, I knew several well and physically met almost all. Their corporeal presence thrilled me even when I had reservations about what they had become. Robert Lowell I thought the most frightful ass (an estimation he reciprocated with all the strength of the dollar) but it was his wonderful early poetry that

I remembered after I had finished laughing at his absurd professions of help-lessness. Lillian Hellman was plainly as corrupt as the corpses of whichever defenceless animals had provided her fur coat, but Dashiell Hammet had once loved her and no doubt I would have too, putting her unrepentant Stalinism down to playfulness. Gore Vidal was dangerously sardonic but charming beyond belief. And to meet a man like Philip Larkin at the peak of his career, fully aware of his own faults yet guarding his greatness like a sacred mystery, was to experience hero worship in its purest form. There they were, all around me. I loved it all. I thought it would go on like that for ever.

As things turned out, my days in Soho were already numbered. In the Greek Street pub that gave my book its name I eventually, and none too soon, had to face the possibility that I was drinking myself sick. Aided by public demand, I took the decision to quit cold. Subtracting myself from temptation with a headlong retreat to respectability, I left the Modish London Literary World, never really to return. Television became my stock in trade. Instead of the writer I might have been and my friends generously expected me to be, I became a different kind of writer altogether, and there are those who doubt whether I am any longer a writer at all. Married to a scholar whose solid brilliance chasteningly reminds me that to serve litera-ture entails self-denial, I am obliged to consider that self-display can go only so far. But there was a time when I made it go as far as it could, and today, when I write outside television at all, this is still the kind of writing I most like to do: with a heart less light now, yet with the same conviction that in response to the writing of others the self will be revealed most usefully, whether in praise or blame. It would be better, of course, to leave the self out of it altogether, but I never had the option, only the wish—and if wishes were horses, beggars would ride.

—London, 1997

Acknowledgements

For this second collection of my critical essays I am once again indebted to the editors and literary editors of various publications. I should like to thank Arthur Crook of the T.L.S.; John Gross of the T.L.S. and earlier of the *New Statesman*; John Sturrock of the T.L.S.; Claire Tomalin and Martin Amis of the *New Statesman*; Anthony Thwaite of *Encounter*; and Donald Trelford, Terence Kilmartin and Miriam Gross of the *Observer*. For their generosity and patience in editing my prose at long range, particular thanks must go to Norman Podhoretz of *Commentary* and Robert Silvers of the *New York Review of Books*.

In addition, I am grateful to Miriam Gross for commissioning the article on Raymond Chandler for her anthology *The World of Raymond Chandler* and to John Wain for inviting me to return to the inexhaustible subject of Edmund Wilson.

One debt of thanks remains: that to Ian Hamilton of *The New Review*, for his editing, companionship and advice. I only wish that the dedication of this book to him were sufficient acknowledgement.

If my first book of essays, combatively dubbed *The Metropolitan Critic*, had a defiant stance, this second one should proclaim a decent modesty even in its title. And in fact it does. For the educated public the Pillars of Hercules might be the Mediterranean gate beyond which it was fatal to sail, but for the London literati—a less romantic breed—the name must always evoke a certain pub in Greek Street, Soho. It is a place the reverse of glorious, reflecting the original legend only in the sense that many a writer, having once entered its doors, gets no further that day. So any heroic overtones seemingly given off by my title page are in the ear of the reader. The writer remains a hard-bitten realist, he likes to think.

Contents

A*

Part One
POETS MAJOR AND MINOR

1. Farewelling Auden

(i) ON *EPISTLE TO A GODSON*

'You don't need me to tell you what's going on:' writes W. H. Auden in his latest book's first piece, 'the ochlocratic media, joint with under-the-dryer gossip, process and vent without intermission all to-day's ugly secrets. Imageable no longer, a featureless anonymous threat from behind, to-morrow has us gallowed shitless: if what is to happen occurs according to what Thucydides defined as "human", we've had it, are in for a disaster that no four-letter words will tardy.'

This passage is highly interesting prose, detectable only in its lexical intensity as the work of a poet: Hazlitt, right on this point as on so many others, long ago laid down the word about that give-away proneness to local effect. An ochlocracy is mob rule; the O.E.D. last noticed 'joint' being used that way in 1727; to gallow is an obsolete form of to gally, which is itself a way of saying to frighten that hasn't been heard for a long time anywhere except in a whaling station; 'tardy' as a verb staggered on a few years past its moment of glory in A *Winter's Tale* only to disappear in 1623. But let's start again.

In the title poem of *Epistle to a Godson*, W. H. Auden writes:

> . . . You don't need me to tell you what's
> going on: the ochlocratic media,
> joint with under-the-dryer gossip,
> process and vent without intermission
> all to-day's ugly secrets. Imageable
> no longer, a featureless anonymous
> threat from behind, to-morrow has us
> gallowed shitless: if what is to happen
> occurs according to what Thucydides
> defined as 'human', we've had it, are in for
> a disaster that no four-letter
> words will tardy.

This passage is highly interesting poetry, but only within the confines of Auden's strictly prosaic later manner. Paying lip service to some dimly apprehensible classical metre, sentences wriggle intricately and at length down the syllabic grid.

Blessed be all metrical rules that forbid automatic responses,
    force us to have second thoughts, free from the fetters of Self.

The greatest modern verse technician, Auden long ago ran out of metrical rules needing more than a moment's effort to conform to. Technically, his later manner—which involves setting up a felt rhythmic progress inside an arbitrary syllabic convention—is really a way of restoring to the medium some of the resistance his virtuosity earlier wiped out. This technical mortification is closely allied with the ethical stand forbidding any irrationalities, all happy accidents. No automatic responses, no first thoughts. Helping to explain the omission of certain poems from his *Collected Shorter Poems 1927–1957*, Auden wrote in 1966:

A dishonest poem is one which expresses, no matter how well, feelings or beliefs which its author never felt or entertained. For example, I once expressed a desire for 'New styles of architecture'; but I have never liked modern architecture. I prefer old styles, and one must be honest even about one's prejudices. Again, and much more shamefully, I once wrote:

> History to the defeated
> may say alas but cannot help nor pardon.

To say this is to equate goodness with success. It would have been bad enough if I had ever held this wicked doctrine, but that I should have stated it simply because it sounded to me rhetorically effective is quite inexcusable.

Glumly reconciling themselves to the loss of *September, 1939*, in its entirety and favourite fragments from other poems engraved in the consciousness of a generation, critics respectfully conceded Auden's right to take back what he had so freely given. It was interesting, though, that no strong movement arose to challenge Auden's assumption that these youthful poetic crimes were committed by the same self being dishonest, rather than a different self being honest. Auden was denying the pluralism of his own personality. It was his privilege to do so if he wanted to, but it was remarkable how tamely this crankily simplistic reinterpretation of his own creative selfhood was accepted.

More remarkable still, however, was the virtual silence which greeted the spectacle of a great modern talent disallowing the automatic response, proclaiming the virtues of knowing exactly what you mean against the vices of letting the poem find out what it wants to mean. Auden had apparently worked his way through to the last sentence of the *Tractatus Logico-Philosophicus*. 'Wovon man nicht sprechen kann', Wittgenstein had written, 'darüber muss man schweigen.' What we cannot speak about we must pass over in silence. It was piquant to find the poet who above all others seemed to command the secret of modern magic occupying this position so very long after the philosopher who thought of it had moved out. Here was a man attacking the validity of his own serendipity, discrediting his own trick of setting up a bewitching resonance. Long before, combining with Louis MacNeice in preparing that seductive lash-up of a book *Letters from Iceland*, Auden had written:

> And the traveller hopes: 'Let me be far from any
> Physician'; And the poets have names for the sea;

But on the way to press this was accidentally transformed into

> And the traveller hopes: 'Let me be far from any
> Physician'; And the ports have names for the sea;

Noting straight away that 'ports' suggested more than 'poets', Auden let the slip stand. The names that ports have for the sea are likely to be functional as well as mythical, mistrustful as well as admiring, many-rooted rather than casually appropriate—in a word, serious. Or so we guess. Or so the unexpected ring of the word, its unpredictability in that context, leads us to conjecture—gives us *room* to conjecture. And this thinking-space, the parkland of imagination that existed in Auden's earlier manner, was what marked it out—and what he annihilated in forming his later manner. There have been artists who possessed some of Auden's magic and who went on to lose it, but it is hard to think of anyone who deliberately suppressed it. All conscious artists feel the urge to refine what is unique in their work, but few interpret this call to refine as a command to eliminate. Unless we are dealing with a self-destructive enthusiast—and Auden on the face of it can scarcely be categorized as one of those—then we are up against that most disciplined of all artistic adventurers, the man who gets sick of his own winning streak.

Pick up a Photostat of the 1928 *Poems* and read it through (it takes about twenty minutes): was there ever a more capacious young talent? It goes beyond precocity.

> We saw in Spring
> The frozen buzzard
> Flipped down the weir and carried out to sea.
> Before the trees threw shadows down in challenge
> To snoring midges.
> Before the autumn came
> To focus stars more sharply in the sky
> In Spring we saw
> The bulb pillow
> Raising the skull,
> Thrusting a crocus through clenched teeth.

Hindsight lends us prescience, but it is permissible to claim that merely on the basis of this passage's first three lines we would have pronounced the writer capable of virtually anything. The way the turn from the second line into the third kinetically matches the whole stated action is perfect and obviously instinctive—what other men occasionally achieve was all there as a gift.

> The sprinkler on the lawn
> Weaves a cool vertigo, and stumps are drawn; . . .

Elated by the effortless lyricism of a coup like this, we need to remember not just Auden's age, but the time. Yeats had not yet finished forming the compact musicality of his last phase, and the authoritative clarities of the first of Eliot's Quartets were still years away. Auden got this sonic drive absolutely from out of the blue. The plainest statement he could make seemed to come out as poetry:

> Nor was that final, for about that time
> Gannets blown over northward, going home . . .

It was a Shakespearian gift, not just in magnitude but in its unsettling—and unsettling especially to its possessor—characteristic of making anything said sound truer than true. In all of English poetry it is difficult to think of any other poet who turned out permanent work so early—and whose work seemed so tense with the obligation to be permanent. In his distinguished essay on Auden, John Bayley penetratingly pointed out that it was not in Auden's creative stance ever to admit to being young. What has not yet sufficiently been noticed is that it was not in the nature of Auden's talent to win sympathy by fumbling towards an effect—to claim the privileges of the not yet weathered, or traffic in the pathos of an art in search of its object. Instant accomplishment denied him a creative adolescence.

As always in Auden, ethics and techniques were bound up together. Barely out of his teens, he was already trying to discipline, rather than exploit, the artistic equivalent of a Midas touch. It is for this reason that the *Scrutiny* group's later limiting judgments and dismissals of Auden were wrong-headed as well as insensitive: they were branding as permanently undergraduate the one major modern gift which had never been content with its own cleverness for a moment. They missed the drama of Auden's career in the 1930s and 1940s, never realizing that the early obscurity and the later bookishness were both ways of distancing, rather than striving after, effect. The moral struggle in Auden was fought out between what was possible to his gift and what he thought allowable to it: the moralists, looking for struggles of a different kind, saw in his work nothing but its declarative self-assurance. The more he worked for ironic poise, the more they detected incorrigible playfulness. Subsequent critical systems, had they been applied, would not have fared much better. Suppose, for example, that our standards of the desirable in poetry are based on the accurate registration of worldly things. We would think, in that case, that a man who had come from the frozen buzzards of 1928 to the etymological fossicking of 1972 had moved from the apex of an art to the base. But suppose the ability to send frozen birds flipping over the mind's weir came too easily to be gone on with? What then?

> Doom is dark and deeper than any sea-dingle.
> Upon what man it fall
> In spring, day-wishing flowers appearing,
> Avalanche sliding, white snow from rock-face,
> That he should leave his house,
> No cloud-soft hand can hold him, restraint by women;
> But ever that man goes
> Through place-keepers, through forest trees,

> A stranger to strangers over undried sea,
> Houses for fishes, suffocating water,
> Or lonely on fell as chat,
> By pot-holed becks
> A bird stone-haunting, an unquiet bird.

Quoted from the first public edition of *Poems*, this stanza was the kind of thing which made Auden the hero of the young intelligentsia. Noteworthy, though, is the way in which the enchanting declarative evocation discussed above is painstakingly avoided. The stanza's rhythmic progress is as dazzlingly erratic as a skyrocket toppled from its bottle. The switchback syntax, the Hardyesque hyphenated compounds—they pack things tight, and the reader is never once allowed to draw an inattentive breath. One of the many triumphs of Auden's first public volume was that this difficult verse came to be regarded as equally characteristic with the simpler felicities that were everywhere apparent.

> Beams from your car may cross a bedroom wall.
> They wake no sleeper; you may hear the wind
> Arriving driven from the ignorant sea
> To hurt itself on pane, on bark of elm
> Where sap unbaffled rises, being spring; . . .

Merely to mention the headlight beams crossing the wall was enough to create them for the reader's dazzled eye. But Auden's maturity had already arrived: he was well aware that such moments were not to be thought of as the high points of poetry—rather as the rest points. Take, for example, these lines from 'Prologue', the opening poem of his 1936 collection *Look, Stranger!*

> And make us as Newton was, who in his garden watching
> The apple falling towards England, became aware
> Between himself and her of an eternal tie.

The apple falling towards England is superb, but poetry which had such effects as a *raison d'être* would be a menace. This very instance has in fact come under critical attack—an accusation of decadence has been levelled. But it should be obvious that Auden had no intention of allowing such facility to become fatal. Set against it were the inhibitors; syntactical, grammatical, lexical. And with them they brought ambiguity, resonance, areas of doubt and discovery—all the things his later poetry was to lose. The suggestiveness of Auden's poetry lay in the tension between his primal lyricism and the means employed to discipline it. The suggestiveness couldn't survive if either term went missing. And eventually it was the lyricism that went.

Looking through the individual collections of Auden's poems, each in succession strikes us as transitional. On each occasion there seems to be a further move towards paraphrasable clarity. Even at the height of his bookish phase (in, say, *New Year Letter*) Auden is still being more narrowly clear than he was before. Gradually, as we read on to the end, we see what kind of progress this has been. It has been a movement away from excitement and towards satisfaction.

Epistle to a Godson is like *About the House* and *City Without Walls* in being utterly without the excitement we recognize as Audenesque. And yet it, like them, gives a peculiar satisfaction : the patriarch grunts, having seen much and come a long way. The book is flat champagne, but it's still champagne. Part of Auden's genius was to know the necessity of chastening his talent, ensuring that his poetry would be something more enduring than mere magic. The resource and energy he devoted to containing and condensing his natural lyricism provide one of the great dramas in modern literary history. Pick up *Look Stranger!* or *Another Time*—they read like thrillers. Every poem instantly establishes its formal separateness from all the others. Through Auden's work we trace not just themes but different ways of getting something unforgettably said : the poem's workings are in the forefront of attention. Finally the contrast between the early and the late manners is itself part of the drama. To understand Auden fully, we need to understand how a man with the capacity to say anything should want to escape from the oppression of meaning too much. Late Auden is the completion of a technical evolution in which technique has always been thought of as an instrument of self-denial. What Auden means by the fetters of Self is the tyranny of an ungoverned talent, and his late poetry is a completed testament to the self-control which he saw the necessity for from the very start—the most commendable precocity of all.

(*T.L.S.*, 12 January 1973)

(ii) ON FOREWORDS AND AFTERWORDS

In the normal way of things a reviewer with no pressing deadline could spend a score of widely scattered hours reading *Forewords and Afterwords*, stimulated always by the vast expanse of what he doesn't know that Auden does. The range of interest, and none of it mechanical! All of it professional in the best sense, amateur in the best sense, free of bluff, full of life. As it turns out, though, this book becomes the last one to have been published in the poet's lifetime.

A collection of all the shorter critical pieces and introductions he wished to preserve—the longer prose is in *The Enchafèd Flood, Secondary Worlds* and his central critical work, *The Dyer's Hand*— *Forewords and Afterwords* could at first sight seem a fair distance from the poetry and scarcely a representative last text. Posthumous verse collections will surely follow at a brisk rate. And yet, as a volume conveying Auden's European magnitude as an artist, this collection of his ancillary prose could scarcely be bettered. In its casual way (casual in the happenstance of its occasions and compilation: there is, of course, nothing casual whatever about its thought and craft) it is a testament not just to Auden's culture but to culture—the European artistic civilization which, we can now see, Auden was as effective as Eliot in comprehending and maintaining. And he was more at ease in it than Eliot. In every sense he was at home.

Literary journalism, then; but an ample demonstration that literary journalism at its height—and even when dictated in its emphases by the preoccupations of a working artist—is the criticism that transmits value. And unlike many synoptic critics who are in the omniscience business full time, Auden does not feel compelled to reinforce his sense of value by pretending that everything worth knowing about the heritage of every tongue finds its confluence in him. Not out of humility, just out of practical necessity, he admits ignorance and follows where it leads. After explaining, for example, that the French alexandrine, even when Racine is writing it, always sounds to him like the anapaestic canter of 'The Assyrian came down like a wolf on the fold' he goes on:

> I have known Valéry's poem *Ebauche d'un serpent* for over twenty-five years, reread it often with increasing admiration and, as I thought, comprehension, only to discover the other day, on

reading a letter by the poet to Alain, that I had missed the whole point, namely, that the tone of the poem is burlesque, that the assonances and alliterations are deliberately exaggerated, and that the serpent is intended to sound like Beckmesser in *Die Meistersinger*.

In such a passage several of Auden's special qualities as a writer of critical prose are simultaneously busy. There is his lightness of touch, as if all these things were workaday affairs and not at all frightening. There is the unintended hint at the vastness of his reading, which extends even to the minor correspondence of the great artists and especially to their correspondence with each other: in Auden's prose all the artists of the past are alive and talking among themselves in a humane (mostly) and engagingly human (always) unanimity of interest—an interest which Auden ensures, by assuming so, that you share. On top of these things there is the insistence that the facts of art are concrete and practical, and that educating yourself in them is a matter of *finding out* about them, and that years might go by before the truth reveals itself. By returning to this point over and over—by always insisting that of finding things out there is no end—Auden creates, unbeatably, the feeling that education is lifelong, addictive, playful. In him there is no element of the self-immolating drudge. He would never have been capable of Eliot's sermon on the necessity for the student to embrace boredom.

For Auden mortification has to do with the disciplines of poetic technique: the acquisition of culture is as natural as breathing, and within the limitations of your propensities you do it to relax. Look at the galleries of knowledge, the number of literatures, the languages penetrated to the rhythm of their roots, that are all present and vividly functioning in Auden's prose. And yet it is only on second thought that the whole thing impresses us, just as we have to live on into adulthood before we realize—if we ever do—that the fairgrounds of childhood are the evolution of the centuries, the designs of studious men. The paintwork, the music and the coloured lights were all thought out, and are more than just a game.

Valéry is continually invoked. One had already realized, reading these pieces as they came out in the magazines and anthologies, that the parallelism of Auden's and Valéry's critical careers was becoming more and more explicit. As well as anthologizing aphorisms (*The Faber Book of Aphorisms*, edited with Louis Kronenberger, and the recent *A Certain World*, concerned with slightly longer but still brief pronouncements, are the key works here), Auden has for a long time been manufacturing gnomic utterances and quiddities of his own. The similarity to Valéry's practice is obvious, and even in the longer pieces Valéry's example is likely to be prominent: there is many a long essay by Auden whose compressions can be clarified by glancing into a short book by Valéry. In both men the talk is of art as the one continuous world. The same is true of Montale. Only in Brecht, the fourth master, does art acknowledge the primacy of politics. Auden's long, curving progress—from his mental entanglement with the German extremist political spectrum of the early 1930s to his gradual adoption of the hallowed, art-idealist role as otherwise exemplified by Valéry and Montale—is a classic example of how the pursuit of mastery leads away from battle. Despite his Austrian domicile and the vital presence of the German language (and German opera) at the centre of his life, Auden's ripest years were devoted to the complete acceptance of his part in the Latin tradition, the Icelandic sagas notwithstanding.

Forewords and Afterwords is dedicated to Hannah Arendt, and appropriately it shares not just the undisputed qualities of her journalism but the questionable qualities of her formal philosophy. One has been puzzling for a long time to recall whom Auden has been echoing when he starts a new essay by declaring that there are three different kinds of compassion, or precisely twelve varieties of contrition. Well, here is the answer. Miss Arendt's proclivity for staking out a philosophical mining operation before ripping up the soil in a declared number of parallel strips has spread to Auden and often involves him in generating an air of faintly bogus rigour. Such a tone goes against the direction of Auden's real effort, which is composed of a refreshing certainty about what he knows to be true, an equally refreshing diffidence about what he has not yet discovered, and a lively, contradiction-ridden dialectical hubbub concerning what lies between. Throughout the book we find him declaring that a poet's private life is his own business, yet delving on the same page into every aspect of a poet's private life he can smell out. That is the multiplicity of approach that makes Auden what he is and which his tendencies to ponderousness might stifle, should he let them. What he was. Might have stifled. If he had let them. Suddenly, unexpectedly, we need the past tense.

(T.L.S., 12 October 1973)

(iii) ON HIS DEATH

For a long time before his death, the fact that a homosexual was the greatest living English poet had the status of an open secret: anybody with better than a passing knowledge of W. H. Auden's writing must have been in on it, and in his later essays (one thinks particularly of the essays on Housman and Ackerley) he was teetering on the verge of declaring himself outright. During E. M. Forster's last decades the intelligentsia was similarly privy to covert information. At Forster's death, however, the obituaries—many of them written by old acquaintances—didn't hesitate to let the cat spring from the bag and dash about among a wider public. It isn't recorded that anybody died of shock at this revelation. One would have thought that a precedent for plain dealing had at long last been set. With Auden's demise, though, there has been a retreat into coy mummery—perhaps to protect his dedicatees still living, but more probably because no respectable *literatus* wants the responsibility of firing the gun that will set the young scholars off on their plodding race to re-explicate what any sensitive reader has long since seen to be one of the more substantial poetic achievements of the modern age. Poor scorned clericals, they will find that their new key turns with bewitching ease, but that it might as well be turning in a lake as in a lock. Auden is long way beyond being a crackable case.

Nevertheless, the truth helps. It was an often-stated belief in Auden's later essays that knowledge of an artist's personal life was of small relevance in understanding his work. Insatiably and illuminatingly inquisitive, Auden transgressed his own rule on every possible occasion. The principle was the right one, but had been incorrectly stated. He was saying that to know the truth will still leave you facing a mystery. What he should have said was that to know the truth will leave you with a better chance of facing the *right* mystery. And it quickly becomes evident, I think, that to accept the truth about Auden's sexual nature does nothing to diminish his poetry—quite the opposite. Acceptance leads in the very short run to the realization that the apparent abstractness of Auden's expressed sensuality is really a lyricism of unique resonance, and in the long run to the conviction that Auden's artistic career, taken as a whole, is a triumph of the moral self living out its ideal progress as a work of art.

Auden's first poems instantly revealed an unrivalled gift for luminous statement. Simply by naming names he could bring anything to life:

> Who stands, the crux left of the watershed,
> On the wet road between the chafing grass
> Below him sees dismantled washing-floors,
> Snatches of tramline running to the wood
> An industry already comatose. . . .

After the withering of 30s illusions it became fashionable to laugh at 'Pylon' poetry, but even though intentions do not make deeds there was always something honourable in the intention of domesticating a technological imagery, and anyway Auden himself had only to intend and the deed was done. So formidable a capacity to elevate facts from the prosaic to the poetic had been seen rarely in centuries, and such fluent gestures in doing it had almost never been seen. Auden's poetry possessed the quality which Pasternak so admired in Pushkin—it was full of *things*. And yet in an epoch when homosexuality was still a crime, this talent was the very one which could not be used unguarded to speak of love.

For that, he was forced from the concrete to the abstract, and so moved from the easy (for him) to the difficult. As Gianfranco Contini definitively said when talking of Dante's dedication to the rhyme, the departure point for inspiration is the obstacle. The need to find an acceptable expression for his homosexuality was the first technical obstacle to check the torrential course of Auden's unprecedented facility. A born master of directness was obliged to find a language for indirection, thus becoming immediately involved with the drama that was to continue for the rest of his life—a drama in which the living presence of technique is the antagonist.

> Doom is dark and deeper than any sea-dingle.
> Upon what man it fall
> In spring, day-wishing flowers appearing,
> Avalanche sliding, white snow from rock-face,
> That he should leave his house,
> No cloud-soft hand can hold him, restraint by women;
> But ever that man goes
> Through place-keepers, through forest trees,
> A stranger to strangers over undried sea,

> Houses for fishes, suffocating water,
> Or lonely on fell as chat,
> By pot-holed becks
> A bird stone-haunting, an unquiet bird.

In this first stanza of Poem II in *Poems* (it was entitled 'The Wanderer' only later, in *Collected Shorter Poems 1930–1944*) the idea of the homosexual's enforced exile is strongly present, although never explicit: the theme lies hidden and the imagery is explicit instead, thereby reversing the priorities of the traditional lyric, and bodying forth an elliptical suggestiveness which rapidly established itself as the new lyricism of an era. But already we are given a foretaste of the voyage that came to an end in Oxford forty years later—a wanderer's return to the Oxford of *Another Time*, the centre of anger which is the only place that is out of danger. Auden never looked for cloistered safety until very late on the last day. The danger and fatigue of his journey were too much of an inspiration.

> There head falls forward, fatigued at evening
> And dreams of home,
> Waving from window, spread of welcome,
> Kissing of wife under single sheet;
> But waking sees
> Birds-flocks nameless to him, through doorway voices
> Of new men making another love.

Only tiredness could make the doomed traveller dream the banalities of hearth and wife: awake, he is once again involved with real love. And real love is a new love, with all political overtones fully intended. Auden's radicalism, such as it was, was at one with his sexuality, with the subsequent result that he spent the 30s experiencing Communism as sensual and sex as political.

As Brecht found his politicized lyricism in sophistication (*In der Asphaltstadt bin ich daheim*), Auden found his in innocence: masturbation in the dormitory, languishing looks between prefects and blond new boys, intimate teas and impassioned lollings on grassy hillsides. The armies and the political parties of the 30s were the thrillingly robust continuation of school rugger and cricket teams, being likewise composed of stubborn athletes and prize competitors. Bands apart, they were all-male and Hellenic—and the neo-Hellenism of the 30s was all Teutonic. Auden's political and intellectual spectrum in the 30s is mainly German, and it's harder than the gullible might think to pick his emotional allegiance between the two sets of muscle-packed shorts, Communist or Nazi. Intellectually, of course, he didn't fool with fascism for a moment; but to his sexual proclivities the blond Northern hero made an appeal which only a poetic embodiment could resolve—it took pearl to silence the irritation set up by those vicious specks of grit.

> Save him from hostile capture
> From sudden tiger's leap at corner;
> Protect his house,
> His anxious house where days are counted
> From thunderbolt protect,
> From gradual ruin spreading like a stain;
> Converting number from vague to certain,
> Bring joy, bring day of his returning,
> Lucky with day approaching, with leaning dawn.

Towards the glamour of the opposing teams—the chaps—Auden's feelings were ambiguous. So were his feelings towards his own homosexuality. Like many homosexuals he seems to have experienced homosexual congress as the only clean kind, and thus had no reason to hesitate in identifying homosexuality with a new political order. Nevertheless guilt remained. In the 30s it was a cultural residue (later on, when Auden returned to Christianity, it became a religious precept), but was no less powerful for that. Just as, in another poem, the 'ruined boys' have been damaged by something more physical than the inculcation of upper-class values which Left readers delightedly assumed, so in this last stanza of 'The Wanderer' the spreading ruin is something closer to home than the collapse of Europe. There was fear in Auden's pride about his condition. Fear of the police and fear that the much-trumpeted corruption might be a fact. He thought that heterosexual people could enjoy security but that only homosexuals could enjoy danger; that the intensity of the homosexual's beleaguered experience was the harbinger of a new unity; but that, nevertheless, the homosexual was unlucky. In the last line of this most beautiful of young poems, he doesn't really expect luck to be granted or his kind of day to dawn. It's yet another mark of Auden's superiority that whereas his contemporaries could be didactic about what they had merely thought or read, Auden could be tentative about what he felt in his bones. (It was marvellous, and continues to be marvellous, that the *Scrutiny* critics never detected in Auden his unwearying preoccupation with the morality of his art, nor realized that a talent of such magnitude—the magnitude of genius—matures in a way that criticism can hope to understand but not prescribe.)

It will be useful, when the time comes, to hear a homosexual critic's conjectures about the precise nature of Auden's sexual tastes. It seems to me, who am no expert, that Auden's analysis of Housman's guilt feelings (he said Housman was so convinced a Hellenist that he felt ashamed of being passive rather than active) was an indirect admission that Auden was passive himself. Even in the earliest poems he seems not to be taking the lead. All too often he is the forsaken one, the one who loves too much and is always asking his beloved to share an impossibly elevated conception of their union.

> You whom I gladly walk with, touch,
> Or wait for as one certain of good,
> We know it, we know that love
> Needs more than the admiring excitement of union,
> More than the abrupt self-confident farewell,
> The heel on the finishing blade of grass,
> The self-confidence of the falling root,
> Needs death, death of the grain, our death,
> Death of the old gang . . .

But as Auden half-guessed that it might turn out, the old gang wouldn't go away: oppression would always be a reality and homosexual lovers would continue to live in fear and fragments. Out of this insecurity as a soldier in a lost army, it seems to me, emerged Auden's unsettling obsession with the leader principle—a version of *führerprinzip* which was in fact no more Hitlerite than Stalinist, but was simply Auden's dream of a puissant redeemer.

> Absence of fear in Gerhart Meyer
> From the sea, the truly strong man.

The Truly Strong Man, the Airman, the Tall Unwounded Leader/ Of Doomed Companions—he occurs and recurs throughout Auden's younger work, forever changing form but always retaining the magic power to convert fear into peace. A tall white god landing from an open boat, a laconic war-bitten captain, the Truly Strong Man is a passive homosexual's dream of equitable domination. He is the authentic figure of good in early Auden just as his half-brother, the Dictator, is the authentic figure of evil, the man swifter than Syrian horses who can throw the bully of Corinth and is seeking brilliant Athens and us.

In the Strong Man's embrace Auden achieves release from terror and a respite from his own admitted ugliness—his post-coital death at the hands of his Hellenic aggressor would appear to have a close visual affinity with the Dying Warrior.

> Acquire that flick of wrist and after strain
> Relax in your darling's arms like a stone.

In this Owenesque half-rhymed couplet the schoolboy vocabulary of mutual masturbation snuggles up with dainty boldness to the image of the narrator coiled in the tall leader's massive embrace. We could be excused for assuming that Auden spent half of his most productive decade fainting dead away: he returns to the image of orgasm over and over, as the lolling bridegroom droops like a dying flower or lapses into a classic fatigue.

Auden's butch hero flying fast aeroplanes or roping his weaker companions up F6 bears an ineluctable resemblance to the Aryan demigod breaking records in his BF 109 or pounding skyward at 45 degrees into the white hell of Pitz Palu. As with heterosexuals, so with homosexuals, sexual fantasizing is the mind's dreariest function. The scholars, when they finally do get started on this tack, would do well to refrain from waxing ecstatic when nosing truffles of ambiguity. Auden started supplying a sardonic critique of his physical ideal almost from the moment of its creation. All generalized desire leads to banality. Auden staved off bathos by transcendence on the one hand and by foolery on the other. It needs always to be understood that the British schoolboys of his generation saw too much homosexuality ever to think of its mere mechanism as a mystery. Auden planted an abundance of gags for the lads.

> Out of the reeds like a fowl jumped the undressed
> German,
> And Stephen signalled from the sand dunes like a wooden
> madman. . . .

Those were the days. Penned during his early time as a schoolmaster, frolicsome lovesick odes to the rugger team are similarly self-aware. Their presence in *Poems* edifyingly reminds us that Auden's exaltation of the third sex (soon to have its internationalism recognized by being sneeringly branded 'the homintern') as a political paradigm was innocent only politically—sexually it was self-analytical to an extent that made Auden's achievement of chaste lyricism a double triumph.

In *Look, Stranger!*, the wonder book of Auden's poetry, the lyricism was carried to its height. On the one hand, there was the perfection of his abstract sweetness—*dolcezza* so neutralized that it could be sung as plighting music for lovers everywhere.

> Moreover, eyes in which I learn
> That I am glad to look, return
>   My glance every day;
> And when the birth and rising sun
> Waken me, I still speak with one
>   Who has not gone away.

On the other hand, there was a deepening admission of vulnerability, of a fateful strangeness which no amount of bravado could usher into its inheritance.

> Whispering neighbours, left and right,
> Pluck us from the real delight;
> And the active hands must freeze
> Lonely on the separate knees.

All lust, Auden now complains, is at once informed on and suppressed: the new political forces will offer outlaws no place. Throughout *Look, Stranger!* the heterosexuals are characteristically pictured as the tireless sentries guarding those lonely roads on which lovers walk to make a tryst, unpitying soldiers

> Whose sleepless presences endear
> Our peace to us with a perpetual threat.

It's the threat which makes the homosexual's peace more poignant than the heterosexual's freedom, as Auden had already stated in *Poems*, XXVI:

> Noises at dawn will bring
> Freedom for some, but not this peace
> No bird can contradict: passing, but is sufficient now
> For something fulfilled this hour,
>   loved or endured.

In *Look, Stranger!*, with the 30s barely half over and the big battles yet to be fought, Auden already knew that for him and his kind the new age, if it ever came, would not come easily. Love would go on being a thing of glances meeting in crowded pubs, risky whispers in lavatories, one night stands in cheap rooms, partings on railway stations, persecution and exile. Rhetorically he still proclaims his confidence; realistically he hints at a maturing doubt; poetically he creates from this dialectic some of the great love poetry of the century. To Poem IX in *Look, Stranger!* (called 'Through the Looking Glass' in *Collected Shorter Poems 1930–1944*) only Lorca's *Llanto por Ignacio Sanchez Mejias* is even an approximate rival. For his compactness, for his mastery of lyricism as a driving force rather than a decoration, for his unstrained majesty of movement, Auden in this phase of his writing is without an equal. The poetry happens like an event in nature, beautiful because it can't help it.

> Your would-be lover who has never come
> In the great bed at midnight to your arms. . . .

Imperfect, ruggedly rounded out, and in places appearing almost uncorrected, the poem creates its effects with a monstrously skilled carelessness that is in every sense superb, as if the mere details had been left to a team of assistants and the haughty master's attention reserved for passages like

> Such dreams are amorous, they are indeed:
> But no one but myself is loved in these,
> And time flies on above the dreamer's head
> Flies on, flies on, and with your beauty flies.

How can we tell the intoxicator from the intoxicated? Lines like these are the loose scrawl of genius in its cups, the helpless, incandescent finale of Auden's meteorite making contact with the atmosphere of realism. Gorgeous fires of defeat.

But Auden's prescient withdrawal into loneliness was pained as well as plangent, as we see in the hard-edged bitterness of *Look, Stranger!*, XXVIII:

> Dear, though the night is gone
> The dream still haunts today
> That brought us to a room,
> Cavernous, lofty as
> A railway terminus

In this enormous room crowded with beds, Auden's lover turns towards someone else. The clarity of the setting belongs less to Lorca's branch of surrealism than to something colder and more northern. The presiding spirits at Lorca's lament are those of Buñuel and Dali. With Auden, it's Magritte.

Poem XXX in *Look, Stranger!* starts with the famous line 'August for the people and their favorite islands' and is dedicated to Christopher Isherwood. In *Collected Shorter Poems 1930–1944* it is called 'Birthday Poem,' and in *Collected Shorter Poems 1927–1957* it does not appear at all—one of that volume's several shattering omissions. The line about the spy's career gains luminosity once we have accustomed ourselves to the close identification in Auden's mind of homosexuality with clandestine activity and all its apparatus of codes and invisible inks. There are lines between the lines of Auden's younger poems which will come to life in the mild heat of knowledge. Beginning far back in the schoolboy mythology of Mortmere, such symbolic cloak-and-dagger men as the Adversary and the Watcher in Spanish defeat all scholarly attempts to place them as political exemplars, but are easily apprehended as madly camp star turns at a drag ball. They are there to brighten the lives of secret men. As Auden wrote years later in 'The Fall of Rome,' all the literati keep an imaginary friend. Auden's artistic indulgence in the 30s vocabulary of espionage—a vocabulary which was a matter of life and death to those from whom he borrowed it—seemed then, and can still seem now, trivial beyond forgiveness. It's worth remembering, though, that Auden was in a war too, and needed to hide himself just as deep. And his war had been going on since time out of mind.

To use his own phrase, the wicked card was dealt: in the face of totalitarianism, homosexuality was no longer a valid image for collective action. The world was not a school and adolescence was at long last over. Auden's exile began in earnest. In New Year Letter we learned that those hunted out of ordinary life are 'wild quarry,' but are granted the privilege of themselves becoming hunters— hunters of the past. New Year Letter is one of the synthetic works by which Auden accepted the responsibility of comprehending European culture—an acceptance which was to lead him in the course of time to his position as the most variously erudite poet since Goethe. The Strong Man had faded out and the Dictator was in control, leaving

> Culture on all fours to greet
> A butch and criminal elite

which is as clear, and personal, an image of violation as you could wish.

The innocence of young love retained its purity through knowledge, of itself and of the multiple past which justified the pluralist political dream—now solely an ideal, and more radiant for that—of the Just City.

> White childhood moving like a sigh
> Through the green woods unharmed in thy
> Sophisticated innocence
> To call thy true love to the dance.

In Another Time, his collection of lyrics from that period, Auden ushered in the new decade with a reiteration of his solitude:

> Ten thousand soldiers marched to and fro:
> Looking for you and me, my dear, looking for you and me.

The sentries were still walking the ridges. During the long decade of warfare and recovery they gradually and mysteriously grew fewer and less imbued with missionary zeal. In the decade between Another Time and Nones Auden seems to have faced the fact that art, politically speaking, has no future, only a past. Whatever Auden the person was up to, Auden the poet had begun to accept and love the world. He no longer thought of homosexuality as newness—just a permanent apartness. From Nones the diligent stylistic analyst will deduce that the poet's studies of the Oxford English Dictionary had got as far as the letter C. The lover of his poetry will find that the period of dialectical tension has come to an end. Often taken as a gratuitous glibness, Auden's later insistence that all his poetry put together had not saved a single Jew was already a plain fact. Poetry, he had said even before the 30s were over, makes nothing happen. In *Nones* there was sardonic realism about love but any idealism about it had been banished. What idealism there was was all about art, and the eternal order which art formed outside history.

As a mind, Auden curved away from the purely Germanic culture and developed a growing kinship with the all-embracing Latin one, of which he is indeed the true modern representative in English after Eliot. Despite his domicile in Austria and his involvement with German opera, his final affinity appears to have been with the thought of Valéry—whose shelf of N.R.F. paperbacks is the closest contemporary parallel to Auden's preoccupations with the aphorism and the ideal order of creativity.

In Christianity Auden found forgiveness for sin. But to redeem the luxuriance of his early cleverness he had to work out his own cure, and as with Dante the cure was *technical*. Holding his art to be a sacrament, Dante acted out his penitence in the form of technical behaviour. For the early sin of rhyming Christ's name with a dirty word he makes recompense in the *Divine Comedy* by never rhyming it with anything except itself—the only word to be so treated. The triadic symmetries of the *Divine Comedy* are a set of disciplines so strict that lyricism has no freedom to indulge itself: when it happens, it happens as a natural consequence of stating the truth. For the educated man, there is a moment of his early acquaintanceship with Dante when he realizes that all he has slowly taught himself to enjoy in poetry is everything that Dante has grown out of. A comparable moment of fear is to be had with Auden, when we understand that his slow change through the 40s entails a renunciation of the art-thrill, and that the Audenesque dazzle is forever gone. For a poet to lose such a talent would have been a misfortune. For a poet to give it up was an act of disciplined renunciation rarely heard of in English.

A brief recapitulation of Auden's innovations in technical bravura is worth making at this point. Unlike Brecht, who wrote both *Die Moritat von Mackie Messer* and *Die Seeräuber-Jenny* in the year of Auden's first privately-printed booklet, Auden never met his Kurt Weill. He met Britten, but the results were meagre. It is no denigration of Isherwood to say that if, of his two admired artistic types, Auden had teamed up with the Composer instead of the Novelist, modern English musical history would have been transformed. As it was, Auden's talent as a lyricist was never developed: the songs for Hedli Anderson had the melody-defeating line-turnovers of ordinary poems, and his activities as a librettist—whether writing originals for Stravinsky or translating *The Magic Flute*—seem to me frustrating in the recognizable modern English manner. Auden had command of a linear simplicity that would have suited the lyric to perfection. As it was, however, he stuck mainly to poetry: and anyway it's probable that the pressure of his homosexual indirectness would have distorted his linear simplicity as thoroughly as, and less fruitfully than, it dislocated his pictorial integrity. Alone with pencil and paper, Auden was free to explore his technical resources. They were without limit, Mozartian. Auden mastered all the traditional lyric forms as a matter of course, bringing to some of them—those which had been imported from rhyme-rich languages and for good reasons had never flourished—the only air of consummate ease they would ever possess. At the same time he did a far more thorough job than even *vers libre* had done of breaking down the last vestiges of the artificial grip the lyric still had on the written poem. He produced apprehensible rhythmic unities which were irregular not only from line to line but within the lines themselves. Finally he penetrated within the word, halting its tendency toward slur and contraction, restoring its articulated rhythmic force. This is the technical secret behind his ability to sustain the trimeter and tetrameter over long distances, driving them forward not along a fixed lattice-work of terminal and internal rhymes but with an incessant modulation across the vowel spectrum and the proliferating concatenated echoes of exploded consonantal groups.

Hazlitt said that Burke's style was as forked and playful as the lightning, crested like the serpent. Everybody sensitive to poetry, I think, has known the feeling that Auden's early work, with its unmatched technical brilliance, is an enchanted playground. The clear proof of his moral stature, however, is the way he left the playground behind when all were agreed that he had only to keep on adding to it and immortality would be his.

Auden's later books are a long—and sometimes long-winded—penitence for the heretical lapse of letting art do his thinking for him. In *Homage to Clio, About the House, City without Walls,* and *Epistle to a Godson* he fulfils his aim of suppressing all automatic responses. A blend of metres and syllabics, his austere forms pro-

gressively empty themselves of all mesmeric flair. Auden conquers
Selfhood by obliterating talent: what is left is the discipline of mechanical accomplishment, supporting the salt conclusions of a lifetime's thinking—cured wisdom. At the same time, Auden claimed
the right to erase any of his early works he now thought were lies.
A generation's favourites fell before his irascible, Tolstoyan scythe.
His friend Louis MacNeice had once written that after a certain time
the poet loses the right to get his finished poems back. Auden didn't
agree with MacNeice's humility, just as he had never agreed with
MacNeice's sense of usefulness: MacNeice had tired himself out
serving the B.B.C. instead of the Muse.

It is a common opinion among the English literati that Auden's
later work is a collapse. I am so far from taking this view that I
think an appreciation of Auden's later work is the only sure test for
an appreciation of Auden, just as an appreciation of Yeats's earlier
work is the only sure test for an appreciation of Yeats. You must
know and admire the austerity which Auden achieved before you
can take the full force of his early longing for that austerity—
before you can measure the portent of his early brilliance. There
is no question that the earlier work is more enjoyable. The question
is about whether you think enjoyability was the full extent of his
aim. Auden, it seems to me, is a modern artist who has lived out his
destiny as a European master to the full, a man in whom all cultural history is present just as the sufferings of all the past were still
alive in his lover's eyes:

> A look contains the history of Man,
> And fifty francs will earn the stranger right
> To warm the heartless city in his arms.

Famed stranger and exalted outcast, Auden served a society larger
than the one in which he hid. In his later work we see not so much
the ebbing of desire as its transference to the created world, until
plains and hills begin explaining the men who live on them. Auden's
unrecriminating generosity toward a world which had served him
ill was a moral triumph. Those who try to understand it too
quickly ought not to be trusted with grown-up books.

I was born in the month after Auden wrote 'September 1, 1939' and
saw him only three times. The first time, in Cambridge, about five
years ago, he gave a poetry reading in Great St. Mary's. The second

time, on the Cambridge-to-London train a year later, I was edging
along to the buffet car when I noticed him sitting in a first-class com-
partment. When the train pulled in I waited for him at the barrier
and babbled some nonsense about being privileged to travel on the
same train. He took it as his due and waved one of his enormous
hands. The third time was earlier this year, in the Martini Lounge
atop New Zealand House in London, where a reception was thrown
for all of us who had taken part in the Poetry International Festi-
val. Auden shuffled through in a suit encrusted with the dirt of
years—it was a geological deposit, an archaeological pile-up like the
seven cities of Troy. I don't think anybody of my generation knew
what to say to him. I know I didn't. But we knew what to think,
and on behalf of my contemporaries I have tried to write some of
it down here. I can still remember those unlucky hands; one of them
holding a cigarette, the other holding a brimming glass, and both
trembling. The mind boggled at some of the things they had been
up to. But one of them had refurbished the language. A few months
later he was beyond passion, having gone to the reward which
Dante says that poets who have done their duty might well enjoy—
talking shop as they walk beneath the moon.

(*Commentary*, October 1973)

2. Robert Lowell's Marble Chips

Of the three new books by Robert Lowell—all of them consisting, like their antecedent *Notebook*, of unrhymed sonnets—only *The Dolphin* contains entirely fresh material. It is dedicated to Lowell's new consort Caroline, and deals with the life they are now leading together. *For Lizzie and Harriet* deals exclusively with the life Lowell has left behind: it isolates and reworks those poems concerning his ex-wife and daughter which were earlier scattered through *Notebook*. The central and bulkiest volume of the current three, *History*, is an extensive reworking and thoroughgoing reordering of all the remaining poems in *Notebook*, with eighty extra ones mixed in.

When we consider that *Notebook* itself had two earlier versions before being published in Britain, it is clear that there is a great deal going on. If mere bustle were creativity, then later Lowell would be the most creative thing in modern poetry. Daunted, the critic is tempted to hand the whole problem directly to the scholar and get the work of collating done before any judgments are hazarded. Unfortunately judgment will not wait—not least because these recent works offer an invitation to scholarship to start up a whole new branch of its industry, an invitation which will be all too eagerly accepted if criticism neglects to mark out the proper, and reasonably discreet, size of the job. Lowell is a giant, but his perimeter is still visible: there is no need to think that he fills the sky.

In so far as it had one, *Notebook*'s structure was rhapsodic—an adjective which, in its technical sense, we associate with the Homeric epic. As the poet stumbled in circles of crisis and collapse, digressions could occur in any direction, sub-sequences of the proliferating sonnets form round any theme. These sequences constituted rhapsodies, and it was easy to sense that the rhapsodies were intent on forming themselves into an epic. At that stage, the Lowell epic resembled John Berryman's *Dream Songs*: its digressions had shape, but there was no clear line of progress initiating them—no simple story for which they could serve as complications. The story was mixed in with them. All of human history was there, and

Lowell's personal history was there too. Both kinds of history jumped about all over the place.

The new books have simplified everything, while simultaneously making a claim to universality that takes the reader's breath away. 'My old title, Notebook, was more accurate than I wished, i.e., my composition was jumbled' writes the poet in a foreword. 'I hope this jumble or jungle is cleared—that I have cut the waste marble from the figure.' Cutting away the marble until the figure is revealed is an idea that reminds us—and is probably meant to remind us—of Michelangelo. As we realize that not even these new books need bring the matter to an end, the idea that the figure need never fully emerge from the marble also reminds us of Michelangelo. Lowell seems intent on having us believe that he is embarked on a creative task which absolves his talent from wasting too much time polishing its own products. He does a lot to make this intention respectable, and we soon see, when reading History, that although thousands of details have been altered since Notebook, the changes that really matter are in the grand structure. It is at this point that we temporarily cease thinking of marble and start thinking about, say, iron filings. Notebook was a random scattering of them. In History a magnet has been moved below, and suddenly everything has been shaken into a startling linear shape.

As rearranged and augmented in History, the sonnets begin at the dawn of creation and run chronologically all the way to recent events in the life of the poet. We have often thought, with Lowell, that history was being incorporated into the self. Here is the thing proved, and the pretension would be insupportable if it were not carried out with such resource. The information which Lowell commands about all cultures in all ages found a ragged outlet in Notebook. Deployed along a simple line of time, it gains in impressiveness—gains just enough to offset the realization that it is Lowell's propensity for reading his own problems into anything at all which makes him so ranging a time-traveller. History is the story of the world made intelligible in terms of one man's psychology. It is a neurotic work by definition. Nobody reasonable would ever think of starting it, and the moment Lowell begins to be reasonable is the moment he will stop. There is no good cause to assume, however, that Lowell any longer thinks it possible to be reasonable about history. Stephen Dedalus said history was a nightmare from which he was trying to awake. Raising the stakes, Lowell seems to

believe that history is something you cannot appreciate without
losing your sanity. This belief releases him into realms of artistic
effect where reason would find it hard to go. That the same belief
might bring inhibition, as well as release, is a separate issue.

Broadly, History's progression is first of all from Genesis through
the Holy Land to the Mediterranean, ancient Greece and Rome,
with diversions to Egypt at the appropriate moments. Medieval
Europe then gives way to the Renaissance and the Enlightenment,
tipping over into the French Revolution. Through the complexities
of the nineteenth century, strict chronological sequence is manfully
adhered to, whether in painting, letters, music or ante and post-
bellum American politics. French symbolism sets the scene for the
twentieth-century arts, while the First World War sets the tone for
the modern politics of crisis and annihilation. The Russian revolution throws forward its divisive shadow, which later on will split
the New York intelligentsia. By this time Lowell's family history
is active in all departments, and soon the poet himself arrives on
stage. Everything that has happened since the dawn of humanity
has tended to sound like something happening to Lowell. From
here on this personal tone becomes intense, and those named—especially if they are artists—are mainly people the poet knows. By
now, unquestionably, he is at the centre of events. But the book
has already convinced us that all events, even the vast proportion of
them that happened before he arrived in the world, are at the centre
of him.

History is a long haul through places, things and, preeminently,
names. Helen, Achilles, Cassandra, Orestes, Clytemnestra, Alex-
ander, Hannibal, Horace, Juvenal, Dante, Villon, Anne Boleyn,
Cranach, Charles V, Marlowe, Mary Stuart, Rembrandt, Milton,
Pepys, Bishop Berkeley, Robespierre, Saint-Just, Napoleon, Beet-
hoven, Goethe, Leopardi, Schubert, Heine, Thoreau, Henry Adams,
George Eliot, Hugo, Baudelaire, Rimbaud, Mallarmé, Lady Cynthia
Asquith, Rilke, George Grosz, Hardy, Al Capone, Ford Madox
Ford, Allen Tate, Randall Jarrell, John Crowe Ransom, F. O. Mat-
theissen, Roethke, Delmore Schwartz, T. S. Eliot, Wyndham Lewis,
MacNeice, William Carlos Williams, Robert Frost, Stalin, Harpo
Marx, Che Guevara, Norman Mailer, Dwight Macdonald, Adrienne
Rich, Mary McCarthy, Eugene McCarthy, Elizabeth Schwarzkopf,
Martin Luther King, Robert Kennedy, De Gaulle, Lévi-Strauss, R. P.
Blackmur, Stanley Kunitz, Elizabeth Bishop, I. A. Richards, John

B*

Berryman, Robert Lowell and many more: a cast of thousands. The range they cover, and the pertinent information Lowell is able to adduce when treating each one—these things are little short of astonishing. But they were already startling in *Notebook*. What makes these qualities doubly impressive now is the new effect of faces succeeding faces in due order. Leaving, of course, a thousand gaps—gaps which the poet seems understandably keen to set about filling.

Lizzie and Harriet's retributive presence in *Notebook* has been eliminated from *History* and given a book of its own. *The Dolphin* likewise enshrines a portion of Lowell's experience which is plainly not going to be allowed to overbalance the future of *History*. It is possible to suggest, given the dispersal of foci represented by these three volumes, that Lowell's 'confessional' poetry is no longer his main thing. The *History* book now embodies his chief effort, and in relation to this effort the ordinary people inhabiting his life don't make the weight. *History* is full of public names, rather than private ones: public names united not so much by prestige as in their undoubted puissance in shaping, exemplifying or glorifying historic moments. In *History* Lowell, alone, joins the great.

And the number of the great grows all the time. Instructive, in this respect, to take a close look at the *History* poem called 'Cleopatra Topless', one of a short sequence of poems concerning her. Where have we seen it before? Was it in *Notebook*? But in *Notebook* it is untraceable in the list of contents. Where was it, then? The answer is that the poem is in *Notebook* but is called simply 'Topless' and has nothing to do with Cleopatra. In the *Notebook* poem she's just a girl in a nightclub:

> She is the girl
> as Renoir, Titian and all full times have left her

To convert her into Cleopatra, it is only necessary to get rid of the inappropriate Renoir and Titian, filling the space with a line or so about what men desire. Throughout *History* the reader is continually faced with material which has apparently been dragged in to fill a specific chronological spot. Nor does this material necessarily have its starting point in *Notebook*: the fact that it appears in that volume, if it does appear, doesn't preclude its having begun its life in an earlier, and often far earlier, Lowell collection. For example, a version of Valéry's 'Hélène' is in *Imitations*, with the inspiration

for it credited to Valéry. By the time it arrives in *History*, it is
credited to no one but Lowell. It is true that the drive of the verse
has been weakened with over-explanatory adjectives:

> My solitary hands recall the kings
> > (*Imitations*)
> My loving hands recall the absent kings
> > (*History*)
> Mes solitaires mains appellent les monarques
> > (Valéry)

But this is incidental. As we can see abundantly in other places,
Lowell's minor adjustments are just as likely to impart point as detract from it. Fundamentally important, however, is the way the
imitation has been saddled with extraneous properties (Agamemnon,
Ulysses) in order to bolster it for the significance it is being asked
to provide in its new slot. Though making regular appearances in
the early sections of *History*, Agamemnon and Ulysses are nowhere
mentioned in Valéry's poem. But then, the poem is no longer
Valéry's: in *History* the source is uncredited.

Trusting to the itch of memory and ransacking the library shelves
in order to scratch it, the reader soon learns that Lowell has been
cannibalizing his earlier works of translation and imitation—cutting them up into fourteen-line lengths and introducing them with
small ceremony first of all into *Notebook* and later, on the grand
scale, into *History*. Usually the provenance of the newly installed
sonnet is left unmentioned. There are exceptions to this: the 'Le
Cygne' of *Notebook*, which the gullible might have attributed to
Lowell, has a better chance of being traceable to its origins now
that it is called 'Mallarmé I. Swan'. It is in fact the second of the
'Plusieurs Sonnets' in *Poésies* and is called—after its first line—'Le
vierge, le vivace et le bel aujourd'hui'. In *Notebook* Lowell had
'blind' for *vivace*, an inscrutable boldness which in *History* has
been softened to 'alive'. Other improvements in the new version are
less welcome: 'the horror of the ice that ties his wings' is a reversal
of Mallarmé's sense, which in the *Notebook* version had been got
right. Mallarmé is saying that the swan *accepts* the ice. Here Lowell
seems to have been improving his first version without reference to
the original. On the other hand, he has now substituted 'wings'
for 'feet' and thereby humbly returned much closer to *plumage*.
The key phrase, *l'exil inutile*, which is ringingly present in the *Note-*

book version, is now strangely absent. Anyone who attempts to
trace poems back through *Notebook* to their sources in foreign
literatures is fated to be involved in these niggling questions at all
times. But at least, with such a clear signpost of a title, there is a
hint that this particular poem *has* such a history. In many cases
even this tenuous condition does not obtain.

When a bright young American scholar produces a properly in-
dexed Variorum Lowell—preferably with a full concordance—it
will be easier to speak with confidence about what appears in *History*
that is not in *Notebook*. A good few poems appear in both with
different titles, and it is difficult for even the keenest student to hold
the entire mass of material clearly in his mind. But if *History's*
'Baudelaire 1. The Abyss' is not in *Notebook*, it was in *Imitations*,
where it was billed as a version of 'Le Gouffre'. There, it reduced
Baudelaire's fourteen lines to thirteen. Now it is back to being a
sonnet again, and the *Êtres* are now rendered as 'being' instead of
'form', which one takes to be a net gain. One is less sure that the
poem's provenance would be so recognizable if it were not for the
memory of the *Imitations* version. The question keeps on cropping
up—are we supposed to know that such material started out in
another poet's mind, or are we supposed to accept it as somehow
being all Lowell's? Is it perhaps that Lowell is putting himself forward as the representative of all past poets? It should be understood that one is not questioning Lowell's right to employ allusion,
or to embody within his own work a unity of culture which he feels
to be otherwise lost. The ethics are not the problem; the aesthetics
are. Because none of these poems carries the same weight, when presented as ordinary Lowell, as it does when its history is clearly seen
to be still surrounding it.

'Baudelaire 2. Recollection' was called 'Meditation' in *Imitations*
and is thus a revision of a version of 'Recueillement'. It is interesting
to see that *va cueillir des remords* now means 'accumulating re-
morse' rather than the previous and unfathomable 'fights off anguish'.
Minor satisfactions like that can be clung to while the reader totals
'Baudelaire 1. The Abyss' and 'Baudelaire 2. Recollection' and
glumly reconciles himself to the fact that that's his lot on Baudelaire—two revamped imitations.

Rimbaud does better. Five sonnets. But all five turn out to have
been in a sequence of eight versions printed in *Imitations*. 'Rimbaud
1. Bohemia' was called 'On the Road' and is a version of 'Ma Bo-

hème'; 'Rimbaud 2. A Knowing Girl' was called 'A Knowing Girl' and is a version of 'La Maline'; 'Rimbaud 3. Sleeper in the Valley' was more expansively called 'The Sleeper in the Valley' and is a version of 'Le Dormeur du Val'; 'Rimbaud 4. The Evil' was less expansively called 'Evil' and is a version of 'Le Mal'; 'Rimbaud 5. Napoleon after Sedan' was called 'Napoleon after Sedan', is a version of 'Rages de Césars', and was the only one of the five to have made an intermediary appearance in *Notebook*, where it was called 'Rimbaud and Napoleon III'. With this last poem, then, we have three separate texts to help send us cross-eyed, but if we can concentrate long enough we will see a characteristic change. The *Imitations* version is shaped like the original and confines itself to the original's material, plus a few scraps of interpolated elucidatory matter (where Rimbaud just said 'Compère' Lowell tactfully adds some explanatory horses) and of course the inevitable intensifying of the verbs. The *Notebook* version is no longer readily identifiable as an imitation: the stanza-breaks have been eliminated, the first four lines are a piece of scene-setting which have nothing to do with the original, and Robespierre's name has been introduced, answering a question—'quel nom sur ses lèvres muettes/Tressaille?'—which Rimbaud had left unanswered. The *History* version gets the fidgets, throwing out Compère but leaving the horses. By this time, you would need to be pretty thoroughly acquainted with Rimbaud if you were to spot the poem as anything but neat Lowell.

Of the other Rimbaud poems, 'La Maline' is now closer to the way Rimbaud wrote it than the *Imitations* version, but Lowell's 'Ma Bohème' misses by just as far as it used to, though in a different way:

> September twilight on September twilight.
> > (*Imitations*)
> September twilights and September twilights
> > (*History*)

A minor alteration to a major aberration: the repetition is not in Rimbaud and does nothing for his meaning whichever way Lowell puts it.

Material which had its starting point in *Imitations* can be changed to any extent from slightly to drastically on its way to a fourteen-line living-space in *History*. Lowell's version of 'L'Infinito' is squeezed by three lines but is otherwise the poem we have come to

recognize as probably the least sympathetic translation of Leopardi
ever committed. 'Hugo at Théophile Gautier's Grave' is a rearrangement of an *Imitations* version of Hugo's 'A Théophile Gautier' which
had already cut the original by more than half. 'Sappho to a Girl' was
in *Notebook* as just 'Sappho', and is a mosaic of bits and pieces which
can be seen in *Imitations* still mounted in their original settings—
i.e. versions of the poem to the bride Anactoria (No. 141 in the *Oxford Book of Greek Verse*) and that tiny, lovely poem to Night (No.
156) which contains the line about the Pleiads. In his *Imitations* version Lowell left the Pleiads out. In the *Notebook* version they were
still out. In the *History* version he put them back in. The cardplayer,
who is in all three versions, seems not to belong to Sappho, but
could conceivably belong to Cézanne.

  Imitations, however, is not the only source of workable stone.
Notebook/*History* is Lowell's Renaissance and like the Renaissance
in Rome it doesn't question its right to use all the monuments of
the ancient city as a quarry. *History*'s 'Horace: Pardon for a Friend'
started life, at twice the length, as a version of Horace's *Odes* II, 7,
in *Near the Ocean*. In the same collection first appeared 'Juvenal's
Prayer', which at that stage constituted the last nineteen lines of a
version of Juvenal's 10th Satire. And to return briefly to Cleopatra,
'Nunc est bibendum, Cleopatra's Death' is (as the title this time
allows) another imitation, or at least a fragment of one—Horace's
Odes I, 37, which in *Near the Ocean* can be found imitated in full.

  And still they come, racing out of the past to find their new
home. *History*'s 'Caligula 2' is part of a much longer Caligula in
For the Union Dead. And from as far back as *Lord Weary's Castle*,
'In the Cage' is an acknowledged reworking, with the attention now
turning from the observed to the observer. But other material from
the same early period is less easily spotted. The sonnet 'Charles V by
Titian', for example, was called 'Charles the Fifth and the Peasant'
in *Lord Weary's Castle*, where it was subtitled 'After Valéry' and
appeared to be a version of his 'César' in which almost every pro-
perty, Titian included, was an interpolation. *History*'s 'Dante 3.
Buonconte' goes back to a poem in *Lord Weary's Castle* called 'The
Soldier', which was modelled on the Buonconte da Montefeltro episode in *Purgatorio* V. Here we have a clear case of the way Lowell's
wide learning has matured with the years: he nowadays quietly and
correctly renders *la croce* as Buonconte's hands folded on his chest,
rather than as a crucifix—a subtly rich textual point of the kind

which Lowell at his best is brilliantly equipped to bring out. Re-
stored from an unwieldy third person to the direct first person of
the original, this poem is easily the best of those devoted to Dante:
'Dante 4. Paolo and Francesca' is a copybook example of how
Lowell's irrepressible extremism of language is unable to match
the flow of lyrical Italian—and unabashed lyricism is a good half
of Francesca's self-deluding personality. Lowell takes Francesca's
side against the oppressors of her flesh. If it has occurred to him that
Dante didn't, he doesn't say so. In the Dante rhapsody as a whole,
we are able to see that below the uniform intensity of Lowell's
language there is a uniform intensity of psychology—a certain
monotony of feeling. Dante's love for Beatrice is presented rather as
if the relationship between work and love bore strong resemblances
to that same relationship in the life of Robert Lowell. Could Lowell
find means, we wonder, to convey the fact that with Dante the consuming, disabling passion was just as likely to be for philosophy as
for sex?

For all the examples cited above, elementary sleuthing suffices to
trace the origins—either the title gives a clue or else the poem is
more or less intact and can't fail to jog the reader's memory. But
it's doubtful if the cannibalizing process stops there, and at this
stage it's probably safer to assume that Lowell regards none of
his earlier work, whether imitative or original, as exempt from re-
quisitioning and a reconstruction ranging from mild to violent. For
example, in a History poem called 'The Spartan Dead at Thermopy-
lae' the lines about Leonidas are lifted straight from the Imitations
version of Rilke's 'Die Tauben'. Pretty well untraceable, if these
lines weren't original Lowell then, they are now.

Lowell's discovery of a linear historical structure for History has
opened the way to a poet's dream—the simple line allowing infinite
complication. The sudden insatiable demand for material has sent
him raiding back over all his past poetry—not necessarily just the
translations—in a search for stuff that fits. A great deal does. On the
other hand, isn't there something Procrustean about carving up all
that past work into fourteen-line chunks? To get back to Michelangelo and the marble, it's as if Michelangelo were to pick up a
power-saw and slice through everything from the Madonna of the
Stairs to the Rondinini Pietà at a height of fourteen inches.

Whatever Procrustes might have thought, trimming things to fit
an arbitrary frame is not a discipline. And without its rhyme-

schemes, the sonnet is an arbitrary frame. There are many times in
Notebook/History when the reader thrills to the impact of an
idea achieving a formal measure almost in spite of itself:

> I hear the catbird's coloratura cluck
> singing fuck, fuck above the brushwood racket.
> The feeder deals catfood like cards to the yearling
> salmon in their stockpond by the falls.

The singing power of the mimesis, the clashing couplings of the
shunting assonance, the muscle of the enjambement: if there were
a single sonnet wholly assembled with such care then one would
not even have to set oneself to learn it—it would teach itself. But
fragments are the most we get. Lowell's later method might allow
some parts of his talent free play but it allows his technique only
child's play. 'I want words meat-hooked from the living steer',
he writes in the course of rebuking Valéry for preferring six passable
lines to one inspired one. He gets what he wants: meat-hooked
words and inspired lines. But what one misses, and goes on missing until it aches, is form.

Still, within the limits he has now set for it—the liberating
limits, as he sees them—Lowell's talent is still operating, and still
majestic. There are times when nothing has happened except language yet you must helplessly concede that the vitality of his language is unique:

> Man turns dimwit quicker than the mayfly
> fast goes the lucid moment of love believed;

And there are times when the language subsides into nothing
special, but the visualizing faculty reveals itself for the hundredth
time as a profound gift:

> coming back to Kenyon on the Ohio local—
> the view, middle distance, back and foreground, shifts,
> silos shifting squares like chessmen—

What an idea! But in all the vast expanse of *Notebook/History*
there are not many times when both things come together, and none
at all when a poem sustains itself in the way to which Lowell once
made us accustomed. There is no doubt that Lowell has abandoned
his old course deliberately. Nor is there any doubt that he has
opened up for himself an acreage of subject-matter which could

never have been reached in the old way. But we still have to decide if what we are being given is poetry or something else. Of some comfort here is that Lowell appears to be still undecided himself.

Setting aside the decisive alteration of structure which turned the circularity of Notebook into the linear stride of History, all the minor changes seem to have been made with the fidgeting lack of direction that you might expect from a writer who somehow feels compelled to refurbish the deliberately formless. Most of the attention has been expended on points of language: it's too late by now to go back to fourteen passable lines, but apparently there is still hope of drumming up the odd inspired one. All too frequently, the striving for intensity results in a further, incomprehensible compression of an idea already tightened to the limit. In the Notebook version of 'In the Forties I':

> Green logs sizzled on the fire-dogs,
> painted scarlet like British Redcoats. . . .

Whereas the History version has:

> greenwood sizzling on the andirons,
> two men of iron, two milk-faced British Redcoats.

Without a knowledge of the first version, it would be hard to guess what the second might mean: the idea of the red paint has become familiar to Lowell, and he has got rid of it without pausing to reflect that we will have trouble following the idea unless it is spelled out to some extent. Scores of these changes for the worse could be adduced. Other changes are simply neutral. In Notebook's 'Harriet 2', the fly is like a plane gunning potato bugs. Appearing again in the sonnet 'Summer, 2' in For Lizzie and Harriet, the fly is like a plane dusting apple orchards. The second version is perhaps preferable for its verb being the more easily appreciated, but on the other hand potato bugs have more verve than apple orchards. It's a toss-up.

Another kind of change is incontestably for the better. In History Robert Frost's voice is 'musical and raw' rather than, as in Notebook, 'musical, raw and raw'. One had always wondered why the repetition was there, and now one finds that Lowell had been wondering the same thing. In Notebook Frost was supposed to have inscribed a volume 'Robert Lowell from Robert Frost, his friend in the art'. In History this becomes 'For Robert from Robert, his friend in

the art'. Much chummier. Was Lowell, for modesty's sake, misquoting the first time? Or is he, for immodesty's sake, misquoting
now? It is impossible to tell, but grappling with the implications
of these minor shifts is one of the involving things about reading
all these books together.

The comparison between *Notebook* and *History* could go on for
ever, and probably will. Discovering that the *Notebook* poem for
Louis MacNeice is reproduced in *History* with one of its lines doubled
and another line dropped—a really thunderous printer's error—one
wonders distractedly if anybody else knows. Does Lowell know? It's
large territory to become familiar with, even for him. Finally one
decides that getting familiar with it is as far as appreciation can go.
To recognize details is possible; but there is small hope of remembering the whole thing. Like Berryman's *Dream Songs*, Lowell's *Note-
book/History/For Lizzie and Harriet* defeats memory. Perhaps *The
Dolphin* is heading back to the way things were, but on examina-
tion it starts yielding the kind of names—Hölderlin, Manet—which
make us think that most of it is fated to end up in the next version
of *History*. In *The Dolphin* the only human, unhistoried, unsigni-
ficant voice occurs in the quoted parts of Lizzie's letters. If Lowell
wrote them, he should write more. But there isn't much point in
saying 'should'. The outstanding American poet is engaged in writing his version of the poem that Pound, Williams and Berryman
have each already attempted—The Big One. Lowell thinks he is
chipping away the marble to get at the statue. It's more likely that
he is trying to build a statue out of marble-chips. Who cares about
history, if poetry gets thrown away? Perhaps he does. And anyway
the poetry was his to throw.

(T.L.S., 10 August 1973)

3. Don Juan in Hull: Philip Larkin

(i) WOLVES OF MEMORY

Larkin collections come out at the rate of one per decade: *The North Ship*, 1945; *The Less Deceived*, 1955; *The Whitsun Weddings*, 1964; *High Windows*, 1974. Not exactly a torrent of creativity: just the best. In Italy the reading public is accustomed to cooling its heels for even longer. Their top man, Eugenio Montale, has produced only five main collections, and he got started a good deal earlier. But that, in both countries, is the price one has to pay. For both poets the parsimony is part of the fastidiousness. Neither writes an unconsidered line.

Now that the latest Larkin, *High Windows*, is finally available, it is something of a shock to find in it some poems one doesn't recognize. Clipping the poems out of magazines has failed to fill the bill—there were magazines one hadn't bargained for. As well as that, there is the surprise of finding that it all adds up even better than one had expected: the poems which one had thought of as characteristic turn out to be more than that—or rather the *character* turns out to be more than that. Larkin has never liked the idea of an artist Developing. Nor has he himself done so. But he has managed to go on clarifying what he was sent to say. The total impression of *High Windows* is of despair made beautiful. Real despair and real beauty, with not a trace of posturing in either. The book is the peer of the previous two mature collections, and if they did not exist would be just as astonishing. But they do exist (most of us could recognize any line from either one) and can't help rendering many of the themes in this third book deceptively familiar.

I think that in most of the poems here collected Larkin's ideas are being reinforced or deepened rather than repeated. But from time to time a certain predictability of form indicates that a pervious discovery is being unearthed all over again. Such instances aren't difficult to spot, and it would be intemperate to betray delight at doing so. Larkin's 'forgeries' (Auden's term for self-plagiarisms) are very few. He is more original from poem to poem than almost any modern poet one can think of. His limitations, such as they are, lie deeper than that. Here again, it is not wise to be happy about spotting them. Without the limitations there would be no Larkin—the beam cuts *because* it's narrow.

It has always seemed to me a great pity that Larkin's more intelligent critics should content themselves with finding his view of life circumscribed. It is, but it is also bodied forth as art to a remarkable degree. There is a connection between the circumscription and the poetic intensity, and it's no surprise that the critics who can't see the connection can't see the separation either. They seem to think that just because the poet is (self-admittedly) emotionally wounded, the poetry is wounded too. There is always the suggestion that Larkin might handle his talent better if he were a more well-rounded character. That Larkin's gift might be part and parcel of his own peculiar nature isn't a question they have felt called upon to deal with. The whole fumbling dereliction makes you wonder if perhaps the literati in this country haven't had things a bit easy. A crash-course in, say, art criticism could in most cases be recommended. Notions that Michelangelo would have painted more feminine-looking sibyls if he had been less bent, or that Toulouse-Lautrec might have been less obsessive about Jane Avril's dancing if his legs had been longer, would at least possess the merit of being self-evidently absurd. But the brain-wave about Larkin's quirky negativism, and the consequent trivialisation of his lyrical knack, is somehow able to go on sounding profound.

It ought to be obvious that Larkin is not a universal poet in the thematic sense—in fact, he is a self-proclaimed stranger to a good half, *the* good half, of life. You wonder what a critic who complains of this imagines he is praising when he allows that Larkin is still pretty good anyway, perhaps even great. What's missing in Larkin doesn't just tend to be missing, it's glaringly, achingly, unarguably *missing*. But the poetry is all there. The consensus about his stature is consequently encouraging, even if accomplished at the cost of a majority of its adherents misunderstanding what is really going on. At least they've got the right man.

The first poem in the book, 'To the Sea', induces a fairly heavy effect of *déjà lu*. Aren't we long used to that massive four-stanza form, that conjectural opening ('To step over the low wall . . .') in the infinitive? Actually we aren't: he's never used them before. It's

the tone that's reminiscent, and the tactics. The opening takes
us back to the childhood and the lost chance of happiness, the shots
that all fell wide—

> The miniature gaiety of seasides.

In the familiar way, sudden brutalities of diction bite back a remembered sweetness—

> A white steamer stuck in the afternoon.

Alienation is declared firmly as the memories build up—

> Strange to it now, I watch the cloudless scene:

Details well up in the mind with Proustian specificity—

>   . . . and then the cheap cigars,
> The chocolate-papers, tea-leaves, and, between
> The rocks, the rusting soup-tins . . .

The mind, off guard, unmanned by recollection, lets slip the delicately expressed lyrical image—

> The white steamer has gone. Like breathed-on glass
> The sunlight has turned milky.

Whereupon, as in 'Church-Going' or 'The Whitsun Weddings', the
poem winds up in a sententious coda.

>   . . . If the worst
> Of flawless weather is our falling short
> It may be that through habit these do best,
> Coming to water clumsily undressed
> Yearly, teaching their children by a sort
> Of clowning; helping the old, too, as they ought.

The happiness we once thought we could have can't be had, but
simple people who stick to time-honoured habits probably get the
best approximation of it. Larkin once said that if he were called in
to construct a religion he would make use of water. Well, here it is,
lapping at the knobbled feet of unquestioning plebs. Such comfort
as the poem offers the reader resides in the assurance that this old
habit of going to the seaside is 'still going on', even if reader and
writer no longer share it. A cold comfort, as always. Larkin tries,

he has said, to preserve experience both for himself and for others, but his first responsibility is to the experience.

The next big poem is the famous three-part effort that appeared in the *Observer*, 'Livings'. A galley-proof of it is still folded into the back of my copy of *The Less Deceived*. I think it an uncanny piece of work. The proof is read to shreds, and I can still remember the day I picked it up in the office. Larkin had the idea—preserved, in concentrated form, in one of the poems in this volume, 'Posterity'—that a young American Ph.D. student called Jake Balokowsky is all set to wrap him up in an uncomprehending thesis. The first part of 'Livings' is full of stuff that Balokowsky is bound to get wrong. The minor businessman who annually books himself into 'the —— Hotel in ——ton for three days' speaks a vocabulary as well-rubbed and subtly anonymous as an old leather couch. Balokowsky will latch on well enough to the idea that the poem's narrator is a slave to habit,

> wondering why
> I keep on coming. It's not worth it. Father's dead:
> He used to, but the business now is mine.
> It's time for change, in nineteen twenty-nine.

What Jake will probably miss, however, is the value placed on the innocuous local newspaper, the worn décor, the ritual chat, the non-challenging pictures and the ex-Army sheets. It's dependable, it's a living, and 'living' is not a word Larkin tosses around lightly. Judging the narrator is the last thing Larkin is doing. On the contrary, he's looking for his secret. To be used to comfort is an enviable condition. Beer, whisky, cigars and silence—the privileges of the old mercantile civilization which Larkin has been quietly celebrating most of his life, a civilization in which a place like Leeds or Hull (see 'Friday night in the Royal Station Hotel') counts as a capital city. There *is* another and bigger life, but Larkin doesn't underestimate this one for a minute.

In fact he conjures it up all over again in the third part of the poem. The setting this time is Oxford, probably in the late 17th century. The beverage is port instead of whisky, and the talk, instead of with wages, tariffs and stock, deals with advowsons, resurrections and regicide. Proofs of God's existence lie uncontested on dusty bookshelves. 'The bells discuss the hour's gradations.' Once again the feeling of indoor warmth is womb-like. Constellations sparkle over the roofs, matching the big sky draining down the estuary in Part I.

The central poem of the trio squirms like a cat caught between two cushions. Its narrator is conducting a lone love-affair with the sea.

> Rocks writhe back to sight.
> Mussels, limpets,
> Husband their tenacity
> In the freezing slither—
> Creatures, I cherish you!

The narrator's situation is not made perfectly clear. While wanting to be just the reverse, Larkin can on occasion be a difficult poet, and here, I think, is a case of over-refinement leading to obscurity. (Elsewhere in this volume 'Sympathy in White Major' is another instance, and I have never been able to understand 'Dry Point' in *The Less Deceived*.) My guess—and a guess is not as good as an intelligent deduction—is that the speaker is a lighthouse keeper. The way the snow ('O loose moth world') swerves against the black water, and the line 'Guarded by brilliance', seem somehow to suggest that: that, or something similar. Anyway, whoever he is, the narrator is right in among the elements, watching the exploding sea and the freezing slither from seventy feet up on a stormy night. But we see at the end that he, too, is safe indoors. On the radio he hears of elsewhere. He sets out his plate and spoon, cherishing his loneliness. In this central panel of his triptych, it seems to me, Larkin is saying that the civilizations described in the side-panels—one decaying, the other soon to lose its confidence—have an essence, and that this is it. The essence can be preserved in the soul of a man on his own. This is not to suggest that there is anything consolingly positive under Larkin's well-known negativism: the only consoling thing about Larkin is the quality of his art.

'High Windows', the next stand-out poem, shows an emotional progression Larkin had already made us used to.

> When I see a couple of kids
> And guess he's fucking her and she's
> Taking pills or wearing a diaphragm,
> I know this is paradise. . . .

Larkin is a master of language-levels and eminently qualified to use coarse language for shock effects. He never does, however. Strong language in Larkin is put in not to shock the reader but to define the narrator's personality. When Larkin's narrator in 'A Study of Reading Habits' (in *The Whitsun Weddings*) said 'Books are a load of crap' there were critics—some of them, incredibly, among his more appreciative—who allowed themselves to believe that Larkin was expressing his own opinion. (Kingsley Amis had the same kind of trouble, perhaps from the same kind of people, when he let Jim Dixon cast aspersions on Mozart.) It should be obvious at long last, however, that the diction describes the speaker. When the speaker is close to representing Larkin himself, the diction defines which Larkin it is—what mood he is in. Larkin is no hypocrite and has expressed envy of young lovers too often to go back on it here. The word 'fucking' is a conscious brutalism, a protective way of not conjuring up what's meant. However inevitable it might be that Jake Balokowsky will identify this opening sentiment as a Mugger-idgean gesture of contempt, it is incumbent on us to realize that something more interesting is going on.

Everyone young is going down 'the long slide' to happiness. The narrator argues that his own elders must have thought the same about him, who was granted freedom from the fear of Hellfire in the same way that the kids are granted freedom from the fear of pregnancy. But (and here comes the clincher) attaining either free-dom means no more than being lifted up to a high window, through which you see

> ... the deep blue air, that shows
> Nothing, and is nowhere, and is endless.

There is no doubt that the narrator is calling these callous sexual activities meaningless. What's open to doubt is whether the nar-rator believes what he is saying, or, given that he does, whether Larkin (wheels within wheels) believes the narrator. Later in the volume there is a poem called 'Annus Mirabilis' which clearly con-tradicts the argument of 'High Windows'.

> Sexual intercourse began
> In nineteen sixty-three
> (Which was rather late for me)—
> Between the end of the Chatterley ban
> And the Beatles' first LP.

Evincing an unexpected sensitivity to tone, Jake could well detect an ironic detachment here. To help him out, there is a suggestion, in the third stanza, that the new liberty was merely license.

> And every life became
> A brilliant breaking of the bank,
> A quite unlosable game.

It all links up with the bleak view of 'High Windows'. What Jake might not spot, however, is that it contrasts more than it compares. 'Annus Mirabilis' is a jealous poem—the fake-naïve rhythms are there for self-protection as much as for ironic detachment. Larkin can't help believing that sex and love ought by rights to have been easier things for his generation, and far easier for him personally. The feeling of having missed out on something is one of his pre-occupations. The thing Balokowsky needs to grasp is that Larkin is not criticizing modern society from a position of superiority. Over the range of his poetry, if not always in individual poems, he is very careful to allow that these pleasures might very well be thought meaningful. That he himself finds them meaningless might have something to do with himself as well as the state of the world. To the reader who has Larkin's poetry by heart, no poet seems more open. Small wonder that he finds it simply incomprehensible when critics discuss his lack of emotion. Apart from an outright yell for help, he has sent every distress signal a shy man can.

'The Old Fools'—even the ex-editor of the *Listener* blew his cool over that one, billing it as 'marvellous' on the paper's mast-head. And marvellous it is, although very scarey. There is a pronounced technical weakness in the first stanza. It is all right to rhyme 'remember' with 'September' if you make it quite clear why September can't be July. Does it mean that the Old Fools were in the Home Guard in September 1939? It's hard to know. Apart from that one point, though, the poem is utterly and distressingly explicit. Once again, the brutalism of the opening diction is a tip-off to the narrator's state of mind, which is, this time, fearful.

> What do they think has happened, the old fools,
> To make them like this? Do they somehow suppose
> It's more grown-up when your mouth hangs open and drools. . . .

Ill-suppressed anger. The crack about supposing 'it's more grown-up' is a copybook example of Larkin's ability to compact his intelligibility without becoming ambiguous. Supposing something to be 'more grown-up' is something children do: ergo, the Old Fools are like children—one of the poem's leading themes stated in a single locution.

Why aren't they screaming?

Leaving the reader to answer: because they don't know what's happening to them. The narrator's real fears—soon he switches to a personal 'you'—are for himself. The second stanza opens with an exultant lyrical burst: stark terror never sounded lovelier.

> At death, you break up: the bits that were you
> Start speeding away from each other for ever
> With no one to see. It's only oblivion, true:
> We had it before, but then it was going to end,
> And was all the time merging with a unique endeavour
> To bring to bloom the million-petalled flower
> Of being here.

The old, he goes on to suggest, probably live not in the here and now but 'where all happened once.' The idea takes some of its force from our awareness that that's largely where Larkin lives already—only his vision could lead to this death. The death is terrifying, but we would have to be like Larkin to share the terror completely. The reader tends to find himself shut out, glad that Larkin can speak so beautifully in his desperation but sorry that he should see the end in terms of his peculiar loneliness. There is always the edifying possibility, however, that Larkin is seeing the whole truth and the reader's defence mechanisms are working full blast.

If they are, 'The Building' will quickly break them down. Here, I think, is the volume's masterpiece—an absolute chiller, which I find myself getting by heart despite a pronounced temperamental aversion. The Building is the house of death, a Dantesque hell-hole— one thinks particularly of *Inferno* V—where people 'at that vague age that claims/The end of choice, the last of hope' are sent to 'their appointed levels'. The ambience is standard modernist hum-drum:

paperbacks, tea, rows of steel chairs like an airport lounge. You can look down into the yard and see red brick, lagged pipes, traffic. But the smell is frightening. In time everyone will find a nurse beckoning to him. The dead lie in white rows somewhere above. This, says Larkin with an undeflected power unique even for him, is what it all really adds up to. Life is a dream and we awake to this reality.

> O world.
> Your loves, your chances, are beyond the stretch
> Of any hand from here! And so, unreal,
> A touching dream to which we all are lulled
> But wake from separately. In it, conceits
> And self-protecting ignorance congeal
> To carry life. . . .

There is no point in disagreeing with the man if that's the way he feels, and he wouldn't write a poem like 'The Building' if he didn't feel that way to the point of daemonic possession. He himself is well aware that there are happier ways of viewing life. It's just that he is incapable of sharing them, except for fleeting moments— and the fleeting moments do not accumulate, whereas the times in between them do. The narrator says that 'nothing contravenes/The coming dark'. It's an inherently less interesting proposition than its opposite, and a poet forced to devote his creative effort to embodying it has only a small amount of space to work in. Nor, within the space, is he free from the paradox that his poems will become part of life, not death. From that paradox, we gain. The desperation of 'The Building' is like the desperation of Leopardi, disconsolate yet doomed to being beautiful. The advantage which accrues is one of purity— a hopeless affirmation is the only kind we really want to hear when we feel, as sooner or later everybody must, that life is a trap.

There is no certain way of separating Larkin's attitude to society from his conception of himself, but to the extent that you can, he seems to be in two minds about what the world has come to. He thinks, on the one hand, that it's probably all up; and on the other hand that youth still has a chance. On the theme of modern life being an unmitigated and steadily intensifying catastrophe he reads like his admired Betjeman in a murderous mood—no banana blush or cheery telly teeth, just a tight-browed disdain and a toxic line of invective. 'Going, Going' is particularly instructive here. In 'How Distant' we hear about

> ... the departure of young men
> Down valleys, or watching
> The green shore past the salt-white cordage
> Rising and falling

Between the 'fraying cliffs of water' (always a good sign when there's a lot of water about) the young adventurers used to sail, in the time of what we might call *genuine newness*. Larkin's objections to modern innovation are centred on its lack of invention—it's all fatally predictable. Jimmy Porter was nostalgic for the future. Larkin is anticipatory about the past. He longs for the time when youth meant the possibility of a new start.

> This is being young,
> Assumption of the startled century
> Like new store clothes,
> The huge decisions printed out by feet
> Inventing where they tread,
> The random windows conjuring a street.

The implication being that the time of adventure is long over. But in 'Sad Steps', as the poet addresses the Moon, youth is allowed some hope.

> One shivers slightly, looking up there.
> The hardness and the brightness and the plain
> Far-reaching singleness of that wide stare
>
> Is a reminder of the strength and pain
> Of being young; that it can't come again,
> But is for others undiminished somewhere.

An elegantly cadenced admission that his own view of life might be neurotic, and excellent fuel for Jake's chapter on the dialectical element in Larkin in which it is pointed out that his poems are judiciously disposed in order to illuminate one another, Yeats-style. The Sun and Moon, like Water, bring out Larkin's expansiveness, such as it is. It's there, but you couldn't call it a bear-hug. Time is running out, as we hear in the wonderfully funny *Vers de Société*:

> Only the young can be alone freely.
> The time is shorter now for company,

And sitting by a lamp more often brings
Not peace, but other things.

Visions of The Building, for example.

The book ends on an up-beat. Its next to last poem, 'Show Saturday', is an extended, sumptuous evocation of country life ('Let it always be there') which has the effect of making the rural goings-on so enviably cosy that the reader feels almost as left out as the narrator. The final piece is an eery lyric called 'The Explosion', featuring the ghosts of miners walking from the sun towards their waiting wives. It is a superb thought superbly expressed, and Larkin almost believes in it, just as in 'An Arundel Tomb' (the closing poem of *The Whitsun Weddings*) he almost believed in the survival of love. Almost believing is all right, once you've got believing out of it. But faith itself is extinct. Larkin loves and inhabits tradition as much as Betjeman does, but artistically he had already let go of it when others were only just realizing it was time to cling on. Larkin is the poet of the void. The one affirmation his work offers is the possibility that when we have lost everything the problem of beauty will still remain. It's enough.

(*Encounter*, June, 1974)

(ii) SMALLER AND CLEARER

Philip Larkin once told Philip Oakes—in a *Sunday Times* Magazine profile which remains one of the essential articles on its subject—how he was going to be a novelist, until the novels stopped coming. First there was *Jill* in 1946, and then there was *A Girl in Winter* in 1947, and after those there were to be several more. But they never arrived. So Philip Larkin became the leading poet who once wrote a brace of novels, just as his friend Kingsley Amis became the leading novelist who occasionally writes poems: the creative labour was divided with the customary English decorum, providing the kind of simplified career-structures with which literary history prefers to deal.

It verges on the unmannerly to raise the point, in Larkin's case, that the novels were in no sense the work of someone who had still to find his vocation. Chronology insists that they were written at a time when his verse had not yet struck its tone—*The North Ship*, Larkin's mesmerized submission to Yeats, had only recently been published, and of *The Less Deceived*, his first mature collection, barely half the constituent poems had as yet been written. But the novels had struck *their* tone straight away. It is only now, by hindsight, that they seem to point forward to the poetry. Taken in their chronology, they are impressively mature and self-sufficient. If Larkin had never written a line of verse, his place as a writer would still have been secure. It would have been a smaller place than he now occupies, but still more substantial than that of, say, Denton Welch, an equivalently precocious (though nowhere near as perceptive) writer of the same period.

The self-sufficient force of Larkin's two novels is attested to by the fact that they have never quite gone away. People serious in their admiration of Larkin's poetry have usually found themselves searching out at least one of them—most commonly *Jill*, to which Larkin prefixed, in the 1964 edition, an introduction that seductively evoked the austere but ambitious Oxford of his brilliant generation and in particular was creasingly funny about Amis. Unfortunately this preface (retained in the current paperback) implies, by its very retrospection, a status of obsolescence for the book itself. Yet the present reissue sufficiently proves that *Jill* needs no apologizing for. And *A Girl in Winter* is at least as good as *Jill* and in some departments conspicuously better. Either novel is guaranteed to jolt any reader who expects Larkin to look clumsy out of his bailiwick. There are times when Larkin *does* look that, but they usually happen when he tempts himself into offering a professional rule of thumb as an aesthetic principle—a practice which can lay him open to charges of cranky insularity. None of that here. In fact quite the other thing: the novels are at ease with a range of sympathies that the later poems, even the most magnificent ones, deal with only piecemeal, although with incomparably more telling effect.

Considering that Evelyn Waugh began a comic tradition in the modern novel which only lately seems in danger of dying out, and considering Larkin's gift for sardonic comedy—a gift which by all accounts decisively influenced his contemporaries at Oxford—it is remarkable how non-comic his novels are, how completely they do not fit into the family of talents which includes Waugh and Powell and Amis. *Jill* employs many of the same properties as an Oxford novel by the young Waugh—the obscure young hero is casually destroyed by his socially superior contemporaries—but the treatment is unrelievedly sad. Larkin's hero has none of the inner strength which Amis gave Jim Dixon. Nor is there any sign of the Atkinson figures who helped Jim through the tougher parts of the maze. Young John comes up to Oxford lost and stays lost: he is not a symbol of his social condition so much as an example of how his social condition can amplify a handicap—shy ordinariness—into tragedy. All the materials of farce are present and begging to be used, but tragedy is what Larkin aims for and what he largely achieves.

The crux of the matter is John's love for Jill—a thousand dreams and one kiss. Jill is a clear forecast of the Larkin dream-girl in the poems. But if John is Larkin, he is hardly the Larkin we know to have dominated his generation at Oxford. He is someone much closer to the author's central self, the wounded personality whose deprivation has since been so clearly established in the poems. What is remarkable, however (and the same thing is remarkable about the poems, but rarely comes into question), is the way in which the hero's desolation is viewed in its entirety by the author. The author sees the whole character from without. The novel does something which very few novels by 21-year-old writers have ever done. It distances autobiographical material and sets events in the global view of mature personality.

As if to prove the point, *A Girl in Winter* is a similar story of callow love, but seen from the girl's angle. The book perfectly catches the way a young woman's emotional maturity outstrips a young man's. Katherine, a young European grappling with England (an inversion of the Larkin-Amis nightmare in which the Englishman is obliged to grapple with Europe), is morally perceptive—sensitive would be the right word if it did not preclude robustness—to an unusual degree, yet Larkin is able to convince us that she is no freak. While still an adolescent she falls in love with her English pen-pal, Robin, without realizing that it is Robin's sister, Jane, who is really interested in her. Time sorts out the tangle, but just when Katherine has fallen out of love Robin shows up on the off-chance of sleeping with her. Katherine quells his importunity with a few apposite remarks likely to make any male reader sweat from the palms, although finally she sleeps with him because it's less trouble than not to. Yet Katherine is allowed small comfort in her new maturity.

The book is as disconsolate as its predecessor, leaving the protagonist once again facing an unsatisfactory prime.

A contributory grace in both novels, but outstanding in A *Girl in Winter*, is the sheer quality of the writing. Larkin told Oakes that he wrote the books like poems, carefully eliminating repeated words. Fastidiousness is everywhere and flamboyance non-existent: the touch is unfaltering. Katherine 'could sense his interest turning towards her, as a blind man might sense the switching on of an electric fire'. Figures of speech are invariably as quiet and effective as that. The last paragraphs of A *Girl in Winter* have something of the cadenced elegance you find at the close of *The Great Gatsby*.

Why, if Larkin could write novels like these, did he stop? To hindsight the answer is easy: because he was about to become the finest poet of his generation, instead of just one of its best novelists. A more inquiring appraisal suggests that although his aesthetic effect was rich, his stock of events was thin. In a fictional texture featuring a sore tooth and a fleeting kiss as important strands Zen diaphanousness always threatened. (What is the sound of *one* flower being arranged?) The master lyric poet, given time, will eventually reject the idea of writing any line not meant to be remembered. Larkin, while being to no extent a dandy, is nevertheless an exquisite. It is often the way with exquisites that they graduate from full-scale prentice constructions to small-scale works of entirely original intensity, having found a large expanse limiting. Chopin is not too far-fetched a parallel. Larkin's two novels are like Chopin's two concertos: good enough to promise not merely more of the same but a hitherto unheard-of distillation of their own lyrical essence.

(*New Statesman*, 21 March 1975)

(iii) YEATS *v.* HARDY IN DAVIE'S LARKIN

In recent months Philip Larkin, based as always in Hull, and Donald Davie, back in Europe from California, have been conducting a restrained slugging-match concerning Larkin's fidelity to the *locus classicus* in modern times, as defined—or distorted, if you are of Professor Davie's persuasion—in *The Oxford Book of Twentieth-Century English Verse*. Important issues have been raised, and it will be some time before any keeper of the peace will be able to still them.

The time is propitious for an assessment of Professor Davie's *Thomas Hardy and British Poetry*, which in a normal climate might be politely—and erroneously—half-praised as a well-bred squib, but for the duration of hostilities demands to be regarded as live, heavy-calibre ammunition.

Professor Davie is a poet of importance—of such importance, indeed that his academic title can safely be set aside for the remainder of this article—and from poets of importance we want works of criticism that are less safe than strange. There is nothing safe about this volume, and a lot that is strange. *Thomas Hardy and British Poetry* is a surprisingly odd book, but it is also a considerable one. In fact, the forces ranged against each other in the current squabble can now be said to be more evenly matched than might at first appear.

A good part of the secret of what Larkin really thinks about art is distributed through the pages of *All What Jazz?*, and if you want to take the weight of Larkin's aesthetic intelligence, it is to that collection (and not so much to his so-far uncollected criticisms of poetry in the magazine *Listen*, although they count) that you must go. On the Davie side, we are given, in this new book, a view of his thought which is at the very least as luminous as the one made available in *Ezra Pound: Poet as Sculptor*. When Davie talks about Hardy he sounds like Larkin talking about jazz. To put it crudely, on their pet subjects they both talk turkey. But this doesn't mean that either man makes himself plain. Larkin worships Bix Beiderbecke and deplores Charlie Parker, believing that Parker destroyed with arid intellectualism the art to which Beiderbecke contributed by lyrical instinct. Conveying this distinction, Larkin apparently makes himself clear; but it would be a suicidally foolish critic who thought that such a distinction could be used unexamined as a light on Larkin's poetry. In poetry, Larkin is Beiderbecke and Parker combined: his criticism chooses sides among elements which are in balance within his complex creative personality. Similarly with Davie: his critical position calls for an even more cautious probing, since he is less aware of self-contradictions by the exact measure that he is more receptive to Literary influence. *Thomas Hardy and British Poetry* raises confusion to the level of criticism: it is a testament to Britain's continuing fertility as an intellectual acreage in which ideas will flourish at rigour's expense, the insights blooming like orchids while the valid syllogisms wither on the vine.

c

Davie starts by proposing Hardy as a more important influence than Yeats on the poetry of this century. The distinction between *is* and *ought* is not firmly made, with the result that we spend a lot of our time wondering whether Hardy has been the big influence all along, or merely should have been. 'But for any poet who finds himself in the position of choosing between the two masters', Davie says, 'the choice cannot be fudged; there is no room for compromise.' The reason why there is no room for compromise is not made as clear as the ordinary reader might require. 'Hardy', it is said, 'has the effect of locking any poet whom he influences into the world of historical contingency, a world of specific places at specific times.' Yeats, apparently, doesn't have this effect: he transcends the linear unrolling of recorded time and attains, or attempts to attain, the visionary. Davie says that the reader can delight in both these approaches, but that the writer has to choose. It is difficult, at first, to see why the writer can't employ the same combinative capacity as the reader. Difficult at first, and just as difficult later.

The other important thing happening at the beginning of the book concerns Larkin. Davie mentions Larkin's conversion from Yeats to Hardy after *The North Ship* in 1946, thus tacitly proposing from the start that Larkin was doing the kind of severe choosing which Davie asserts is essential. Neither at this initial point, nor later on when Larkin is considered at length, is the possibility allowed that Yeats's influence might have lingered on alongside, or even been compounded with, Hardy's influence. One realizes with unease that Davie has not only enjoyed the preface to the re-issue of *The North Ship*, he has been utterly convinced by it: instead of taking Larkin's autobiographical scraps as parables, he is treating them as the realities of intellectual development. Larkin conjures up a young mind in which Hardy drives out Yeats, and Davie believes in it.

But Davie's main comments about Larkin are postponed until some sturdy ground-work has been put in on Hardy. We are told that Hardy's technique is really engineering, and that he is paying a formal tribute to Victorian technology by echoing its precisioned virtuosity. A little later on we find that Davie doesn't wholly approve of this virtuosity, and is pleased when the unwavering succession of intricately formed, brilliantly matched stanzas is allowed to break down—as in 'The Voice', where, we are assured, it breaks down under pressure of feeling.

A crucial general point about technique has bulkily arisen, but Davie miraculously succeeds in failing to notice it. At one stage he is almost leaning against it, when he says that Hardy was usually 'highly skilled indeed but disablingly modest', or even 'very ambitious technically, and unambitious every other way.' For some reason it doesn't occur to Davie that having made these admissions he is bound to qualify his definition of technique in poetry. But not only does he not qualify it—he ups the stakes. Contesting Yeats's insistence that Hardy lacked technical accomplishment, Davie says that 'In sheer *accomplishment*, especially of prosody, Hardy beats Yeats hands down' (his italics). Well, it's a poser. Yeats's critical remark about Hardy doesn't matter much more than any other of Yeats's critical remarks about anybody, but Davie's rebuttal of it matters centrally to his own argument. He is very keen to set Yeats and Hardy off against each other: an opposition which will come in handy when he gets to Larkin. But keenness must have been bordering on fervour when he decided that Hardy had Yeats beaten technically in every department except something called 'craft'— which last attribute, one can be forgiven for thinking, ought logically to take over immediately as the main subject of the book.

Davie argues convincingly that we need to see below the intricate surface form of Hardy's poems to the organic forms beneath. But he is marvellously reluctant to take his mind off the technical aspects of the surface form and get started on the problem of what technical aspects the organic form might reasonably be said to have. 'We must learn to look through apparent symmetry to the real asymmetry beneath.' We certainly must, and with Hardy Davie has. But what Davie has not learnt to see is that with Yeats the symmetry and asymmetry are the same thing—that there is no distance between the surface form and the organic form, the thing being both all art and all virtuosity at the same time. Why, we must wonder, is Davie so reluctant to see Yeats as the formal master beside whom Hardy is simply an unusually interesting craftsman? But really that is a rephrasing of the same question everybody has been asking for years: the one about what Davie actually means when he praises Ezra Pound as a prodigious technician. Is it written in the stars that Donald Davie, clever in so many others matters, will go to his grave being obtuse in this? Why can't he see that the large, argued Yeatsian strophe is a technical achievment thoroughly dwarfing not only Pound's imagism but also Hardy's tricky stanzas?

Davie is continually on the verge of finding Hardy deficient as a working artist, but circumvents the problem by calling him a marvellous workman whose work tended to come out wrong for other reasons. In 'During Wind and Rain' he detects a 'wonderfully fine ear', which turns out to be a better thing than 'expertise in prosody'—the wonderfully fine ear being 'a human skill' and not just a 'technical virtuosity'. It ought to follow that knowing how to get the ear working while keeping the virtuosity suppressed is of decisive importance to poetic technique. It ought to follow further that because Hardy couldn't do this—because he wasn't even aware there was a conflict—he spent a lot of his time being at odds with himself as a poet. What Davie is struggling to say is that Hardy wasn't enough of an artist to make the best of the art that was in him. But the quickness of the pen deceives the brain, and Davie manages to say everything but that.

The strictures Davie *does* put on Hardy are harsh but inscrutable. There is in Hardy a 'crucial selling-short of the poetic vocation'. In the last analysis, we learn, Hardy, unlike Pound and Pasternak (and here Yeats, Hopkins and Eliot also get a mention), doesn't give us a transformed reality—doesn't give us entry 'into a world that is truer and more real than the world we know from statistics or scientific induction or common sense'. This stricture is inscrutable for two main reasons. First, Hardy spent a lot of his time establishing a version of reality in which, for example, lovers could go on being spiritually joined together after death: nothing scientific about that. Second, even if he had not been at pains to establish such a version of reality—even if his themes had been resolutely mundane—his poetry, if successful, would have done it for him. In saying that Hardy's poetry doesn't transform statistical, scientific reality, Davie is saying that Hardy hasn't written poetry at all.

It should be obvious that Davie, while trying to praise Hardy as an artist, is actually diminishing him in that very department. Less obviously, he is also diminishing art. To look for a life-transforming theme, surely, is as self-defeating as to look for a life-enhancing one. Good poetry transforms and enhances life *whatever it says*. That is one of the reasons why we find it so special. In this case, as in so many others, one regrets the absence in English literary history of a thoroughly nihilistic poet. The Italians had Leopardi, who in hating existence could scarcely be said to have been kidding. Faced with his example, they were obliged at an early date to realize that there is poetry which can deny a purpose to life and yet still add to its point.

Larkin, Davie insists, follows Hardy and not Yeats. 'Larkin has testified to that effect repeatedly', he announces, clinching the matter. Yeats's influence was 'a youthful infatuation'. The ground is well laid for a thorough-going misunderstanding of Larkin on every level, and after a few back-handed compliments ('The narrowness of range . . . might seem to suggest that he cannot hear the weight of significance that I want to put on him, as the central figure in English poetry over the past twenty years'—narrowness of range as compared with whom? With people who write worse?) Davie buckles down to the task.

Hardy, we have already learnt, was neutral about industrialism because his technique mirrored it: his skill as a constructor implicated him. With Larkin it is otherwise. Larkin can feel free to hate industrialism because he has no special sense of himself as a technician: 'The stanzaic and metrical symmetries which he mostly aims at are achieved skilfully enough, but with none of that bristling expertise of Hardy which sets itself, and surmounts, intricate technical challenge.'

By this stage of the book it is no longer surprising, just saddening, that Davie can't draw the appropriate inferences from his own choice of words. Being able to quell the bristle and find challenges other than the kind one sets oneself—isn't that the true skill? The awkward fact is that unless we talk about diction, and get down to the kind of elementary stylistic analysis which would show how Larkin borrowed Hardy's use of, say, hyphenated compounds, then it is pretty nearly impossible to trace Larkin's technical debt to Hardy. Not that Davie really tries. But apart from understandably not trying that, Davie clamorously doesn't try to find out about Larkin's technical debt to Yeats. And the inspiration for the big, matched stanzas of 'The Whitsun Weddings' is not in Hardy's 'intricacy' but in the rhetorical majesty of Yeats. In neglecting to deal with that inspiration, Davie limits his meaning of the word 'technique' to something critically inapplicable. Technically, Larkin's heritage is a combination of Hardy and Yeats—it can't possibly be a substitution of the first by the second. The texture of Larkin's verse is all against any such notion.

Mistaking Larkin's way of working is a mere prelude to mistaking his manner of speaking, and some thunderous misreadings follow as a consequence. In Larkin, we are told, 'there is to be no historical perspective, no measuring of present against past'. Applied to the author of 'An Arundel Tomb', this assertion reminds us of the old Stephen Potter ploy in which a reviewer selected the characteristic for which an author was most famous and then attacked him for not having enough of it.

According to Davie, Larkin is a Hardyesque poet mainly in the sense that he, too, 'may have sold poetry short'. With Larkin established as such a baleful influence, the problem becomes how to 'break out of the greyly constricting world of Larkin'. Davie enlists the poetry of Charles Tomlinson to help us do this, but it might have been more useful to linger awhile and ask if Larkin isn't already doing a good deal by himself to help us get clear of his dreary mire—by going on writing, that is, with the kind of intensity which lit up the gloom and made us notice him in the first place. Here again, and ruinously, Davie is dealing in every reality except the realities of art. He cannot or will not see that Larkin's grimness of spirit is not by itself the issue. The issue concerns the gratitude we feel for such a grimness of spirit producing such a beauty of utterance.

Near the end of the book, Davie draws a useful distinction between poets and prophets. The prophet is above being fair-minded: the poet is not. The poet helps to shape culture, with which the prophet is at war. Prophetic poetry is necessarily an inferior poetry.

To this last point one can think of exceptions, but generally all this is well said, and leaves the reader wondering why Davie did not then go back and find something centrally and vitally praiseworthy in the limitations of the Hardy tradition. Because it is the Hardy tradition which says that you can't be entirely confident of knowing everything that reality contains, let alone of transcending it. The Hardy tradition is one of a mortal scale. It does not hail the superhuman. As Larkin might put it, it isn't in the exaltation business. That is the real point which Davie has worriedly been half-making all along. In a striking way, Thomas Hardy and British Poetry is an eleventh-hour rejection of Davie's early gods. Somewhere in there among the dust and hubbub there is a roar of suction indicating that the air might soon be cleared.

(T.L.S., 13 July 1973)

(iv) THE NORTH WINDOW

To stay, as Mr. Larkin stays, back late
Checking accessions in the Brynmor Jones
Library (the clapped date-stamp, punch-drunk, rattling,
The sea-green tinted windows turning slate,
The so-called Reading Room deserted) seems
A picnic at first blush. No Rolling Stones
Manqués or Pink Floyd simulacra battling
Their way to low-slung pass-marks head in hands:
Instead, unpeopled silence. Which demands

Reverence, and calls nightly like bad dreams
To make sure that that happens. Here he keeps
Elected frith, his thanedom undespited,
Ensconced against the mating-mandrill screams
Of this week's Students' Union Gang-Bang Sit-in,
As wet winds scour the Wolds. The Moon-cold deeps
Are cod-thronged for the trawlers now benighted,
Far North. The inland cousin to the sail-maker
Can still bestride the boundaries of the way-acre,

The barley-ground and furzle-field unwritten
Fee simple failed to guard from Marks and Spencer's
Stock depot some time back. (Ten years, was it?)
Gull, lapwing, redshank, oyster-catcher, bittern
(Yet further out: sheerwater, fulmar, gannet)
Police his mud-and-cloud-ashlared defences.
Intangible revetments! On deposit,
Chalk thick below prevents the Humber seeping
Upward to where he could be sitting sleeping,

So motionless he lowers. Screwed, the planet
Swivels towards its distant, death-dark pocket
He opens out his notebook at a would-be
Poem, ashamed by now that he began it.
Grave-skinned with grief, such Hardy-hyphened diction,
Tight-crammed as pack ice, grates. What keys unlock it?
It's *all gone wrong.* Fame isn't as it should be—

No, nothing like. 'The town's not been the same'
He's heard slags whine, 'since Mr. Larkin came.'

Sir John arriving with those science-fiction
Broadcasting pricks and bitches didn't help.
And those Jap Ph.Ds, their questionnaires!
(Replying 'Sod off, Slant-Eyes' led to friction.)
He conjures envied livings less like dying:
Sharp cat-house stomp and tart-toned, gate-mouthed yelp
Of Satchmo surge undulled, dispersing cares
Thought reconvenes. In that way She would kiss,
The Wanted One. But other lives than this—

Fantastic. Pages spread their blankness. Sighing,
He knuckles down to force-feed epithets.
Would Love have eased the joints of his iambs?
He can't guess, and by now it's no use trying.
A sweet ache spreads from cramp-gripped pen to limb:
The stanza next to last coheres and sets.
As rhyme and rhythm, tame tonight like lambs,
Entice him to the standard whirlwind finish,
The only cry no distances diminish

Comes hurtling soundless from Creation's rim
Earthward—the harsh *recitativo secco*
Of spaces between stars. He hears it sing,
That voice of utmost emptiness. To him.
Declaring he has always moved too late,
And hinting, its each long-lost blaze's echo
Lack-lustre as a Hell-bent angel's wing,
That what—as if he needed telling twice—
Comes next makes this lot look like Paradise.

(T.L.S., 26 July 1974)

4. Supplier of Verses: John Betjeman

Collections of John Betjeman's verse don't change, they merely become more appropriate. Betjeman poems have always watched the old England die, the self age, believed fearlessly in the gentle virtues and tremulously in salvation. Neither his earlier nor his later work has required to be falsified in order to achieve such remarkable consistency. Betjeman was simply born old, thereby ruling out the prospect of immaturity; or else is still infantile, with maturity never to arrive; or perhaps both. The co-existence of sage and toddler keeps predictability at bay. The only risk he has run as an artist is of being repetitive.

Everything in *A Nip in the Air* has occurred before. But still the ambiguities linger, making the best loved and most cuddly of Poets Laureate a permanent oddball. Familiarity is deceptive, although very familiar. Really he was already By Appointment in the Thirties, as in 'Death of King George V' from *Continual Dew*:

> Spirits of well-shot woodcock, partridge, snipe
> Flutter and bear him up the Norfolk sky . . .

While Edward landed hatless from the air on the runway hemmed in by a new suburb. Material change threatened the fruitful continuities. The voice of the old middle class was calling on the aristocracy to conserve its ways, and still is: the poems to Charles and Anne in this volume were written by a born monarchist, not a convert. The disappearing social order whose details he so lovingly records was the only certain good. Modernism holds no place for his kind. It would be—well, it is—a message acceptable to any thinking Tory. Opportunistic rapacity has done for the old order. But it is only lately, at the eleventh hour, that Betjeman has begun to examine the possibility of the old middle class and the new rapists being close kin. It would be a subversive conclusion to most of what he has always said, so it is no surprise that the conclusion is not quite reached. But 'County' is still an unusually abrasive effort:

c*

> God save me from the Porkers,
>   God save me from their sons
> Their noisy tweedy sisters
>   Who follow with the guns ...

Porker is a *faux-bonhomme* and dull with it, evading taxes while blasting the pheasants. He is all pedigree and purse (and his womenfolk are worse). The Porkers set a bad example to the new rich. As the poet waxes wroth, the reader waxes stunned: it is unusual to find that the Porkers are not themselves new. For destruction to emanate from somewhere in the poet's own background is an odd concession from Betjeman. Perhaps the Porkers, without being really new, are yet newish. Anyway, the matter is not pursued beyond that, and for most of the volume the villains are the planners and communicators we have come to know and loathe.

In 'Executive' the hero is a peach of his genus. Essentially he integrates, and is basically viable. He does some 'mild developing' on the side. And Rex, the P.R.O. of 'Shattered Image', is a trapped paedophil who finds his fellow smoothies dumping him. The new, usurping middle class doesn't pull together except for advantage. They find their unity in legalized vandalism, creating nothing but a wilderness, in which the disinherited working class aimlessly sheds litter. The caravans of the milling proles jam the shoreline and the wrappings of their potato crisps non-biodegradably choke the surf.

'Let us keep what is left of the London we knew,' Betjeman sighs in 'Meditation on a Constable Picture', but by now he is more resigned than desperate. We remember that in his superlative television programme on Metroland he had already half-waved his goodbye to England. Much of the energy has gone out of his theme: a poignant mark of the enemy's triumph. But for the greater part of his creative life the urge to preserve supplied him with his most important creative impulse. To him and the few writers in his league, the onset of chaos meant the necessity of turning recollection into art. For some time yet it will be an act of critical daring to call Betjeman or Osbert Lancaster anything more lofty than exquisite, but in fact they have transmuted a fleeting reality into a tangible fiction during the moment of its vanishing, and when the vanishing is completed will be easily seen to have performed a service.

Not that they didn't enjoy performing it. The younger Betjeman elegantly lamented an old building even when it was still upright. In 'On Seeing An Old Poet In The Café Royal' from *Old Lights for New Chancels* he wept delightedly for smells gone by—'Scent of Tutti-Frutti-Sen-Sen/And cheroots upon the floor'. But apart from the lamps, not much about the place had changed. It was just that the people were gone. Betjeman would still have been nostalgic if not a single gasolier had ever been uprooted anywhere in the realm. He is cast back neurotically. His macaronic threnodies, crowded with the names of things remembered, are charms, like the coincidental gatherings of characters in Anthony Powell.

Self-revelation has come slowly in Betjeman's work and there are still many puzzles for those of us not in the know. But in the aggregate of his lyrics—and more clearly than in the avowedly autobiographical *Summoned by Bells*—we can by now clearly see the bitter heritage of his early traumata. Whatever the wounds were, they left him nuzzling his woolly bear for ever, while yearning for that most engulfing of all women, the Betjeman Girl. She survives in this new book as Laurelie Williams, Queen of the Hunt Ball, but her strapping reign of glory started early on. In *Old Lights for New Chancels* she was Pam, the 'great big mountainous sports girl' with the hairy arms, or else Myfanwy, the bikey, dikey Valkyrie, 'chum to the weak'. In *New Bats in Old Belfries* she was Joan Hunter Dunn, the horny-handed tennis-girl of 'A Subaltern's Love-song', who returned, still in those redolent white shorts, as Bonzo Trouncer in *Selected Poems*. In *A Few Late Chrysanthemums* she was equipped with 'the strongest legs in Pontefract' and made yet another appearance as a tennis champ—'The Olympic Girl' who stared down from a great height and whose racket he would like to have been, so as 'to be press'd/With hard excitement to her breast'. (Of girl cyclists he is on record as desiring to be the saddle.) All this is poised, distanced, suave and funny, but you can see very clearly the regressive hurt.

'You're to be booted. Hold him steady chaps!' The childhood memory was one of the late chrysanthemums. He was slow to take revenge, never quite realizing that it was his class-mates, in both senses, who had a mission to rip up his world. Betjeman puzzled at the inscrutable doings of the *hoi polloi* formiculating in 'the denser suburbs' but never faced the genuine paradox of a civilized order hastening its own ruin. He identified himself with a class at a time when it was not yet fully clear that the class would fail to identify itself with him. They would buy his books while tearing down anything beautiful that stood in their way. Betjeman's audience *are* the developers. He was, from the beginning, in a historical fix. From *Selected Poems* onwards, the apocalypse began to roll in—the sea, which will send its waves for centuries to come, 'when England is not England'.

The sea, 'consolingly disastrous', recurred in his poetry all through the Fifties and is loud in this volume, rustling with campers' jetsam. Betjeman doesn't see a future: he is elegiac to the end of the line—elegiac where his admirer Larkin is tragic, since at least Betjeman is longing for an existence he once led. The past is gone and the future is not worth having—it would be a hell of a message if message were all there was. But the poetry is a cornucopia of cherished things, and the pessimism is all too easily traceable to its author's personality. He fears the loss of his life as he feared the loss of his way of life—he feels unprotected. Death is all through this new book but it was all through the old books too, as vivid as the sadistic threats of his bent nursery-maid. He can be called light-minded only by the thick-witted, and this remains true even though the well-placed find him comforting.

(*New Statesman*, 22 November 1974)

5. Kenneth Slessor's Importance

With all that matters of him occupying no more than two not very bulky volumes—one of verse, called *Poems*, another of prose, called *Bread and Wine*—Kenneth Slessor nevertheless continues to be one of the really substantial Australian poets. Substantial and, beyond that, promising even more: hinting towards greatness. He lived his full three score and ten years and died five years ago, yet somehow seemed still to be only on the verge of accomplishing what was in him.

Slessor's was a remarkable gift. Between Christopher Brennan, for whom the claims made are usually too high but whose individuality was unmistakable, and A. D. Hope, who was an international poet from the beginning even though resolutely chauvinistic, Slessor's is the bridging talent. He raised all the problems about the relationship of the Australian poet to European culture. He never found Hope's solutions but on the other hand he did not succumb to Brennan's neuroses: he wrote to the limits set for him by an insoluble dilemma, and then stopped. You cannot read his poems without pondering the might-have-beens. On the other hand, what he did achieve is of permanent value.

Graham Burns's little book *Kenneth Slessor* is a commendable introduction. Without presuming to answer it, Mr. Burns knows the abiding question about Slessor: why does his poetry so often suggest that the full force of his imagination has not been committed? It is easy to go overboard about Slessor's work, but finally it is more edifying to stay disenchanted, since a full appreciation of his achievement depends on realizing that to some extent it remained potential. Mr Burns is always ready to withhold astonishment, paying Slessor the larger tribute of treating him as an artist who was rather beyond the lyric poems he left us, even when those lyrics were masterpieces.

And masterpieces some of them are, even though generations of Australian schoolboys—it was already happening while Slessor was alive, to his great embarrassment—have been told to think so. Slessor's language at its easy height has an unforced richness, an understated but pervasive musicality, that must be any young poet's ideal. 'Five Bells', his most famous poem, has every kind of interest in its ambitious design, but the first thing that always strikes any sensitive reader is the confident originality of its local imagery, carried forward by a deceptively natural iambic pulse—quite literally unforgettable.

> You have no suburb, like those easier dead
> In private berths of dissolution laid—
> The tide goes over, the waves ride over you
> And let their shadows down like shining hair. . . .

Ducking under the breakers and watching their shadows on the sand below, there must have been scores of times in my student years when I recalled that last line. The first two lines might have been written by Wilfred Owen or indeed any latter-day Georgian who had learnt Owen's lessons, but that last idea is Slessor's very own, and seems to me even now to be expressed in the uniquely Australian language which so many Australian poets sought, and still seek, in vain.

'Australianness' has always been the philosopher's stone, or poet's stone, of Australian culture. Every means has been tried in order to attain it. Incomprehensible vocabularies composed of arcane references to flora, fauna and aboriginal folkways have burgeoned, withered and died. The arbitrary symbolism of the apocalyptic 1940s in British poetry was a miracle of tautness compared to its Australian equivalent, which had all that plus home-grown totemism. The aim has always been to make a fresh start free from the dragging weight of the European heritage.

Language is a continuity and in a continuity there can be no such thing as a fresh start, but for a long time the fact could not be faced—the nationalistic urge was too powerful. As Mr. Burns points out, Slessor managed to break free of this bind. His early poetry shows a certain amount of European culture being absorbed, without any doomed attempts at transcendence. Pretending in a dramatic monologue to be Heine, he sounds more like Browning, but even more than that he begins to sound like himself.

All kinds of influences are detectable (Mr. Burns might have mentioned Flecker, whose sickle moon surely provides the illumination on much of the early romanticism about the sea) but the important thing is that when Slessor turned towards Australian subjects he was already maturing beyond the self-destructive ambition to talk about them in a nationalist language. At first he strained for effect, trying to achieve it as most gifted (and all giftless) young poets do, by novelty of expression. But he soon grew out of that, to the point where his originality of diction emerged naturally out of his originality of observation—the desirable order of events, since if originality of diction is the first aim then originality of observation tends not to happen, being usurped by mannerist posturings.

Slessor began as a King's Cross bohemian who worshipped Norman Lindsay and ended as a leader writer for *The Daily Telegraph*, a newspaper of stridently conservative views. It was not a particularly distinguished intellectual record. He was never a scholar as Hope is a scholar. All the more extraordinary, then, that he should have surmounted his early pretensions, fighting his way free of them by creative instinct.

'Five Bells', 'Captain Dobbin'—most of Slessor's finest poems are about Sydney Harbour. Yet when we look into *Bread and Wine* we see that his prose on the same subject is at least as wealthy in vision, and often more so. His dispatches from El Alamein—war correspondence which far outstrips Hemingway's in the evocation of battle—make his anthology-piece poem about the war in the desert, 'Beach Burial', look a bit impoverished. The transfigurative potentiality of Slessor's poetry was never fully realized, perhaps because he was not notably interested in society as such—he was a lyric poet by the circumscription of his personality.

But over and above that consideration there is the fact that his full resources as a writer were for some reason held back from his poetry. When a poet's prose manifests qualities that his verse is starved of, we are entitled to suspect that he has not taken his final risks as an artist. Why Slessor did not take those risks is still something of a mystery, which Mr. Burns's pamphlet does not pretend to clear up. Ultimately, I am convinced, Slessor's diffidence had something to do with the uncertainty of his role as an Australian poet—a role which he was too intelligent to fulfil uncritically, but not intellectually formidable enough to transform. He lived it as a problem, and was restricted by it. Nevertheless he left us a generous legacy, which Mr. Burns is well qualified to discuss, although no educated man should ever use the expression 'life-style' except in jest.

(T.L.S., 9 April 1976)

6. The Poetry of Edmund Wilson

Apart from *Poets, Farewell!*, which was published in 1929 and has been unobtainable for most of the time since, the two main collections of Edmund Wilson's verse are *Note-Books of Night* and *Night Thoughts*. Of these, *Note-Books of Night* was published in America in 1942, took three years to cross the Atlantic (Secker & Warburg brought it out in May 1945) and has since become fairly unobtainable itself, although it is sometimes to be found going cheap in the kind of second-hand book shop that doesn't know much about the modern side. *Night Thoughts*, published in America in 1961 and in Britain a year later, is still the current collection. It regroups most of the work in *Note-Books of Night* into new sections, interspersing a good deal of extra matter, ranging from lyrics written in youth to technical feats performed in age. The final effect is to leave you convinced that although *Night Thoughts* is good to have, *Note-Books of Night* remains the definitive collection of Wilson's verse. Less inclusive, it is more complete.

Being that, it would be an interesting book even if Wilson's verse were negligible—interesting for the sidelight it threw on the mind of a great critic. But in fact Wilson's verse is far from negligible. Just because Wilson's critical work is so creative doesn't mean that his nominally creative work is a waste of time. Even without *Memoirs of Hecate County* and *I Thought of Daisy*, the mere existence of *Note-Books of Night* would be sufficient evidence that Wilson had original things to say as a writer. It is a deceptively substantial little book which looks like a slim volume only by accident. There are more than seventy pages of solid text, with something memorable on nearly every page. Thirty pages are given to prose fragments and the rest to poetry. It isn't major poetry, but some of it is very good minor poetry—and in an age of bad major poetry there is very little good minor poetry about.

Wilson was no shrinking violet, but he knew his limitations. He knew that his touch with language wasn't particularly suggestive so he went for precision instead. He possessed a lot of information to be precise with. Where his verse is excessive, it is the excess of the seed catalogue—a superfluity of facts. He never usurps the lyrical genius's prerogative of saying more than he knows. Nor did he ever consider himself talented enough to be formless—his formal decorum always reminds us that he stems from the early 20th-century America which in retrospect seems more confident than Europe itself about transmitting the European tradition. The work is all very schooled, neat, strict and assured. And finally there is his gift for parody, which sometimes led him beyond mere accomplishment and into the realm of inspiration. In 'The Omelet of A. MacLeish', for example, the talent of his verse is reinforced by the genius of his criticism, with results more devastating critically than his essays on the same subject, and more vivid poetically than his usual poems.

In *Note-Books of Night* the poems are arranged in no chronological scheme. From the rearrangement in *Night Thoughts* it is easier to puzzle out when he wrote what, but even then it is sometimes hard to be sure. Eventually there will be scholarly research to settle the matter, but I doubt if much of interest will be revealed touching Wilson's development as a writer of verse. After an early period devoted to plangent lyricism of the kind which can be called sophomoric as long as we remember that he was a Princeton sophomore and an exceptionally able one into the bargain, Wilson quickly entered into his characteristic ways of seeing the world. Like other minor artists he matured early and never really changed. Indeed he was writing verse in the thirties which forecast the mood of the prose he published in the early seventies, at the end of his life. The desolate yearning for the irretrievably lost America which makes *Upstate* so sad a book is already there in *Note-book of Night*, providing the authentic force behind the somewhat contrived Arnoldian tone of poems like 'A House of the Eighties'.

> —The ugly stained-glass window on the stair,
> Dark-panelled dining-room, the guinea fowl's fierce clack,
> The great gray cat that on the oven slept—
> My father's study with its books and birds,
> His scornful tone, his eighteenth-century words,
> His green door sealed with baize
> —Today I travel back
> To find again that one fixed point he kept
> And left me for the day

> In which this other world of theirs grows dank, decays,
> And founders and goes down.

Wilson's poetry of the thirties frequently deals with houses going to rack and ruin. The houses are in the same condition that we find them in forty years later, in *Upstate*. They are in the same places: Talcottville, Provincetown, Wilson's ancestral lands. Houses pointing to the solid old New England civilization which once found its space between the sea and the Adirondacks and was already being overtaken by progress when the poet was young. In his essays of the thirties (notably 'The Old Stone House' collected in *The American Earthquake*) Wilson wrote optimistically about an America 'forever on the move'. But if his essays were true to his then-radical intellect, his poetry was true to his conservative feelings. His dead houses are metaphors for a disappearing way of life.

> And when they found the house was bare
> The windows shuttered to the sun
> They woke the panthers with a stare
> To finish what they had begun

The poem is called 'Nightmare'. As we know from his great essay of 1937, 'In Honour of Pushkin' (collected in *The Triple Thinkers* and rightly called by John Bayley the best short introduction to Pushkin—a generous tribute, considering that Bayley has written the best long one) Wilson was particularly struck by the supreme poetic moment in *Evgeny Onegin* when Lensky is killed in a duel and his soulless body is compared to an empty house, with whitewashed windows. The image is one of the climactic points in all poetry—it is like Hector's address to Andromache, or Eurydice holding out her useless hands, or Paolo kissing Francesca's trembling mouth—so it is no wonder that Wilson should have been impressed by it. But you also can't help feeling that the image was congenial to his personal psychology. Although in books like *Europe Without Baedecker* Wilson did his best to secede from the weight of the European heritage, the fact always remained that by his education—by his magnificent education—and by his temperament he was inextricably committed to an American past which owed much of its civilized force to the European memory. This was the America which was dying all the time as he grew older. One of the several continuous mental struggles in Wilson is between his industrious loyalty to the

creative impulse of the new America and his despairing sense—
which made itself manifest in his poetry much earlier than in his
prose—that chaos could in no wise be staved off. The decaying houses
of his last books, with their cherished windows broken and highways
built close by, are all presaged in the poetry of his early maturity.

But in some respects maturity came too early. Coleridge, perhaps because he had trouble growing up, favoured a slow ripening
of the faculties. There was always something unsettling about the
precocity of Wilson's mimetic technique: his gift as a parodist was
irrepressibly at work even when he wanted it not to be, with the
result that his formally precise early lyrics tend towards pastiche—
they are throwbacks to the end of the century and beyond. The
tinge of Arnold in 'A House of the Eighties'—the pale echo of his
melancholy, long withdrawing roar—is compounded even there, it
seems to me, by memories of Browning. At other times you can hear
Kipling in the background. Wilson's attempts at plangent threnody
call up the voices of other men.

Wilson's elegaic lyrics are never less than technically adroit:
their high finish reminds us forcibly not only of the standards which
were imposed by Christian Gauss's Princeton (standards which we
can see otherwise in the poetry of John Peale Bishop) but of a whole
generation of American poets, now not much thought about, who
had complete command of their expressive means, even if they did
not always have that much to express. Edna St. Vincent Millay and
Elinor Wylie have by now retreated into the limbo of the semi-read—
Eleanor Farjeon and Ruth Pitter might be two comparable examples
from this side of the water—but when you look at the work of
Elinor Wylie, in particular, it is astonishing how accomplished she
was. Wilson's criticism helped American writing grow out of its
self-satisfaction at mere accomplishment, but he knew about the
certain losses as well as the possible gains. In his poetry he committed himself to the past by synthesizing its cherishable tones,
but he paid the penalty of mimetic homage in not sounding enough
like himself. In 'Disloyal Lines to an Alumnus' he satirized the
poetry of Beauty—

> And Beauty, Beauty, oozing everywhere
> Like maple-sap from maples! Dreaming there,
> I have sometimes stepped in Beauty on the street
> And slipped, sustaining bruises blue but sweet . . .

But his own lyric beauty was not different enough from the Beauty
he was satirizing. These lines from 'Riverton' take some swallowing
now and would have needed excuses even then.

> —O elms! O river! aid me at this turn—
> Their passing makes my late imperative:
> They flicker now who frightfully did burn,
> And I must tell their beauty while I live.
> Changing their grade as water in its flight,
> And gone like water; give me then the art,
> Firm as night-frozen ice found silver-bright,
> That holds the splendour though the days depart.

Give me then the art, indeed. He had the artifice, but the art was
mainly that of a pasticheur. When consumed by Yeats's business of
articulating sweet sounds together, Wilson was the master of every
poetic aspect except originality. Listen to the judiciously balanced
vowel-modulations in 'Poured full of thin gold sun':

> But now all this—
> Peace, brightness, the browned page, the crickets in the grass—
> Is but a crust that stretches thin and taut by which I pass
> Above the loud abyss.

A virtuoso is only ever fully serious when he forgets himself.
Wilson is in no danger of forgetting himself here. In his later
stages, which produced the technical games collected in *Night
Thoughts*, his urge to jump through hoops clearly detached itself
from the impulse to register feeling; but it should also be noted that
even early on the division existed. His penchant for sound effects,
like his ear for imitation, usually led him away from pure expression.
On occasions, however, when consciously schooled euphuistic bravura was lavished on a sufficiently concrete subject, Wilson got
away from tricksy pastoralism and achieved a personal tone—urban,
sardonic, tongue-in-cheek, astringent. The consonant-packed lines of
'Night in May'

> Pineapple-pronged four-poster of a Utica great-great

were a portent of what Wilson was able to do best. Such a line is
the harbinger of an entire, superb poem: 'On Editing Scott Fitz-

gerald's Papers', which first appeared in the preliminary pages of *The Crack-Up* and stands out in *Note-Books of Night* as a full, if regrettably isolated, realization of the qualities Wilson had to offer as a poet.

Speaking personally for a moment, I can only say that it was this poem, along with certain passages in Roy Campbell's bloody-minded satires, which first convinced me that the rhyming couplet of iambic pentameter was still alive as a form—that in certain respects it was *the* form for an extended poem. Wilson, like Campbell, by accepting the couplet's heritage of grandeur was able somehow to overcome its obsolescence: once the effect of archaic pastiche was accepted, there was room for any amount of modern freedom. In fact it was the fierce rigour of the discipline which made the freedom possible. And Wilson was more magnanimous than Campbell: his grandeur really *was* grandeur, not grandiloquence.

> Scott, your last fragments I arrange tonight. . . .

The heroic tone is there from the first line. (It is instructive, by the way, that only the tone is heroic: the couplets themselves are not heroic but Romance—i.e. open rather than closed.) It would have been a noble theme whatever form Wilson had chosen, because Wilson's lifelong paternal guardianship of Fitzgerald's talent is a noble story. Fitzgerald was the Princeton alumnus who *didn't* benefit from the education on offer. From Wilson's and Fitzgerald's letters to Christian Gauss we can easily see who was the star student and who the ineducable enthusiast. But Wilson, like Gauss, knew that Fitzgerald was destined to make his own way according to a different and more creative law. Wilson called *This Side of Paradise* a compendium of malapropisms but knew that it had not failed to live. When the masterpieces arrived he saw them clearly for what they were. Much of his rage against Hollywood was on Fitzgerald's behalf: he could see how the film world's sinister strength was diabolically attuned to Fitzgerald's fatal weakness. He understood and sympathized with Fitzgerald even in his most abject decline and guarded his memory beyond the grave.

Such a story would be thrilling however it was told. But the couplets are ideal for it: the elegaic and narrative strains match perfectly, while the meretricious, Condé Nast glamour of the imagery is entirely appropriate to Fitzgerald's debilitating regard for the high life—the well-heeled goings on to which, as Wilson well knew,

Fitzgerald sacrificed his soul but which he superseded with his talent.
Hence Wilson evokes the memory of Fitzgerald's eyes in terms of a
Vogue advertisement. Passing their image on to what they mint,
they

> . . . leave us, to turn over, iris-fired,
> Not the great Ritz-sized diamond you desired
> But jewels in a handful, lying loose :
> Flawed amethysts; the moonstone's milky blues;
> Chill blues of pale transparent tourmaline;
> Opals of shifty yellow, chartreuse green,
> Wherein a vein vermilion flees and flickers—
> Tight phials of the spirit's light mixed liquors;
> Some tinsel zircons, common turquoise; but
> Two emeralds, green and lucid, one half-cut,
> One cut consummately—both take their place
> In Letters' most expensive Cartier case.

The consummately cut emerald is obviously *The Great Gatsby*;
the half-cut emerald is probably *Tender Is The Night*; and we suppose that the tinsel zircons are the hack stories Fitzgerald turned out
in order to pay his bills. But apart from the admittedly preponder-
ant biographical element, what strikes you is the assured compression
of the technique. In lines like 'Tight phials of the spirit's light mixed
liquors' Wilson was forging a clear, vital utterance: that he was to
take it no further is a matter for regret. In this poem his complicated
games with language are confined within the deceptively simple
form and serve the purpose. Here is the public voice which Wilson
so admired (and by implication adumbrated for our own time) in the
artistry of Pushkin. In 'On Editing Scott Fitzgerald's Papers' his
playfulness, his seriousness, his severe humour and his sympathetic
gravitas are all in balance. The proof of Wilson's mainly fragmentary
achievement as a poet is the conspicuous force he attained on the
few occasions when his gifts were unified. The artist who is all
artist—the artist who, even when he is also a good critic, is nevertheless an artist first of all—can recognize this moment of unity
within himself and lives for nothing else but to repeat it. Wilson had
too many other interests: which, of course, it would be quixotic to
begrudge him.

There are other narrative poems by Wilson but they lack the
transforming discipline of the couplet. Similarly he has other

strong subjects—especially sex—but as with most revelations their interest has became with time more historical than aesthetic. Yet other poems are full of named things, but the names deafen the vision. Three different kinds of deficiency, all of them interesting.

The first deficiency is mainly one of form. Wilson's narrative poems are an attempt at public verse which certainly comes off better than comparable efforts by more recognized American poets. Nobody now could wade through Robinson Jeffers' *Roan Stallion*, for example. Wilson's 'The Good Neighbour' is the story of Mr and Mrs. Pritchard, who become obsessed with defending their house against invaders. Wilson guards against portentousness by casting the tale in hudibrastics, but the results, though very readable, are less popular than cute. The technique is too intrusive. Another narrative, 'The Woman, the War Veteran and the Bear', is an outrageous tale of a legless trapeze artist and a girl who married beneath her. It is full of interesting social detail but goes on too long: a glorified burlesque number that should have been a burlesque number. The stanzas are really ballad stanzas, but the poem wants to be more than a ballad. 'Lesbia in Hell' is better, but again the hudibrastics are the wrong form: they hurry you on too fast for thought and leave you feeling that the action has been skimped. Doubly a pity, because the theme of Satan falling in love with Lesbia involves Wilson in one of his most deeply felt subjects—sexual passion.

It still strikes the historically minded reader that *Note-Books of Night* is a remarkably sexy little book for its time. Wilson, we should remember, had a share in pioneering the sexual frankness of our epoch. *Memoirs of Hecate County* was a banned book in Australia when I was young. Wilson lived long enough to deplore pornographic licence but never went back on his liberal determination to speak of things as they were. Poems like 'Home to Town: Two Highballs' convey something of the same clinical realism about sex which made Wilson's prose fiction extraordinary and which still gives it better than documentary importance. In *Memoirs of Hecate County* Wilson drew a lasting distinction between the high society lady, who appealed to the narrator's imagination but left his body cold, and the low-born taxi-dancer who got on his nerves but fulfilled him sexually. The chippie seems to be there again in 'Two Highballs'.

And all the city love, intense and faint like you—
The little drooping breasts, the cigarettes,
The little cunning shadow between the narrow thighs. . . .

Paul Dehn, mentioning this passage when the poem was reprinted
in Night Thoughts, found it ridiculous, but I don't see why we
should agree. Wilson's attempts at a bitter urban poetry—

And the El that accelerates, grates, shrieks, diminishes,
        swishing, with such pain—
To talk the city tongue!

are at least as memorable, and certainly as frank about experience,
as the contorted flights of Hart Crane. Of Crane, when I search
my memory, I remember the seal's wide spindrift gaze towards Paradise and the bottles wearing him in crescents on their bellies. There
were things Crane could do that Wilson couldn't—the wine talons,
the sublime notion of travelling in a tear—but on the whole Wilson
did at least as good a job of reporting the city. And in matters of
sex he was more adventurous than anybody—ahead of his time, in
fact.

But if you are ahead of your time only in your subject, then
eventually you will fall behind the times, overtaken by the very
changes in taste you helped engender. So it is with Wilson's sexual
poetry: all the creativity goes into the act of bringing the subject
up, with no powers of invention left over for the task of transforming it into the permanence of something imagined. Ideally, Wilson's
sexual themes should have been a natural part of a larger poetic
fiction. But as we see in 'Copper and White' (not present in Note-
Books of Night, but Night Thoughts usefully adds it to the canon)
what they tended to blend with was greenery-yallery fin de siècle
lyricism.

I knew that passionate mouth in that pale skin
Would spread with such a moisture, let me in
To such a bareness of possessive flesh!—
I knew that fairest skin with city pallor faded,
With cigarettes and late electric light,
Would shield the fire to lash
The tired unblushing cheeks to burn as they did—
That mouth that musing seemed so thin,
Those cheeks that tired seemed so white!

It is as if Ernest Dowson and Lionel Johnson had been asked to versify Edith Wharton's discovery of passion as revealed in her secret manuscript *Beatrice Palmato*. The very tones of out-of-dateness. But the informing idea—of loneliness in love—is still alive. It should have been the poem's field of exploration, but Wilson was content to arrive at the point where his much admired Proust began. Wilson was protective about his selfhood, as major artists never can be.

As to the naming of names—well, he overdid it. Great poetry is always full of things, but finally the complexity of detail is subordinated to a controlling simplicity. Wilson wrote some excellent nature poetry but nature poetry it remains: all the flowers are named but the point is seldom reached when it ceases to matter so much what kind of flowers they are. In 'At Laurelwood', one of the prose pieces in *Note-Books of Night*, he talks of how his grandfather and grandmother helped teach him the names of everyday objects. His range of knowledge is one of the many marvellous things about Wilson. In poems like 'Provincetown, 1936' he piled on the detail to good effect:

> Mussels with broken hinges, sea crabs lopped
> Of legs, black razor-clams split double, dried
> Sea-dollars, limpets chivied loose and dropped
> Like stranded dories rolling on their side:

But in the long run not even concrete facts were a sufficient antidote to the poetry of Beauty. Humour was a better safeguard. On the whole, it is the satirical verse which holds up best among Wilson's work. Quite apart from the classic 'The Omelet of A. MacLeish', there are 'The Extrovert of Walden Pond' with its *trouvé* catch-phrase 'Thoreau was a neuro' and 'The Playwright in Paradise', a minatory ode to the writers of his generation which borrows lines from 'Adonais' to remind them that in Beverly Hills their talents will die young. In these poems Wilson's critical intelligence was at work. If he had possessed comic invention to match his scornful parodic ear, he might have equalled even E. E. Cummings. But 'American Masterpieces' (which makes its only appearance in *Night Thoughts*) shows what Cummings had that Wilson hadn't: in mocking the clichés of Madison Avenue, Wilson can win your allegiance, but Cummings can make you laugh. At the last, Wilson's jokes are not quite funny enough in themselves—they don't take

off into the self-sustaining Empyrean of things you can't help re-
citing. His humour, like his frankness, ought ideally to have been
part of a larger fiction.

Useless to carp. A minor artist Wilson remains. But it ought to
be more generally realized that he was a very good minor artist,
especially in his poetry. Of course, Night Thoughts didn't help.
Inflated with juvenilia and senescent academic graffiti even duller
than Auden's, the book blurred the outlines of Wilson's achievement—although even here it should be noted that its closing poem,
'The White Sand', is one of Wilson's most affecting things, a despairing celebration of late love so deeply felt that it almost over-
comes the sense of strain generated by the internally-rhymed elegiacs
in which it is cast.

What has worked most damagingly against Wilson's reputation as
a poet, however, is his reputation as a critic. It is hard to see how
things could be otherwise. As a critical mind, Wilson is so great
that we have not yet taken his full measure. He is still so prominent as to be invisible: people think they can know what he said
without having to read him. When he is read again, it will soon be
found that he saw both sides of most of the arguments which continue to rage about what literature is or ought to be. Among these
arguments is the one about modern poetry and its audience. Nobody was more sympathetic than Wilson to the emergence of a
difficult, hermetic poetry or better-equipped to understand its origins. But equally he was able to keep the issue in perspective. First
of all, his standards were traditional in the deepest sense: knowing
why Homer, Virgil, Dante, Shakespeare and Pushkin were permanently modern, he knew why most of modern poetry was without
the value it claimed for itself. Secondly, he had an unconquerable
impulse towards community. All his writings are an expression of it,
including his verse. He would have liked to read fully intelligible
works while living in an ordered society. As things turned out, the
works he admired were not always fully intelligible and the society
he lived in was not ordered. But at least in his own creative writings,
such as they were, he could try to be clear. So his poems are as they
are, and the best of them last well.

(1977)

7. After Such Knowledge: T. S. Eliot

Great Tom: Notes towards the definition of T. S. Eliot
by T. S. Matthews

I saw him when distaste had turned to nightmare
  Near the end of this interminable book:
  As if the terraced cloudscape were a staircase
And he himself yet palpable, his sandals,
  Achillean by asphodel uplifted,
  Propelled their burden's effortless ascent—
A tuft of candid feathers at each shoulder
  Proclaiming him apprentice, cherished fledgling
  To overhanging galleries of angels.
And so, the poet first and I behind him,
  But only he a freedman hieing homeward,
  My quarry turned towards me. I cried 'Master!
We all knew you could make it!' and embraced him—
  Since, being both Sordello and Odysseus,
  I forgot my teacher's substance was a shadow,
And gathered uselessly the empty air.
  'Just passing through?' he chuckled as I teetered,
  Perhaps to ease the anguish of my gesture.
'If I were you I wouldn't plan on staying,
  Unless you don't mind falling through the scenery.'
  His smile, admonitory yet seraphic,
Suggested Pentecost, the truce of Advent,
  The prior taste unspeakably assuaging
  Of the ineluctable apotheosis.
'You remember T. S. Matthews, Sir?' I asked.
  'T. S. Who?' 'He's written your biography.'
  'Matthews . . . I suppose I knew him vaguely.
A *Time* man. Is it awful?' A platoon
  Of cherubim flashed past us on the banister,
  Posteriors illumined by the marble:
The welcoming committee for Stravinsky,

As yet some years below but toiling skyward.
'Not quite as bad as most have said, but still
A pretty odious effort.' Here I wavered.
    Around his neck, the excalfactive Order
    Of Merit infumated, argentine,
But the gaze above, both placent and unsleeping,
    Entlastende without tergiversation,
    Compelled the apprehension it prevented.
And I: 'It hasn't got that many facts
    Which can't be found in places more reputed—
    Notably your widow's thoughtful preface
To the MS of *The Waste Land*. That aside,
    The speculative content can add little
    To the cairn of innuendo stacked already
By Sencourt's *T. S. Eliot: A Memoir*.'
    I paused. And he: 'Poor Robert was a pest,
    I'm sad to say. Well, all right: what's the fuss then?'
I caught a sudden flicker of impatience,
    Familiar yet ineffable. 'Sir, nothing;
    For nothing can come of nothing. Matthews puzzles
Repellently about those thousand letters
    You wrote to Emily Hale, but has no answers.'
    And he, diverted: 'Nor will anybody,
For another fifty years. I can't believe, though,
    A full-blown book enshrines no more than these
    Incursions void of judgement. Therefore speak.'
And I: 'He rates his chances as a critic—
    Allowing you your gift, he dares to offer
    Conjectures that your ear verged on the faulty.
You said, for instance, of St. Magnus Martyr,
    Its walls contained inexplicable splendour.
    He calls that adjective cacophonous.'
'He calls it *what*?' 'Cacophonous.' 'I see.'
    And I: 'The strictures go beyond irreverence.
    His animus is manifest. Your consort
He terms "robust" at one point; elsewhere, "ample";
    Yet cravenly endorses in his foreword
    Her telling him in such a forthright manner
To render himself scarce.' A gust of laughter,
    Subversive of his sanctity, perturbed him.

He conjured from the gold strings of his harp
An autoschediastic lilt of love
  Which might have once been whistled by Ravel.
  And he: 'She did that, did she? Excellent.'
I said 'The pride you feel is not misplaced.
  Your wish that no biography be written
  Will not be lightly flouted. Forced to yield,
Your wife will choose her author with great scruple
  Yet most of us who wish your memory well
  By now share the opinion that permission
To undertake the task must soon be granted
  Lest unofficial books like this gain ground,
  Besmirching the achievement of a lifetime.'
And he: 'I'm sure the lass will do what's best.
  One's not allowed to give advice from here
  And care for earthly fame is hard to summon.
It may, perhaps, however, please Another
  To whisper in her ear.' He turned away,
  Declaring as he faded 'It's surprising,
But this place isn't quite as Dante said—
  It's like the escalator at High Holborn,
  Except there's no way down.' So he departed,
Dissolving like a snowflake in the sun,
  A Sybil's sentence in the leaves lost—
  Yet seemed like one who ends the race triumphant.

(*New Statesman*, 6 September 1974)

Part Two
THE AESTHETIC ASPECT

8. In Homage to Gianfranco Contini

Esercizî di lettura sopra autori contemporanei con un'appendice su testi non contemporanei, nuova edizione aumentata di 'Un anno di letturatura';
Una lunga fedeltà, scritti su Eugenio Montale

The welcome reissue of *Esercizî di lettura* brings to a logical fruition Gianfranco Contini's typically meticulous efforts in the past few years to gather and arrange some of the essays which for almost four decades have been bestowed on learned journals and critical magazines, read out as addresses to learned societies, conferred as prefaces on critical editions, sent as letters to foreign countries, contributed to Festschrifts for fellow philologists or (which is virtually the same thing) simply handed out to friends. *Esercizî di lettura* takes its place beside the previously issued *Altri esercizî di lettura* of 1972 and the massive, inexhaustibly enriching *Varianti e altra linguistica* of 1970. I hope Professor Contini will forgive the pun—and Dante's grim shade the blasphemy—if I suggest that we can now see bound into these three volumes, if not into one, the leaves that were before-hand scattered through the universe.

Viewed in all their implications, the 1,500-plus pages of this extraordinary trilogy should convince the appropriately receptive lay reader that Contini is the heir of Ernst Robert Curtius as a scholar and critic of European literature. I recall how once, in Cambridge, a notoriously able young don engagingly admitted that he had sent back Erich Auerbach's *Mimesis* to a learned journal with a covering note saying that he did not know how to review it: the book was so learned it was beyond him. Square the distance of that gap and you will judge how far the reading which underlies Contini's major writings is beyond the present reviewer. But there is at least one crumb of comfort to be had when facing the failure inevitably consequent on trying to sum up work so unsummable. It is the common reader who is likely to see common significance.

The specialist reader already knows about Contini's central importance to Italian scholarship and appreciates the living nature of his erudition. But the specialists' awareness of Contini has so far resulted only in a very slight common awareness. For this, perhaps, there are two main reasons. First, the exceptional difficulty of translating his style into thinkable, let alone readable, English: the compression is such that even Italians have trouble with it. Second, the fact that until these volumes appeared Contini had no book to show which could possibly exercise influence on the same scale as *Mimesis* or Curtius's great *European Literature and the Latin Middle Ages*, each of which had a large but comfortably ascertainable continuity of theme. With Contini the organic unity is both smaller and larger: smaller in the sense that he tackles particular problems individually, larger in the sense that these particular problems are brought together only in the scope of his learning.

Contini's erudition is therefore central to his character both as critic and philologist. Indeed his is a mind in which scholarship and criticism can be seen to be united, and the ordinary professional critic (who in this country especially is as likely to be an artist as an academic) can expect to be at best disturbed, and at worst disabled, by the example Contini provides of seemingly fathomless preparation combined with the most intelligent receptivity possible. For the pragmatic composer and dismantler of *ad hoc* critical principles, a challenge to values is guaranteed. Salvation lies in the realization that the full contents of a mind like Contini's can be transferred only to another mind like Contini's. We must content ourselves with absorbing what we can.

As its full title indicates, *Esercizî di lettura* consists of two smaller, earlier collections. The first edition of the proto-*Esercizî* was published in Florence in 1939 and there was a new edition after the war, in 1947. *Un anno di letteratura* was published, also in Florence, in 1942. In the new Einaudi compilation, the *esercizî* for the first time contain the essay on Umberto Saba which was censored in 1939 and ended up being published in *Un anno*. The essay on Thomas Mann was also censored in 1939 but was included in the *esercizî* in the 1947 edition. (Between 1939 and 1942, doubts as to the perfection of Saba's Aryan background had apparently—Contini slyly hints—moderated. Mann, however, continued to be an unperson.) The essays take their proper place with as little fuss as when they lost it. Contini fought his battles with Fascism the same way he now lectures, in a whisper. There are no grand gestures, just a steady determination to get on with preserving and extending civilized values. It was a measure, of course, of Fascism's relative moderation vis-à-vis Nazism that scholarship was allowed to continue at all.

For many years these two books were the only volumes to which a student of Contini's work could have recourse, and it was an elementary obligation to make them once again readily available. The author's tardiness on this point is no doubt partly due to his feeling, expressed when the *esercizi* first came out, that it was a posthumous book. His reason, he now says, for devoting such care as he has done (entirely sufficient, needless to say) to the job of reissuing these (and, by implication, his other) writings is further to reinforce their nature as objects, 'come di sassi da gettare dietro le spalle'—like stones you toss over your shoulder. Not the worst way, he might have added, to mark a trail.

The *esercizi* within the new *Esercizi di lettura* still begin with a series of fundamental essays on Contini's then contemporary poets; contemporary in the sense that he was the younger man putting the century's work in order for his own generation. The essays devoted to Clemente Rèbora and Dino Campana first appeared in 1937, and are grouped under the heading 'Due poeti degli anni vociani'.

It is worth noting at this point that one of the several tasks Contini undertook in the pre-Second World War period was to assess, on behalf of the periodical *Letteratura*, the poets of the pre-First World War period who were associated with the periodical *La Voce*. As usually happens in such cases, the critical power passed to the younger men as a necessary consequence of defining the older men's creativity.

The essay on Saba dates from 1934, as does 'La verità sul caso Cardarelli', which connects with the postwar 'Lettera da non spedire' (Letter not to be sent) 'a Vincenzo Cardarelli' in *Altri esercizi*. It can be seen from these datings that the placing of the first two essays is strategic, not chronological: *La Voce* set out to raise Italian culture to the European plane and that was the aim which Contini wanted to bring under review in 1939. He then went on to discuss other still-developing poets.

There are three essays on Ungaretti. The first ('Ungaretti, o dell'-Allegria') concerns the so-called 'first' Ungaretti, the second ('Materiali sul "secundo" Ungaretti') the 'second' Ungaretti, i.e., the author of *Sentimenta del tempo* rather than of *L'allegria*. These two essays date from 1932 and 1933 respectively—early, brilliant work. The third essay, 'Ungaretti in francese' of 1939, is more mature. Two of Con-

tini's first essays on Eugenio Montale round out this first, search-
ingly argumentative section of the book. Montale was the finest poet
of the new generation and Contini (some years the younger) was its
finest critical mind, but both things were yet to be proved.

Forty years later their ascendancy is beyond question. These two
early appreciations of Montale, like the other essays on that gratify-
ing subject which appear in Un anno and in Altri esercizî, are now
separately collected in the other, smaller but equally concentrated
book, Una lunga fedeltà, where they gain from being set with their
successors, but lose something by being separated from equivalently
occasional writings devoted to other poets. It goes beyond instruction—it is close to inspiring—to see the young critic defining the
qualities of the outstanding poet's early work, when the fact that he
was outstanding had yet to be fully established. (It should be pointed
out in fairness that Sergio Solmi wrote an important notice—now
amplified and collected in his Scrittori negli anni—when Ossi di
seppia first appeared in 1925.) At that point Contini, the philologist,
the man of Italy's past, was conspicuously a man of its present—the
contemporary man of letters. That the two roles only apparently conflict is a first principle in his idea of his own activity: an idea which
he has lived to the full.

There are almost a score of comparable essays on other contemporary figures—Emilio Cecchi, Antonio Baldini, Nino Savarese,
Georgio Vigolo, and so on—but perhaps it will be more useful to
sample Contini's commentary on one or two of the poets already
mentioned whose reputations are international. The first noticeable
characteristic of Contini's criticism is his ability to make a general
statement about an author which the reader sees to be both widely
applicable and original. This quality is the heavily condensed residuum of Croce's requirement that the critic should give an account
of the poet's stato d'animo—his condition of mind. When Contini
says that Campana was an anarchist who did not know how to liberate the man of order within himself ('Questo anarchico, questo "bo-
hémien" non seppe liberare l'uomo d'ordine ch'era in lui . . .') he is
producing something better than an epigram. Of the 'first' Ungaretti
he says (and the awkwardness is all in my translation) that the background on which the poems are incised is a vivid feeling of concreteness combined with an insatiable regard for far-off things: a distance
opens and a self-sufficient lyrical unit ('quella che si vorrebbe chia-
mare la monade lirica') immediately introduces itself. His analysis is

both definitive and evocative: that, we feel, is the way Ungaretti writes about the world.

Of the 'second' Ungaretti he says that the poet's weakness tends to be the underlying (*sottolinearità* is one of the early Contini's favourite words) of everything about a subject in the desire to exhaust it impressionistically. The argument is mature in all except its tendency to deny the poet a future—from young critics, the prognosis of a poet's condition is nearly always gloomy. Here I can recommend turning to the 1942 essay on Ungaretti in *Altri esercizî*, where Contini puts these two preliminary essays in perspective by conceding his early urge to be dialectical about the two volumes *L'allegria* and *Sentimento del tempo*: the young critic, he ruefully admits, ideally wants his subject-poet to die. Not having yet had a career of his own, he finds it hard to see how the poet could want one either. As a bonus Contini adds a highly illuminating remark emanating from the territory where the philological shades into the critical: Ungaretti's obsession with corrections negated inspiration as a fundamental characteristic (a denial which Contini thinks can never be rooted in fact) but was also his safeguard against an a priori sweetness. Tracing these essays through the two books we reap the benefit of a concern continuing in time. It is usually the way with Contini: he stays with a subject for as long as it is creatively alive. The extreme case among his contemporaries has been Montale. But the same applies to the past.

Writing of a poet, Contini produces phrases so densely apposite that they definitively influence the reader's view. He says of Saba's seeming clichés ('vista dilettoso', 'campagne grate', etc.) that they are not literary furniture but genuine optimism. It would be hard to think of a more suitable qualifying introduction to Saba's deceptive ease. But, as often as he says something which attaches itself permanently to the immediate subject, Contini says something else which leads us on to his total scope. Linking Ungaretti's 'consolation' with Leopardi's, he writes of the release which Leopardi found in setting the hammered phrase in the singable scheme. A point of style in the present leads to a point of style in the past—and with this critic, for whom taste is objective, all poetic problems are eventually problems of style. Criticism leads back to philology as surely as it first emerges from it.

In the nine essays constituting the "Appendice su testi non contemporanei' of the proto-*esercizî* at least two should catch the immediate attention of the general reader. Both are philological essays, but as always with Contini cogent criticism is abundant. 'Come lavorava l'Ariosto' (how Ariosto worked) shows how the variations and editions of *Orlando Furioso* embody the relationship of poetic 'being' to 'not-being'—again it is a Crocean distinction, the famous opposition between *poesia* and *non poesia* which Contini was already subtilizing and modifying. Contini welcomed the editing of Ariosto which had been carried out by Santorre Debenedetto, who confirmed that Ariosto did not make prose sketches of his stanzas (tradition had always held that he did) but narrated and reflected directly in verse. Poetic education, says Contini succinctly, had completely penetrated habit.

'Una lettura su Michelangelo' (1937) is an inquiry into Michelangelo's sonnets from the stylistic viewpoint—which is always Contini's viewpoint, but is here made usefully explicit. Style, says Contini, is the author's way of knowing things. For what he means by Michelangelo's Petrarchism it is advisable to consult the essays on Petrarch in *Varianti*, which form, along with the essays on Dante in the same volume, one of Contini's most weighty contributions to the understanding of poetry.

Un anno gives an early indication (the year was 1939-40) of the variety and solidity of work the mature Contini has since become accustomed to getting through in twelve months. There are six essays on contemporary writers, three 'almost philological' essays, and a piece on Le Corbusier which besides being as interesting as Walter Benjamin on the subject of Paris is presciently disinclined to welcome the benefits promised to that city by modern architecture. Here we are given a glimpse of the critic of the plastic arts Contini might have become. But he seems to have been content to leave that side of things to Roberto Longhi, whose writings he later selected and edited to form a critical history of Italian art and whose status as a *prosatore* he has always been concerned to emphasize—e.g., with the three essays ('Contributi longhiani') in *Altri esercizî*, in the first of which ('Sul metodo', 1949) he defined the quality inherent in Longhi's memory, which was already famous for quantity: 'la memoria, per quanto eccezionalissima, di Longhi è la facoltà di seriare l'immagine fra le immagini prossime, in ogni direzione, secondo linee il più posibile complete.' ('Longhi's memory, besides being exceptional, is the ability to arrange an image in series with its neighbours along lines as complete as they can possibly be—in every direction.') Contini calls this a scientific gift; before the facts, to the extent that they are facts, there are no two methods.

Longhi, of all the writers connected with *La Voce* (although his maturity came later), is perhaps the one whose influence on Contini was formative. Contini praises in Longhi qualities he could legitimately value in himself, if modesty allowed. He calls Longhi's *Piero della Francesca* of 1927 a classic of contemporary letters and its author a true writer. It is interesting that he should feel the need to insist. (Longhi's writings on art bristle with references to literature. Contini's writings on literature are not quite so replete with references to art, but they occur often enough, are always illustrative, and reveal a profound culture. One of his few appearances as an out-and-out art historian is easily obtainable in the popular Rizzoli series *Classici dell'Arte*, No 43: *Simone Martini*. He wrote the introduction, 'Simon Martini gotico intellettuale'—tough going for the casual dabbler.)

Near the end but at the heart of *Un anno* is a reply to an inquiry about *ermetismo*. While defending the poet's right to difficulty, Contini shows that hermeticism as an ideal is a logical mistake. Hermeticism, if it could really be attained, would involve isolation, and so, like every poetry of the Absolute, deny the possibility of individuality, which can arise only where collaboration is possible: i.e., in society. Contini's compliments to other scholars are no mere logrolling. He has always had a sense of the cooperative venture remarkable in one so outstandingly gifted.

And now, with *Esercizî di lettura* ranked alongside *Altri esercizî* and *Varianti*, we can see more clearly just how extraordinary that gift is. The two *esercizî* volumes are the epitome of his writings on the present and near past. The *varianti* volume is the epitome of his writings on the far past. Each epitome lends the other force. Together they show a scope which brings up the whole question of erudition.

In 'L'influenza culturale di Benedetto Croce', a long essay written in 1966 to introduce the Ricciardi anthology of Croce's writings and now included in *Altri esercizî*, Contini gives an intensely compressed account of Croce's intellectual history which contains by implication all he thinks on the question of his own inheritance from the great philosopher. The problem, says the younger man, is to be post-Crocean without being anti. Croceanism, in the pejorative sense, he defines as the diffuse monograph-mongering of those who append their nests and cobwebs to Croce's trunk. Of the epigones one has to be dismissive. But there is no justifiable way of dismissing Croce himself.

Croce deserves something better—criticism. And one of the many vulnerable points Contini finds in Croce concerns erudition. There was a contradiction in Croce between his urge to deal with particular problems and his voracity for omniscience, a hunger which—especially in the late stages—often got out of control. It is important here to realize that Contini is not talking about volume of knowledge so much as relevance. That knowledge could be even more voluminous than Croce's and still be relevant is shown by the 'Memoria di Ramón Menéndez Pidal' which Contini read as a commemorative address to the Accademia dei Lincei and which is also collected in Altri esercizî. Menéndez Pidal was one of Contini's great masters: a scholar who, the pupil says, spontaneously longed for the totality of knowledge. The emphasis is on the spontaneity. In Menéndez Pidal, says Contini, we saw the acceptable limit of intellectual curiosity, an exact symbiosis of the folkloristic collector, the textual critic, the palaeographer, the grammarian, and the historian of language, culture, institutions and politics.

Contini's separation from Croce is perhaps more simply illustrated elsewhere in the Altri esercizî in the 1944 letter to France called Introduction à l'étude de la littérature italienne contemporaine. Here Contini is summing up his ideas for a French audience which necessarily knows less about Croce than an Italian one, so the argument is less compressed (and Contini's French is a good deal easier to follow than his Italian anyway). Croce wasn't interested in scholarship as Contini conceives it: he called it the study of waste paper. For Croce, the study of a poem began after it was finished. Contini asserts his right to study a poem on its way to being born. Such an approach has to link art with life. For Croce the temptation (backed up by his fundamental theoretical separation of categories) was to divorce the two beyond reconciliation. Croce thought that nothing of interest in poetry had happened after Carducci. But Contini could see that scholarship meant nothing if it denied art a present.

On this last point Contini has enjoyed throughout his critical life the privilege of access to a contemporary poet whose eminence is difficult to argue with. Una lunga fedeltà collects six pieces on

Montale ranging from *Introduzione a Ossi di seppia* of 1933 to *Sul Diario del '71 e del '72*—which latter is actually the blurb from the wrapper of the book. There is little on the *Diario* and hardly anything on *Satura*, but the first three collections (the *Ossi*, *Le occasioni* and *La bufera*) inspired some superb critical writing. Montale grew to greatness before the eyes of Contini's generation, assuring them (and thereby reassuring them) that in an age of rhetoric the classical retreats to a hidden world—and survives. Anyone with an interest in Montale's poetry can consult this miniature book and see Contini's critical intellect working at full force: to borrow one of Montale's most famous lines, *qui tocca anche a noi poveri la nostra parte di ricchezza*. Here even we poor get a share of the wealth.

(T.L.S., 22 November 1974)

9. Poetry's Ideal Critic: Randall Jarrell

As a figure representing the Poet's Fate, Randall Jarrell bulks large in the necrology of the American heavies: the patchwork epics of both John Berryman and Robert Lowell are liberally embroidered with portentous musings on his death. Is this, one wonders, what Jarrell's name now mainly means? The thought is enough to chill the bones.

Luckily Jarrell's publishers are now doing what they can to dispel the graveyard mists. Whether his *Complete Poems* did much for his reputation is debatable: his poetry, though he would have hated to hear it said, was a bit light on those Blakean 'minute particulars' he thought good poetry should have a lot of—there was a tendency to the prosaic which rigorous selection did something to disguise. He once said that even a good poet was a man who spent a lifetime standing in a storm and who could hope to be struck by lightning only half a dozen times at best. Disablingly true in his case. One would memorize a needle-thrust like 'The Death of the Ball Turret Gunner' and wonder why someone who could command that kind of penetration should spend so much time lapsing into a practised, resourceful, elegant but in the end faintly wearying expansiveness. He thought that writing came first and that the Age of Criticism—i.e., of writing about writing—was a bad dream from which we needed to pinch ourselves awake. A bitter truth then, that his writing was merely distinguished whereas his writing-about-writing was inspired. Jarrell is poetry's ideal critic, and the current reissue of *Poetry and the Age* couldn't be more welcome. If ever there was a necessary book, this is it. A few more like it and there would still be a chance of saving the humanities for humanity.

A Shaw rather than a Beerbohm, a Sickert rather than a Wyndham Lewis, Jarrell had one of those rare critical minds which are just as illuminating in praise as in attack. We never feel, when reading him, that he is at his most concentrated when he is being most destructive. It is in the effort to draw our attention to merit that he achieves real intensity, and there are very few critics of whom that can be said. Yet there was nothing indulgent about his capacity for admiration. In his definitive essay on Frost, he grants—indeed rubs in—the poet's defects of personality with an epigrammatic disgust which would dominate the argument, were it not for his insistence that Frost's cracker-barrel Wisdom shouldn't distract us from the fact that being wise about life is nevertheless one of the things his poems do supremely well. Jarrell can see clearly that the best of Frost is the best critic of the worst, and that the Critical Task (a locution which would never have crossed his lips) is to demonstrate how good that best is—the best which we tend to reduce to the level of the unremarkable by being so knowing about the worst. Jarrell was against knowingness, and possessed the antidote: knowledge. His wide knowledge of literature impresses you at every turn. He alludes without effort, compares without strain, and makes being simple seem easy.

John Crowe Ransom and Walt Whitman are as well served as Frost. Speaking for myself, Jarrell's remarks helped give me the courage of my secret convictions about Ransom (I had thought it would be intellectual suicide to admit that his luxuriant diction struck me as a kind of strength); they were also instrumental in dismantling a self-designed, home-constructed apparatus of formalistic priggery that had kept me from Whitman for ten years. Better introductions to such a brace of obfuscation-ridden poets couldn't be imagined. Opening his Whitman essay, for example, Jarrell typically outlines the kind of misunderstanding he thinks needs to be eradicated:

> But something odd has happened to the living, changing part of Whitman's reputation: nowadays it is people who are not particularly interested in poetry, people who say that they read a poem for what it says, not for how it says it, who admire Whitman most. Whitman is often written about, either approvingly or disapprovingly, as if he were the Thomas Wolfe of 19th-century democracy. . . .

True when it was said, and true now. That Whitman was read by people who couldn't read seemed to me to be sufficient reason for refraining from reading much of him myself. Jarrell, though, had the confidence and independence to insist that to defend your taste by such a refusal is simply to connive at philistinism and encourage the view that Whitman was an ordinary rhetorician. On the contrary, he was an extraordinary one, whose worst language was not just awful, but unusually awful ('really *ingeniously* bad'), and whose finest flights were poetry about which there could be no argument. ('If the reader thinks that all this is like Thomas Wolfe he *is* Thomas Wolfe; nothing else could explain it.') Quoting the passage from 'I understand the large hearts of heroes' down to 'I am the man, I suffered, I was there', Jarrell says that Whitman has reached a point at which criticism seems not only unnecessary but absurd, since the lines are so good that even admiration feels like insolence. Jarrell's use of quotations approaches the mark Walter Benjamin set for himself, of writing a critical essay consisting of nothing but. The catch—that the quality of the quotation is self-demonstrating only to the reader who doesn't need telling—was one Jarrell recognized and was worried by. Luckily he didn't let it stop him.

The essay on Wallace Stevens is as important as the others already mentioned. Written as a review of *The Auroras of Autumn*, it measures the aridity of Stevens's later work by evoking the exfoliating fruitfulness of the earlier, and gets the whole of the poet's career into proportion without even a hint of cutting him down to size. But the strictures are gripping when they come. Of *The Auroras of Autumn* Jarrell says that one sees in it

> the distinction, intelligence, and easy virtuosity of a master—but it would take more than these to bring to life so abstract, so monotonous, so overwhelmingly *characteristic* a book.

Italics his, and transfixingly placed.

With Jarrell, the urge to share a discovered excellence leads to a mastery of critical language which can only be called creative. The forms of Marianne Moore's poems, he writes,

> have the lacy, mathematical extravagance of snowflakes, seem as arbitrary as the prohibitions in fairy tales; but they work as those work—disregard them and everything goes to pieces.

Not satisfied with that, he goes on:

> Her forms, tricks and all, are like the aria of the Queen of the Night: the intricate and artificial elaboration not only does not conflict with the emotion but is its vehicle.

If his experience had not been so rich, he could not have been so right: it takes range to achieve such a fine focus.

Scattered throughout this book are minor moments of the trouble which in a later collection of essays, A Sad Heart at the Supermarket, coalesced into a persistent anxiety. The foe of academic crassness and critical arrogance, Jarrell was obliged to rely on the good sense of those who read books for love. He knew they were in a minority but was too much of an American fully to accept the fact that this had something to do with inequality: he seemed to think that if you could just speak plainly enough you would break through. There is a distressing moment in A Sad Heart at the Supermarket when he tries to tell his popular-magazine audience that the word 'intellectual' is not one to be frightened of since a mechanic or carpenter is just as much an intellectual about practical things as a poet is about literature. He chose not to notice that the two states of mind are not interchangeable, and probably never began to realize that his own critical writings, among the most readily intelligible of the century, depend for a good part of their clarity on a scope of cultural reference so broad that only the educated can take it in. Too much of a democrat to take pride in his own uniqueness, Jarrell hungered for an egalitarian society with uniformly high standards. Wishful thinking, but of a noble kind. Those sensitive to literature can be taught literature, but sensitivity to literature cannot be taught—a point which should be borne in mind by anyone who runs away with the idea that setting Poetry and the Age as a first-year text would humanize our university English schools overnight. It wouldn't, but it's a measure of Jarrell's gifts that even the most level-headed reader suddenly finds himself suspecting that it could.

(New Statesman, 26 October 1973)

10. Wittgenstein's Dream

Letters to Russell, Keynes and Moore by Ludwig Wittgenstein

Wittgenstein never did much to encourage the fossicking of amateurs, and in particular loathed phrase-making dilettantes. Yet people of a literary turn with no training in or indeed capacity for rigorous philosophy (let me hasten to include myself among them) will probably go on finding him of high interest. He said that we shouldn't be seduced by language—an admonition which will continue being useful to those whose business it is to be seduced by language every day of the week. Wittgenstein is The Cure. He is a rhetorician's way of going on the wagon.

This new volume of letters to Russell, Keynes and Moore is a companion piece for the slim collection of letters to Ogden and Ramsay. Those, being mainly technical, were stiff going for the non-professional. These—especially the substantial sheaf of letters to Russell—are of much more various interest. The reader will find himself drawn to speculate about all aspects of Wittgenstein's strange life. The problem of his personality is, I am sure, eventually insoluble, but that doesn't mean people are going to stop trying.

Most of the letters to Russell stem from the years 1912-21—i.e., from the first Cambridge period up until the publication of the *Tractatus*. In 1922 came a break in their relationship, of the same kind that severed Wittgenstein from G. E. Moore in Norway in 1914. (Apparently he also quarrelled with Russell in 1914, but Russell's part of that exchange is not available.) All the intensity of Wittgenstein's focussed intellect is there from the first moment: 'There is nothing more wonderful in the world than the *true* problems of Philosophy.' Engelmann was quite right in saying that thinking was Wittgenstein's poetry. 'I feel like mad.' He accuses himself of having 'half a talent' for thought.

Fearing that he will die before being able to publish his ideas, he begs Russell to meet him so that he can explain. But explanation is difficult (it is always encouraging for those of us puzzled by the *Tractatus* to find that Russell found it hard reading as well) and he has the poet's reluctance to explicate: 'It bores me BEYOND WORDS to explain . . . it is INTOLERABLE for me to repeat a written explanation which even the first time I gave only with the *utmost repugnance*.'

A letter from Norway evokes the identikit Wittgenstein whose components everybody knows from Norman Malcolm's excellent memoir. 'My day passes between logic, whistling, going for walks, and being depressed.' *Angst* is a continuing theme, screwed to fever pitch by the suspicion that his fellow thinkers don't find him clear: '*Dass Moore meine Ideen Dir nicht hat erklären können, ist mir unbegreiflich*'—'I find it inconceivable that Moore wasn't able to explain my ideas to you.' (Letters written in German are given in the original as well as in translation, and like all Wittgenstein's German writings are so transparent they flatter the reader into believing he knows that language quite well.) In December 1919 Russell met Wittgenstein in The Hague and discussed the *Tractatus* with him for a week. There is a useful quotation from a hitherto unedited letter to Ottoline Morrell: 'I told him I could not refute it, and that I was sure it was either all right or all wrong.' It was difficult to get the book published—a frustration treated more fully in the letters to Engelmann than here. An introduction by Russell was meant to smooth the book's path to publication, but Wittgenstein did not like what Russell wrote and characteristically did not forbear to say so. He said that once the elegance of Russell's style had been lost in translation, only 'superficiality and misunderstanding' were left.

Wittgenstein was incapable of diplomatic flattery, as of any form of give and take: he was, to that extent, anti-social. It is useful, on this point, to look up the letters to Ogden and see how Wittgenstein found himself unable to say the merest of kind words about *The Meaning of Meaning*, even after Ogden had knocked himself out translating the *Tractatus*. Friendship with Wittgenstein was almost impossibly difficult, the demands were so heavy. ('What a maniac you are!' wrote Keynes.) But he could be generous with his mental treasure, as long as you submitted. He was one of those mentors a pupil has to knuckle under to and eventually break free from. But even the proudest could temporarily forgo their liberty if it meant gaining access to a mind like his.

There are many reminders here of a great truth about Wittgenstein which has taken a long time to emerge. His spiritual life was extraordinarily rich. When he said you had to be silent about what you couldn't speak of he didn't mean that it wasn't important—only that it wasn't philosophical. He himself made the point very clearly in one of his *Briefe an Ludwig von Ficker* (Salzburg, 1969), when he said that his work (i.e., the book that was later to be the *Tractatus*) fell into two parts, what was there and what was not—and that the second part was the important one. In English, Wittgenstein devoured pulp fiction and worshipped Carmen Miranda and Betty Hutton, two of the most off-putting stars ever to burden Hollywood. This kind of slumming—which is anyway quite common among people who do intellectual work at high intensity—tends to obscure the profundity of his culture. But we need only to hear him conducting Russell through the major German poets ('if you've *really* enjoyed Mörike, you should see the light about G O E T H E') to see how poetry—and he meant the poetry where the words used did not exceed the thing said—bulked large in his mind and formed the touchstone for his thought.

Poetry, and of course music. Moore was a musician as Russell was not, so the most enchanting moment in this volume occurs in a letter to Moore, when he is instructed to purchase an arrangement of the Brahms *Schicksalslied* for four hands and bring it to Norway. The picture of the two philosophers tickling the ivories side by side is one to be filed with the image of Chopin and Delacroix discussing counterpoint or Dr. Johnson and Baretti running their footrace in Paris. To Russell in 1912 Wittgenstein said Mozart and Beethoven were 'the actual sons of God' and to Moore in 1945 he said that the Schubert C Major Quintet had 'a *fantastic* kind of greatness'. In so far as he could find solace, he seems to have found it in music, but it would probably be a mistake to cut him down to size—to make him 'human'—by pointing to a source of consolation. For the unsentimental reader, it is the inhuman element in Wittgenstein which is likely to remain the most striking. He had, for example, the depressive's knack of doing a quick fade. The Trattenbach episode, which William Warren Bartley found the key to his sexuality, seems to me more interesting when linked to his other disappearing tricks, such as his late-flowering career as a hospital orderly in World War II. The Aircraftman Shaw aspect of Wittgenstein is a clear indication, I think, that he suffered from a periodic inability to detect his own personality. If he was homosexual (and there are plenty of hints to support this) then he was Michelangelesque rather than Leonardian—guilty rather than serene. But I don't see how guilt covers the case. I think protean depressives should recognize one of their kind.

Wittgenstein is turning into a myth. People now bandy his name about who once would have been tinkering with Gurdjieff and Ouspensky. For what grappling with Wittgenstein on a professional level actually involves, it is informative to look into *Understanding Wittgenstein*, Volume 7 of the Royal Institute of Philosophy Lectures, where the professionals are to be seen worrying at the problems: a cold douche for dabblers. Obviously it is a vocation to read work like Wittgenstein's at the level of its writing. But for those of us whose propensities lie in other directions, or who are just not quite clever enough, it is still legitimate to find his career instructive. We need to be careful, though, not to turn his incidental remarks into slogans. In a recent television play about a producer making a film on Wittgenstein, the bemused hero was to be heard muttering 'Death is not an event in life' as if it were an edifying insight. Wittgenstein himself would have been quick enough to point out that St. Augustine goes into the subject more deeply in *The City of God*, or to recommend the texts of Tolstoy and Dostoievsky which helped sustain him during the First World War. Wittgenstein is not a substitute for the culture from which he grew, and a poet would do well to regard him as an enemy, not a friend. But he is the necessary enemy. There is something about his mental landscape, its tungsten outcrops and cryogenic lakes, which quenches one's thirst for austerity. *Seven Types of Ambiguity* and *The Structure of Complex Words* will do more for a poet's understanding of how language works than anything written by Wittgenstein: we read those books and feel that anything is possible. We read Wittgenstein and feel that nothing is—so little can be said. A salutary disenchantment, out of which his finely honed lyricism rings with uncanny beauty. 'We are asleep. Our life is like a dream,' he wrote to Engelmann, 'But in our better hours we wake up just enough to realise that we are dreaming.'

(New Statesman, 18 October 1974)

Part Three
PRISONERS OF CLARITY

11. The Sherlockologists

Sir Arthur Conan Doyle wrote little about Sherlock Holmes compared with what has been written by other people since. Sherlock has always been popular, on a scale never less than world-wide, but the subsidiary literature which has steadily heaped up around him can't be accounted for merely by referring to his universal appeal. Sherlockology—the adepts call it that, with typical whimsy—is a sort of cult, which has lately become a craze. The temptation to speculate about why this should be is one I don't propose to resist, but first there is the task of sorting the weighty from the witless in the cairn of Sherlockiana—they say that, too—currently available. What follows is a preliminary classification, done with no claims to vocational, or even avocational, expertise. Most decidedly not: this is a field in which all credentials, and especially impeccable ones, are suspect. To give your life, or any significant part of it, to the study of Sherlock Holmes is to defy reason.

It is also to disparage Doyle, as John Fowles pointed out in his introduction to *The Hound of the Baskervilles*, one of the four Sherlock Holmes novels handsomely reissued in Britain early last year, each as a single volume. This is an expensive way of doing things, but the books are so good-looking it is hard to quarrel, although the childhood memory of reading all the Sherlock Holmes 'long stories' in one volume (and all the short stories in another volume), well printed on thin but opaque paper, dies hard. Still, the new books look splendid all lined up, and the introductions are very interesting. Apart from Fowles, the men on the case are Hugh Greene (*A Study in Scarlet*), his brother Graham Greene (*The Sign of Four*), and Len Deighton (*The Valley of Fear*). What each man has to say is well worth hearing, even if not always strictly relevant to the novel it introduces. When you add to this four-volume set of the novels the five-volume reissue of the short story collections, it certainly provides a dazzling display.

To follow the order in which Doyle gave them to the world, the short story collections are *The Adventures of Sherlock Holmes* (introduced by Eric Ambler), *The Memoirs of Sherlock Holmes* (Kingsley Amis), *The Return of Sherlock Holmes* (Angus Wilson), *His Last Bow* (Julian Symons), and *The Case-Book of Sherlock Holmes* (C. P. Snow). The dust-wrappers of all nine volumes are carried out in black and gold, a colour combination which in Britain is supposed to put you in mind of John Player Specials, a ritzy line in cigarettes. Doing it this way, it will set you back £21.20 in English money to read the saga through.

A less crippling alternative would be to purchase the Doubleday omnibus introduced by the old-time (in fact, late) Sherlockian Christopher Morley, which reproduces the whole corpus—four novels and fifty-six short stories—on goodish paper for slightly under nine bucks, the contents being as nourishing as in the nine-volume version. The question of just how nourishing that is is one that begs to be shirked, but honour demands I should stretch my neck across the block and confess that Holmes doesn't seem quite so fascinating to me now as he once did. Perhaps only an adolescent can get the full thrill, and the price of wanting to go on getting it is to remain an adolescent always. This would explain a lot about the Sherlockologists.

The best single book on Doyle is *Sir Arthur Conan Doyle, l'homme et l'oeuvre*, a thoroughgoing monograph by Pierre Nordon which came out in its original language in 1964 and was translated into English as *Conan Doyle* a couple of years later. By no coincidence, it is also the best thing on Sherlock. In his chapter on 'Sherlock Holmes and the Reading Public' Nordon says most of what requires to be said about the bases of Sherlock's contemporary appeal. On the sociological side our nine introducers can't do much more than amplify Nordon's points, but since all of them are working writers of fiction (with the exception of Hugh Greene, who has, however, a profound knowledge of the period's genre literature) they usually have something of technical moment to add—and disinterested technical analysis is exactly what the Sherlock saga has for so long lacked. The Sherlockologists can't supply it, partly because most of them are nuts, but mainly because the deficiencies of Doyle's stories are what they thrive on: lacunae are what they are in business to fill, and they see Doyle's every awkwardness as a fruitful ambiguity, an irrevocable licence for speculation. The professional scribes, even when they think highly of Doyle, aren't like that. They haven't the time.

Hugh Greene reminds us that the Sherlock stories were head and shoulders above the yellow-back norm. This is still an essential point to put: Doyle was the man who made cheap fiction a field for creative work. Greene also says that A *Study in Scarlet* is broken-backed, which it is. Graham Greene calls one of Doyle's (brief, as always) descriptive scenes 'real writing from which we can all draw a lesson' but doesn't forget to insist that the subplot of *The Sign of Four* is far too like *The Moonstone* for comfort. (He also calls the meeting of Holmes and Watson in A *Study in Scarlet* unmemorable, an accurate perception denied to the Sherlockians who gravely installed a plaque in St. Bartholomew's hospital to commemorate it.)

Of *The Hound of the Baskervilles*, the only successful Sherlock novel, John Fowles gives an unsparing critical analysis, on the sound assumption that anything less would be patronizing. He sees that Doyle's great technical feat was to resolve 'the natural incompatibility of dialogue and narration' but isn't afraid to call Doyle's inaccuracy inaccuracy. (He is surely wrong, however, to say that if Doyle had really wanted to kill Holmes he would have thrown Watson off the Reichenbach Falls. It is true that Sherlock couldn't exist without Watson, but there is no possible question that Doyle was keen to rub Holmes out.)

Len Deighton, a dedicated amateur of technology, assures us that Doyle really *did* forecast many of the police methods to come—the business with the typewriter in 'A Case of Identity,' for example, was years ahead of its time. Since Nordon, eager as always to demystify Sherlock, rather downrates him on this point, it is useful to have the balance redressed. Unfortunately Deighton says almost nothing pertaining to *The Valley of Fear*, the novel which he is introducing. It seems likely that there was no editor to ask him to.

So it goes with the introductions to the short story collections. All of them are informative, but some of them tell you the same things, and only one or two illuminate the actual book. Kingsley Amis, as he did with Jane Austen and Thomas Love Peacock, gets down to fundamentals and admits that the Sherlock stories, for all their innovations in space and compression, are seldom 'classical' in the sense of playing fair with the reader. Eric Ambler talks charmingly about Doyle's erudition; Angus Wilson pertinently about the plush Nineties (1895-1898, the years of *The Return*, were Sherlock's times of

triumph); Julian Symons penetratingly about how Doyle shared out
his own personality between Holmes and Watson; and C. P. Snow—
well, he, of all the nine, it seems to me, is the one who cracks the
case.

His personality helps. Lord Snow not only sees but admits the at-
tractions of the high position in society to which Sherlock's qualities eventually brought him, with Watson striding alongside. It
might have been Sherlock's bohemianism that pulled in the crowds,
but it was his conservatism that glued them to the bleachers. This
was Pierre Nordon's salient observation on the sleuth's original
appeal, but Lord Snow has outsoared Nordon by realizing that the
same come-on is still operating with undiminished force. Sherlock
was an eccentrically toothed but essential cog in a society which
actually functioned.

The life led by Holmes and Watson in their rooms at 221B Baker
Street is a dream of unconventionality, like Act 1 of La Bohème. (A
Sherlockologist would step in here to point out that Henri Murger's
Scènes de la Vie de Bohème, the book on which the opera was later
based, is perused by Watson in A Study in Scarlet.) Although Len
Deighton is quite right to say that the busy Sherlock is really running the kind of successful medical consultancy which Doyle never
enjoyed, it is equally true to say that Holmes and Watson are
living as a pair of Oxbridge undergraduates were popularly thought
to—and indeed did—live. Holmes is a maverick scientist who treats
science as an art, thereby conflating the glamour of both fields while
avoiding the drudgery of either. He is free of all ties; he does what
he wants; he is afraid of nothing. He is above the law and dispen-
ses his own justice. As with Baudelaire, boredom is his only enemy.
If he can't escape it through an intellectual challenge, he takes
refuge in drugs.

Sherlock in The Sign of Four was fixing cocaine three times a day
for three months: if he'd tried to snort it in those quantities, his
aquiline septum would have been in considerable danger of dropping
off. Morphine gets a mention somewhere too—perhaps he was also
shooting speedballs. Certainly he was a natural dope fiend: witness
how he makes a cocktail of yesterday's cigarette roaches in 'The
Speckled Band.' In The Valley of Fear he is 'callous from over-
stimulation.' All the signs of an oil-burning habit. Did he quit cold
turkey, or did Watson ease him down? Rich pickings for the ex-
Woodstock Sherlockologists of the future. All of this must have

been heady wine for the contemporary reader endowed by the Education Act of 1870 with just enough literacy to read the *Strand* Magazine, helped out by a Sidney Paget illustration on every page.

George Orwell thought Britain needed a boys' weekly which questioned society, but Sherlock, for all his nonconformity, set no precedent. He fitted in far more than he dropped out. Sherlock was the house hippie. His latter-day chummings-up with crowned heads (including the private sessions with Queen Victoria which drive card-carrying Sherlockologists to paroxysms of conjecture) were merely the confirmation of a love for royalty which was manifest as early as 'A Scandal in Bohemia.' 'Your Majesty had not spoken,' announces Holmes, 'before I was aware that I was addressing Wilhelm Gottsreich Sigismond von Ormstein, Grand Duke of Cassel-Felstein, and Hereditary King of Bohemia.' The language, as so often in the Holmes stories, is part-way a put-on, but the relationship is genuine: Sherlock is as eager to serve as any of his cultural descendants. From Sanders of the River and Bulldog Drummond down to Pimpernel Smith and James Bond, all those gifted amateur soldiers can trace their ancestry to Sherlock's bump of reverence. Physically a virgin, spiritually he spawned children numberless as the dust.

At least 30 per cent of London's population lived below the poverty line in Sherlock's heyday, but not very many of them found their way into the stories. Doyle's criminals come almost exclusively from the income-earning classes. They are clinically, not socially, motivated. There is seldom any suggestion that crime could be a symptom of anything more general than a personal disorder. Doyle's mind was original but politically blinkered, a condition which his hero reflects. When Watson says (in 'A Scandal in Bohemia') that Holmes loathes 'every form of society with his whole Bohemian soul', it turns out that Watson means socializing. Society itself Holmes never queries. Even when he acts above the law, it is in the law's spirit that he acts. Nordon is quite right to insist that Sherlock's London, for all its wide social panorama and multiplicity of nooks and crannies, shouldn't be allowed to get mixed up with the real London. (He is quite wrong, though, to suppose that Orwell—of all people—mixed them up. Orwell said that Doyle did, but Nordon has taken Orwell's paraphrase of Doyle's view for Orwell's own opinion. He was helped to the error by a misleading French translation. Pan-culturalism has its dangers.)

Holmes was an nonconformist in a conformist age, yet still won all the conformist rewards. It was a double whammy, and for many people probably works the same magic today. I suspect that such reassurance is at the centre of the cosy satisfaction still to be obtained from reading about Sherlock, but of course there are several things it doesn't explain. The first of these is the incessant activity of the hard-core Sherlockologists, the freaks who are on the Baker Street beat pretty well full time. Most of them seem to be less interested in getting things out of the Sherlock canon than in putting things in. Archness is the keynote: coyly pedantic about imponderables, they write the frolicsome prose of the incorrigibly humourless. The opportunity for recondite tedium knows no limit. This playful racket has been going on without let-up since well before Doyle died. The output of just the last few months is depressing enough to glance through. Multiply it by decades and the mind quails.

Here is *Sherlock Holmes Detected*, by Ian McQueen. It is composed of hundreds of such pseudo-scholarly points as the contention that 'A Case of Identity' might very well be set in September, even though Holmes and Watson are described as sitting on either side of the fire—because their landlady Mrs. Hudson is known to have been conscientious, and would have laid the fire ready for use even before winter. And anyway, Mr. McQueen postulates cunningly, Holmes and Watson would probably sit on either side of the fire *even if it were not lit*. Apparently this subtle argument puts paid to other Sherlockologists who hold the view that 'A Case of Identity' can't possibly be set in September. Where that view originated is lost in the mists of fatuity: these drainingly inconsequential debates were originally got up by Ronald Knox and Sydney Roberts and formalized as an Oxford *vs.* Cambridge contest in dead-pan whimsy, which has gradually come to include the less calculated ponderosity of interloping enthusiasts who don't even realize they are supposed to be joking. Mr. McQueen's book sounds to me exactly the same as Vincent Starrett's *The Private Life of Sherlock Holmes*, which came out in 1933 and seems to have set the pace in this particular branch of the industry.

Two other volumes in the same Snark-hunting vein are the *London of Sherlock Holmes* and *In the Footsteps of Sherlock Holmes*: both written by Michael Harrison, both published recently, and both consisting of roughly the same information and photographs. Both bear the imprint of the same publishing house, which must have an editor whose blindness matches the blurb-writer's illiteracy. Mr. Harrison goes in for the same brand of bogus precision as Mr. McQueen. We hear a lot about what 'must have' happened. We are shown a photograph of the steps which Sherlock's brother Mycroft 'must have used' when going to his job at the Foreign Office. This music hall 'must have been visited' by Sherlock. There is the usual interminable speculation about the whereabouts of 221B, coupled with the usual reluctance to consider that Doyle himself obviously didn't give a damn for the plausibility of its location. The only authentic problem Mr. Harrison raises is the question of which of his two books is the sillier.

Messrs McQueen and Harrison are toddling in the giant footsteps of W. S. Baring-Gould, who compiled *The Annotated Sherlock Holmes*, which went into such scholastic minutiae with the determination of mania. Baring-Gould was also the father of yet another branch of the business—fake biographies. In his *Sherlock Holmes: A Biography of the World's First Consulting Detective* (1962) Baring-Gould sent Sherlock to Oxford. In her contribution to H. W. Bell's *Baker Street Studies* thirty years earlier, Dorothy Sayers sent him to Cambridge. Doyle sent him to neither.

Current biographical efforts are in the same footling tradition. Here is an untiringly industrious novel by John Gardner called *The Return of Moriarty*, in which the Greatest Schemer of All Time returns alive from the Reichenbach. It doesn't daunt Mr. Gardner that he is transparently ten times more interested in Moriarty than Doyle ever was. In 'The Final Problem' Sherlock tells Watson that the silent struggle to get the goods on Moriarty could be the greatest story of all, but Doyle never wrote it. The reason, as Angus Wilson divines, is that Moriarty was a less employable villain than his side-kick, Moran. Moriarty was merely the Napoleon of Crime, whereas Moran was the 'best heavy game shot that our Eastern Empire has ever produced'—which at least *sounded* less vague.

But the vagueness in Doyle is what the speculators like. And here is *The Seven-Per-Cent Solution*, pretending to be 'a reprint from the reminiscences of John H. Watson, M.D., as edited by Nicholas Meyer.' This time Sherlock and Mycroft turn out to be repressing a shameful, nameless secret. In books like this, speculation is supposed to be veering towards the humorous. The transgression would be funny, if only it made you laugh. Mr Meyer's comic invention, however, is thin. But at least he is *trying* to be silly.

The most foolish book of the bunch, and quite frankly the loopiest stretch of exegesis since John Allegro dug up the sacred mushroom, is *Naked is the Best Disguise*, by Samuel Rosenberg, which has been welcomed in the United States with reviews I find inexplicable. Mr. Rosenberg's thesis, briefly, is that Moriarty is Nietzsche and that Doyle is acting out a psycho-drama in which Sherlock is his super-ego suppressing his polymorphous perversity. Even if it had been reached by a convincing show of reasoning, this conclusion would still be far-fetched: fetched, in fact, from halfway across the galaxy. But it has been reached by no kind of reasoning except casuistry. Mr. Rosenberg argues in one place that if a Sherlock Holmes adventure is set in a house with two storeys, that means there are two *stories*— i.e., two levels of meaning. His arguing is of the same standard in every other place.

It seems that Mr. Rosenberg used to work as a legal eagle for a film studio, protecting it from plagiarism suits by finding a common literary ancestor who might have influenced both the plaintiff's script and the script the studio had in the works. He must have been well worth his salary, because he can see similarities in anything. (His standards of accuracy spring from the same gift: he spells A. J. Ayer's name wrongly on seven occasions.) It would be overpraising the book to call it negligible, yet both *Time* and *The New York Times*, among others, seem to have found it a meaty effort.

Though *Naked is the Best Disguise* considers itself to be high scholarship, it reveals itself instantly as Sherlockology by worrying over the importance of minor detail in stories whose major action their author could scarcely be bothered to keep believable. The chronology of the Holmes saga is indefinitely debatable because Doyle didn't care about establishing it. Early on, Sherlock was ignorant of the arts and didn't know the earth went around the sun: later, he quoted poetry in several languages and had wide scientific knowledge. Sherlock was a minor occupation for Doyle and he was either content to leave such inconsistencies as they were or else he plain forgot about them. Mysteries arising from them are consequently unresolvable, which is doubtless their attraction. Programs for explicating Sherlock are like Casaubon's Key to All Mythologies, which George Eliot said was as endless as a scheme for joining the stars.

Uniquely among recent Sherlockiana, *The Sherlock Holmes Scrapbook*, edited by Peter Haining, is actually enjoyable. It reproduces playbills, cartoons, production stills, and—most important—some of the magazine and newspaper articles which set Sherlockology rolling. (One of them is a piece of joky speculation by Doyle himself—a bad mistake. If he wanted to trivialize his incubus, he couldn't have chosen a worse tactic.) Basil Rathbone easily emerges as the most likely looking movie incarnation of Holmes. Sidney Paget's drawings are better than anything else then or since. (What we need is a good two-volume complete *Sherlock Holmes* with all of Paget and none of Baring-Gould.) The whole scrapbook is a great help in seeing how the legend grew, not least because it shows us that legends are of circumscribed interest: too many supernumeraries—belletrist hacks and doodling amateurs with time to burn—contribute to them. As you leaf through these chronologically ordered pages you can see the dingbats swarming aboard the bandwagon.

Doyle's brainchild could scarcely survive this kind of admiration if it did not possess archetypal attributes. Sherlockology is bastardized academicism, but academicism is one of the forces which Doyle instinctively set out to fight, and Sherlock, his Sunday punch, is not yet drained of strength. Sherlock was the first example of the art Dürrenmatt later dreamed of—the art which would weigh nothing in the scales of respectability. Doyle knew that Sherlock was cheap. What he didn't guess before it was too late to change his mind was that the cheapness would last. The only coherence in the Holmes saga is a coherence of intensity. The language is disproportionate and therefore vivid. 'He was, I take it, the most perfect reasoning and observing machine that the world has seen.' The images are unshaded and therefore flagrant. 'I took a step forward: in an instant his strange headgear began to move, and there reared itself from among his hair the squat diamond-shaped head and puffed neck of a loathsome serpent.'

But Sherlock's world was all fragments, and no real world could or can be inferred from it. In *The Valley of Fear* the Scourers work mischief to no conceivable political purpose. Moriarty machinates to no ascertainable end. The Sherlockologists would like to believe that this abstract universe is concrete, and that large questions of good and evil are being worked out. But the concreteness is only in the detail; beyond the detail there is nothing; and the large questions must always lack answers.

Doyle asked and tried to answer the large questions elsewhere, in the spiritualist faith which occupied his full mental effort. Eventually his seriousness went out of date, while his frivolity established itself as an institution. But since his mind at play could scarcely have played so well if it had not been so earnest a mind, there is no joke.

(New York Review of Books, 20 February 1975)

12. The Country Behind the Hill: Raymond Chandler

'In the long run', Raymond Chandler writes in *Raymond Chandler Speaking*, 'however little you talk or even think about it, the most durable thing in writing is style, and style is the most valuable investment a writer can make with his time.' At a time when literary values inflate and dissipate almost as fast as the currency, it still looks as if Chandler invested wisely. His style has lasted. A case could be made for saying that nothing else about his books has, but even the most irascible critic or most disillusioned fan (they are often the same person) would have to admit that Chandler at his most characteristic is just that—characteristic and not just quirky. Auden was right in wanting him to be regarded as an artist. In fact Auden's tribute might well have been that of one poet to another. If style is the only thing about Chandler's novels that can't be forgotten, it could be because his style was poetic, rather than prosaic. Even at its most explicit, what he wrote was full of implication. He used to say that he wanted to give a feeling of the country behind the hill.

Since Chandler was already well into middle-age when he began publishing, it isn't surprising that he found his style quickly. Most of the effects that were to mark *The Big Sleep* in 1939 were already present, if only fleetingly, in an early story like 'Killer in the Rain', published in *Black Mask* magazine in 1935. In fact some of the very same sentences are already there. This from 'Killer in the Rain':

> The rain splashed knee-high off the sidewalks, filled the gutters, and big cops in slickers that shone like gun barrels had a lot of fun carrying little girls in silk stockings and cute little rubber boots across the bad places, with a lot of squeezing.

Compare this from *The Big Sleep*:

> Rain filled the gutters and splashed knee-high off the pavement. Big cops in slickers that shone like gun barrels had a lot of fun

carrying giggling girls across the bad places. The rain drummed hard on the roof of the car and the burbank top began to leak. A pool of water formed on the floorboards for me to keep my feet in.

So there is not much point in talking about how Chandler's style developed. As soon as he was free of the short-paragraph restrictions imposed by the cheaper pulps, his way of writing quickly found its outer limits: all he needed to do was refine it. The main refining instrument was Marlowe's personality. The difference between the two cited passages is really the difference between John Dalmas and Philip Marlowe. Marlowe's name was not all that more convincing than Dalmas's, but he was a more probable, or at any rate less improbable, visionary. In *The Big Sleep* and all the novels that followed, the secret of plausibility lies in the style, and the secret of the style lies in Marlowe's personality. Chandler once said that he thought of Marlowe as the American mind. As revealed in Chandler's *Notebooks* (edited by Frank McShane and published by the Ecco Press, New York), one of Chandler's many projected titles was *The Man Who Loved the Rain*. Marlowe loved the rain.

Flaubert liked tinsel better than silver because tinsel possessed all silver's attributes plus one in addition—pathos. For whatever reason, Chandler was fascinated by the cheapness of L.A. When he said that it had as much personality as a paper cup, he was saying what he liked about it. When he said that he could leave it without a pang, he was saying why he felt at home there. In a city where the rich were as vulgar as the poor, all the streets were mean. In a democracy of trash, Marlowe was the only aristocrat. Working for 25 dollars a day plus expenses (Jim Rockford in the T.V. series *The Rockford Files* now works for ten times that and has to live in a trailer), Marlowe was as free from materialistic constraint as any hermit. He saw essences. Chandler's particular triumph was to find a style for matching Marlowe to the world. Vivid language was the decisive element, which meant that how not to make Marlowe sound like too good a *writer* was the continuing problem. The solution was a kind of undercutting wit, a style in which Marlowe mocked his own fine phrases. A comic style, always on the edge of self-parody—and, of course, sometimes over the edge—but at its best combining the exultant and the sad in an inseparable mixture.

For a writer who is not trying all that hard to be funny, it is remarkable how often Chandler can make you smile. His conciseness can strike you as a kind of wit in itself. The scene with General Sternwood in the hot-house, the set-piece forming Chapter Two of *The Big Sleep*, is done with more economy than you can remember: there are remarkably few words on the page to generate such a lasting impression of warm fog in the reader's brain. 'The air was thick, wet, steamy and larded with the cloying smell of tropical orchids in bloom.' It's the rogue verb 'larded' which transmits most of the force. Elsewhere, a single simile gives you the idea of General Sternwood's aridity. 'A few locks of dry white hair clung to his scalp, like wild flowers fighting for life on a bare rock.' The fact that he stays dry in the wet air is the measure of General Sternwood's nearness to death. The bare rock is the measure of his dryness. At their best, Chandler's similes click into place with this perfect appositeness. He can make you laugh, he gets it so right—which perhaps means that he gets it *too* right. What we recognize as wit is always a self-conscious performance.

But since wit that works at all is rare enough, Chandler should be respected for it. And anyway, he didn't always fall into the trap of making his characters too eloquent. Most of Marlowe's best one-liners are internal. In the film of *The Big Sleep*, when Marlowe tells General Sternwood that he has already met Carmen in the hall, he says: 'She tried to sit in my lap while I was standing up.' Bogart gets a big laugh with that line, but only half of the line is Chandler's. All that Chandler's Marlowe says is: 'Then she tried to sit in my lap.' The film version of Marlowe got the rest of the gag from somewhere else—either from William Faulkner, who wrote the movie, or from Howard Hawks, who directed it, or perhaps from both. On the page, Marlowe's gags are private and subdued. About Carmen, he concludes that 'thinking was always going to be a bother to her.' He notices—as no camera could notice, unless the casting director flung his net very wide—that her thumb is like a finger, with no curve in its first joint. He compares the shocking whiteness of her teeth to fresh orange pith. He gets you scared stiff of her in a few sentences.

Carmen is the first in a long line of little witches that runs right through the novels, just as her big sister, Vivian, is the first in a long line of rich bitches who find that Marlowe is the only thing money can't buy. The little witches are among the most haunting of Chandler's obsessions and the rich bitches are among the least. Whether little witch or rich bitch, both kinds of woman signal their availability to Marlowe by crossing their legs shortly after sitting down and regaling him with tongue-in-the-lung French kisses a few seconds after making physical contact.

All the standard Chandler character ingredients were there in the first novel, locked in a pattern of action so complicated that not even the author was subsequently able to puzzle it out. *The Big Sleep* was merely the first serving of the mixture as before. But the language was fresh and remains so. When Chandler wrote casually of 'a service station glaring with wasted light' he was striking a note that Dashiell Hammett had never dreamed of. Even the book's title rang a bell. Chandler thought that there were only two types of slang which were any good: slang that had established itself in the language, and slang that you made up yourself. As a term for death, 'the big sleep' was such a successful creation that Eugene O'Neill must have thought it had been around for years, since he used it in *The Iceman Cometh* (1946) as an established piece of low-life tough talk. But there is no reason for disbelieving Chandler's claim to have invented it.

Chandler's knack for slang would have been just as commendable even if he had never thought of a thing. As the *Notebooks* reveal, he made lists of slang terms that he had read or heard. The few he kept and used were distinguished from the many he threw away by their metaphorical exactness. He had an ear for depth—he could detect incipient permanence in what sounded superficially like ephemera. A term like 'under glass', meaning to be in prison, attracted him by its semantic compression. In a letter collected in *Raymond Chandler Speaking*, he regards it as self-evident that an American term like 'milk run' is superior to the equivalent British term 'piece of cake'. The superiority being in the range of evocation. As it happened, Chandler *was* inventive, not only in slang but in more ambitiously suggestive figures of speech. He was spontaneous as well as accurate. His second novel, *Farewell, My Lovely* (1940)—which he was always to regard as his finest—teems with show-stopping metaphors, many of them dedicated to conjuring up the gargantuan figure of Moose Malloy.

In fact some of them stop the show too thoroughly. When Chandler describes Malloy as standing out from his surroundings like 'a tarantula on a slice of angel food' he is getting things backwards, since the surroundings have already been established as very sordid indeed. Malloy ought to be standing out from them like a slice of angel food on a tarantula. Chandler at one time confessed to Alfred A. Knopf that in *The Big Sleep* he had run his metaphors into the ground, the implication being that he cured himself of the habit later on. But the truth is that he was always prone to overcooking a simile. As Perelman demonstrated in *Farewell, My Lovely Appetizer* (a spoof which Chandler admired), this is one of the areas in which Chandler is most easily parodied, although it should be remembered that it takes a Perelman to do the parodying.

'It was a blonde', says Marlowe, looking at Helen Grayle's photograph, 'A blonde to make a bishop kick a hole in a stained-glass window.' I still laugh when I read that, but you can imagine Chandler jotting down such brain-waves *à propos* of nothing and storing them up against a rainy day. They leap off the page so high that they never again settle back into place, thereby adding to the permanent difficulty of remembering what happens to whom where in which novel. The true wit, in *Farewell, My Lovely* as in all the other books, lies in effects which marry themselves less obtrusively to character, action and setting. Jessie Florian's bathrobe, for example. 'It was just something around her body.' A sentence like that seems hardly to be trying, but it tells you all you need to know. Marlowe's realization that Jessie has been killed—'The corner post of the bed was smeared darkly with something the flies liked'—is trying harder for understatement, but in those circumstances Marlowe *would* understate the case, so the sentence fits. Poor Jessie Florian. 'She was as cute as a washtub.'

And some of the lines simply have the humour of information conveyed at a blow, like the one about the butler at the Grayle house. As always when Chandler is dealing with Millionaires' Row, the place is described with a cataloguing eye for ritzy detail, as if F. Scott Fitzgerald had written a contribution to *Architectural Digest*. (The Murdock house in *The High Window* bears a particularly close resemblance to Gatsby's mansion: *vide* the lawn flowing 'like a cool green tide around a rock'.) Chandler enjoyed conjuring up the grand houses into which Marlowe came as an interloper and out of which he always went with a sigh of relief, having hauled the family skeletons out of the walk-in cupboards and left the beautiful, wild elder daughter sick with longing for his uncorruptible countenance. But in several telling pages about the Grayle residence, the sentence that really counts is the one about the butler. 'A man in a striped vest and gilt buttons opened the door, bowed, took my hat and was through for the day.'

In the early books and novels, before he moved to Laurel Canyon, when he still lived at 615 Cahuenga Building on Hollywood Boulevard, near Ivar, telephone Glenview 7537, Marlowe was fond of Los Angeles. All the bad things happened in Bay City. In Bay City there were crooked cops, prostitution, drugs, but after you came to (Marlowe was always coming to in Bay City, usually a long time after he had been sapped, because in Bay City they always hit him very hard) you could drive home. Later on the evil had spread everywhere and Marlowe learned to hate what L.A. had become. The set-piece descriptions of his stamping-ground got more and more sour. But the descriptions were always there—one of the strongest threads running through the novels from first to last. And even at their most acridly poisonous they still kept something of the wide-eyed lyricism of that beautiful line in Farewell My Lovely about a dark night in the canyons—the night Marlowe drove Lindsay Marriott to meet his death. 'A yellow window hung here and there by itself, like the last orange.'

There is the usual ration of overcooked metaphors in The High Window (1942). Lois Morny gives forth with 'a silvery ripple of laughter that held the unspoiled naturalness of a bubble dance.' (By the time you have worked out that this means her silvery ripple of laughter held no unspoiled naturalness, the notion has gone dead.) We learn that Morny's club in Idle Valley looks like a high-budget musical. 'A lot of light and glitter, a lot of scenery, a lot of clothes, a lot of sound, an all-star cast, and a plot with all the originality and drive of a split fingernail.' Tracing the club through the musical down to the fingernail, your attention loses focus. It's a better sentence than any of Chandler's imitators ever managed, but it was the kind of sentence they felt able to imitate—lying loose and begging to be picked up.

As always, the quiet effects worked better. The back yard of the Morny house is an instant Hockney. 'Beyond was a walled-in garden containing flower-beds crammed with showy annuals, a badminton court, a nice stretch of greensward, and a small tiled pool glittering angrily in the sun.' The rogue adverb 'angrily' is the word that registers the sun's brightness. It's a long step, taken in a few words, to night-time in Idle Valley. 'The wind was quiet out here and the valley moonlight was so sharp that the black shadows looked as if they had been cut with an engraving tool.' Saying how unreal the real looks make it realer.

'Bunker Hill is old town, lost town, shabby town, crook town.' *The High Window* has many such examples of Chandler widening his rhythmic scope. Yet the best and the worst sentences are unusually far apart. On several occasions Chandler is extraordinarily clumsy. 'He was a tall man with glasses and a high-domed bald head that made his ears look as if they had slipped down his head.' This sentence is literally effortless: the clumsy repetition of 'head' is made possible only because he isn't trying. Here is a useful reminder of the kind of concentration required to achieve a seeming ease. And here is another: 'From the lay of the land a light in the living room . . .' Even a writer who doesn't, as Chandler usually did, clean as he goes, would normally liquidate so languorous an alliterative lullaby long before the final draft.

But in between the high points and the low, the general tone of *The High Window* had an assured touch. The narrator's interior monologue is full of the sort of poetry Laforgue liked—*comme ils sont beaux, les trains manqués.* Marlowe's office hasn't changed, nor will it ever. 'The same stuff I had had last year, and the year before that. Not beautiful, not gay, but better than a tent on the beach.' Marlowe accuses the two cops, Breeze and Spangler, of talking dialogue in which every line is a punch-line. Criticism is not disarmed: in Chandler, everybody talks that kind of dialogue most of the time. But the talk that matters most is the talk going on inside Marlowe's head, and Chandler was making it more subtle with each book.

Chandler's descriptive powers are at their highest in *The Lady In The Lake* (1943). It takes Marlowe a page and a half of thoroughly catalogued natural detail to drive from San Bernardino to Little Fawn Lake, but when he gets there he sees the whole thing in a sentence. 'Beyond the gate the road wound for a couple of hundred yards through trees and then suddenly below me was a small oval lake deep in trees and rocks and wild grass, like a drop of dew caught in a curled leaf.' Hemingway could do bigger things, but small moments like those were Chandler's own. (Nevertheless Hemingway got on Chandler's nerves: Dolores Gonzales in *The Little Sister* is to be heard saying 'I was pretty good in there, no?' and the nameless girl who vamps Marlowe at Roger Wade's party in *The Long Goodbye* spoofs the same line. It should be remembered, however, that Chandler admired Hemingway to the end, forbearing to pour scorn even on *Across the River and Into the Trees*. The digs at Papa in Chandler's novels can mainly be put down to self-defence.)

The Little Sister (1949), Chandler's first post-war novel, opens with Marlowe stalking a bluebottle fly around his office. 'He didn't want to sit down. He just wanted to do wing-overs and sing the prologue to *Pagliacci*.' Ten years before, in *Trouble Is My Business*, John Dalmas felt like singing the same thing after being sapped in Harriet Huntress's apartment. Chandler was always ready to bring an idea back for a second airing. A Ph.D thesis could be written about the interest John Dalmas and Philip Marlow take in bugs and flies. There is another thesis in the tendency of Chandler's classier dames to show a startling line of white scalp in the parting of their hair: Dolores Gonzales, who throughout *The Little Sister* propels herself at Marlowe like Lupe Velez seducing Errol Flynn, is only one of the several high-toned vamps possessing this tonsorial feature. 'She made a couple of drinks in a couple of glasses you could almost have stood umbrellas in.'' A pity about that 'almost'—it ruins a good hyperbole. Moss Spink's extravagance is better conveyed: 'He waved a generous hand on which a canary-yellow diamond looked like an amber traffic light.'

But as usual the would-be startling images are more often unsuccessful than successful. The better work is done lower down the scale of excitability. Joseph P. Toad, for example. 'The neck of his canary-yellow shirt was open wide, which it had to be if his neck was going to get out.' Wit like that lasts longer than hyped-up similes. And some of the dialogue, though as stylized as ever, would be a gift to actors: less supercharged than usual, it shows some of the natural balance which marked the lines Chandler has been writing for the movies. Here is Marlowe sparring with Sheridan Ballou.

'Did she suggest how to go about shutting my mouth?'
'I got the impression she was in favour of doing it with some kind of heavy blunt instrument.'

Such an exchange is as playable as anything in *Double Indemnity* or *The Blue Dahlia*. And imagine what Laird Cregar would have done with Toad's line 'You could call me a guy what wants to help out a guy that don't want to make trouble for a guy.' Much as he would have hated the imputation, Chandler's toil in the salt-mines under the Paramount mountain had done things for him. On the other hand, the best material in *The Little Sister* is inextricably bound up with the style of Marlowe's perception, which in turn depends on Chandler's conception of himself. There could be no complete screen rendition of the scene with Jules Oppenheimer in the studio patio. With peeing dogs instead of hot-house steam, it's exactly the same lay-out as Marlowe's encounter with General Sternwood in *The Big Sleep*, but then there was no filming *that* either. The mood of neurotic intensity—Marlowe as the soldier-son, Sternwood/Oppenheimer as the father-figure at death's door—would be otiose in a film script, which requires that all action be relevant. In the novels, such passages are less about Marlowe than about Chandler working out his obsessions through Marlowe, and nobody ever wanted to make a film about Chandler.

In *The Long Goodbye* (1953) Marlowe moves to a house on Yucca Avenue in Laurel Canyon and witnesses the disintegration of Terry Lennox. Lennox can't control his drinking. Marlowe, master of his own thirst, looks sadly on. As we now know, Chandler in real life was more Lennox than Marlowe. In the long dialogues between these two characters he is really talking to himself. There is no need to be afraid of the biographical fallacy: even if we knew nothing about Chandler's life, it would still be evident that a fantasy is being worked out. Worked out but not admitted—as so often happens in good-bad books, the author's obsessions are being catered to, not examined. Chandler, who at least worked for a living, had reason for thinking himself more like Marlowe than like Lennox. (Roger Wade, the other of the book's big drinkers, is, being a writer, a bit closer to home.) Nevertheless Marlowe is a day-dream—more and more of a day-dream as Chandler gets better and better at making him believable. By this time it's Marlowe v. the Rest of the World. Of all Chandler's nasty cops, Captain Gregorius is the nastiest. 'His big nose was a network of burst capillaries.' But even in the face of the ultimate nightmare Marlowe keeps his nerve. Nor is he taken in by Eileen Wade, superficially the dreamiest of all Chandler's dream girls.

It was a near-run thing, however. Chandler mocked romantic writers who always used three adjectives but Marlowe fell into the same habit when contemplating Eileen Wade. 'She looked exhausted now, and frail, and very beautiful." Perhaps he was tipped off when Eileen suddenly caught the same disease and started referring to 'the

wild, mysterious, improbable kind of love that never comes but once'.
In the end she turns out to be a killer, a dream-girl gone sour like
Helen Grayle in *Farewell, My Lovely*, whose motherly clutch
('smooth and soft and warm and comforting') was that of a strangler.
The Long Goodbye is the book of Marlowe's irretrievable disil-
lusion.

> I was as hollow and empty as the spaces between the stars. When
> I got home I mixed a stiff one and stood by the open window in
> the living-room and sipped it and listened to the ground swell of
> the traffic on Laurel Canyon Boulevard and looked at the glare
> of the big, angry city hanging over the shoulder of the hills
> through which the boulevard had been cut. Far off the banshee
> wail of police or fire sirens rose and fell, never for very long com-
> pletely silent. Twenty-four hours a day somebody is running,
> somebody else is trying to catch him.

Even Marlowe got caught. Linda Loring nailed him. 'The tip of
her tongue touched mine.' His vestal virginity was at long last
ravished away. But naturally there was no Love, at least not
yet.

Having broken the ice, Marlowe was to be laid again, most notably by the *chic*, leg-crossing Miss Vermilyea in Chandler's next
novel, *Playback* (1958). It is only towards the end of that novel that
we realize how thoroughly Marlowe is being haunted by Linda
Loring's memory. Presumably this is the reason why Marlowe's
affair with Miss Vermilyea is allowed to last only one night. (' "I
hate you," she said with her mouth against mine. "Not for this, but
because perfection never comes twice and with us it came too soon.
And I'll never see you again and I don't want to. It would have to
be for ever or not at all." ') We presume that Miss Vermilyea wasn't
just being tactful.

Anyway, Linda Loring takes the prize, but not before Marlowe
has raced through all his usual situations, albeit in compressed form.
Once again, for example, he gets hit on the head. 'I went zooming
out over a dark sea and exploded in a sheet of flame.' For terseness
this compares favourably with an equivalent moment in *Bay City
Blues*, written twenty years before.

> Then a naval gun went off in my ear and my head was a large
> pink firework exploding into the vault of the sky and scattering

and falling slow and pale, and then dark, into the waves. Blackness ate me up.

Chandler's prose had attained respectability, but by now he had less to say with it—perhaps because time had exposed his daydreams to the extent that even he could see them for what they were. The belief was gone. In *The Poodle Springs Story*, his last, unfinished novel, Marlowe has only one fight left to fight, the war against the rich. Married now to Linda, he slugs it out with her toe to toe. It is hard to see why he bothers to keep up the struggle. Even heroes get tired and not even the immortal stay young forever. Defeat was bound to come some time and although it is undoubtedly true that the rich are corrupt at least Linda knows how corruption ought to be done: the classiest of Chandler's classy dames, the richest bitch of all, she will bring Marlowe to a noble downfall. There is nothing vulgar about Linda. (If that Hammond organ-*cum*-cocktail bar in their honeymoon house disturbs you, don't forget that the place is only rented.)

So Marlowe comes to an absurd end, and indeed it could be said that he was always absurd. Chandler was always dreaming. He dreamed of being more attractive than he was, taller than he was, less trammelled than he was, braver than he was. But so do most men. We dream about our ideal selves, and it is at least arguable that we would be even less ideal if we didn't. Marlowe's standards of conduct would be our standards if we had his courage. We can rationalize the discrepancy by convincing ourselves that if we haven't got his courage he hasn't got our mortgage, but the fact remains that his principles are real.

Marlowe can be hired, but he can't be bought. As a consequence, he is alone. Hence his lasting appeal. Not that he is without his repellent aspects. His race prejudice would amount to outright fascism if it were not so evident that he would never be able to bring himself to join a movement. His sexual imagination is deeply suspect and he gets hit on the skull far too often for someone who works largely with his head. His taste in socks is oddly vile for one who quotes so easily from Browning ('the poet, not the automatic'). But finally you recognize his tone of voice.

It is your own, day-dreaming of being tough, of giving the rich bitch the kiss-off, of saying smart things, of defending the innocent, of being the hero. It is a silly day-dream because anyone who could

E*

really do such splendid things would probably not share it, but without it the rest of us would be even more lost than we are. Chandler incarnated this necessary fantasy by finding a style for it. His novels are exactly as good as they should be. In worse books, the heroes are too little like us : in better books, too much.

(1977)

13. The Effective Intelligence of Nigel Balchin

'He is, in fact,' reads the standard Biographical Note in Nigel Balchin's publicity file at Collins, 'in many ways a survival of the days before specialisation became a fetish, and everybody had to be given a convenient label.' There are good reasons for thinking that Balchin wrote this Note himself. The blurbish prose might lack his characteristic rhythm, but the pride in his own versatility is unmistakable. 'To be unlabellable in the modern world', the Note concludes, 'is rare enough to be interesting.' In his time Balchin did manage to dodge most labels, but a fatal one sought him out, applied itself lovingly, and stuck. He was called a brilliant popular novelist.

To be a brilliant popular novelist rather than a pedestrian serious one—to be glittering thin rather than dull solid—implies an impermeable surface, a level below which aesthetic interest does not run. But it seems to me that Balchin is aesthetically interesting in the last analysis as well as the first, and that his reputation ought not to be allowed to remain in its present state of unfocussed semi-respectability. In many ways he is the missing writer of the Forties. The intense illumination of his fame made him a ghost while he was still alive. Often by his admirers, and on a few embarrassing occasions by himself, his intelligibility was used as a stick to beat the highbrows with. In such circumstances it might well have appeared philistine to contend that his clarity had shown certain kinds of artistic ambition to be unfruitful. But there is no reason to be afraid of that imputation now. Not only is Balchin still widely read, but the conflict between the art novel and the top-flight popular novel can now more easily be seen to be permanent. There ought no longer to be any question of either competitor suppressing the other. A more useful question to ask is whether the dialectic between them, far from being inimical to culture, is not essential to it.

The peak of Balchin's success, and of his critical acceptability as a writer of importance, lay in the War period. Before and after, his career leads up to that long moment and then away. He was born in

1908 and spent the years 1919–27 at Dauntsey's School, where he
demonstrated his innate omnicompetence by becoming Captain of
Cricket, Hockey, Rugby and the School itself. At Cambridge he was
a Natural Sciences Exhibitioner and Prizeman in Peterhouse, con-
triving to play county cricket while still an undergraduate. His
published biographical sketches mention an Honours degree but don't
specify the class. In the Biographical Note in his publisher's files
the words First Class are scratched out—the only words apart from
his first wife's name to be eliminated from the text. Balchin took
pride in not being an 'academic' (his adjective) scientist: on leaving
Cambridge he became an industrial consultant on the staff of the
National Institute of Industrial Psychology, and his literary interests
for ever afterwards ran a parallel course with non-literary ones—a
course rare in Britain, and one by which Balchin obviously set
great, if sometimes defensive, store. He was married in 1933: the
marriage produced three children, all daughters, and lasted until
the end of the Forties. Its dissolution.at the beginning of the Fifties
was to be a turning point, as far as one can tell, in his career. Certainly nothing was the same after that.

While things were going well, though, they went very well. As a
contributor to *Punch* in the early Thirties Balchin wrote satirical
sketches about industry, under the name of Mark Spade. They
were collected into books (*How to Run a Bassoon Factory* and *Business for Pleasure*) and gained some reputation. During all this pre-
war period his private business connections seem to have been with
Rowntrees—a relationship he tended to soft-pedal in future interviews. He also wrote three barely noticed novels.

Balchin was prosperous, but hardly exploring his full potential.
The War changed that overnight. He entered it as a Civil Servant,
spending two years at the Ministry of Food. His experiences at the
Ministry provided the background for his novel *Darkness Falls From
the Air*, which came out in 1942 and was a distinct critical success.
Like most of Balchin's better-known novels this one now goes on
selling in Pan paperback, but even when you ignore the later Pan
figures, the earlier sales—in Collins hardback, service editions, and
so on—are impressive enough. *Darkness Falls From the Air* did
14,000 hard-back and at least 99,000 in cheap editions up until the
late Fifties. The Balchin pattern was established: critical success and
big sales all rolled into one.

From the Ministry of Food Balchin went as an officer into the department of the Scientific Adviser to the Army Council. The job, back-room and hush-hush, by all accounts brought the very best out of him. A wartime friend, Denis McMahon, recalled in his obituary for Balchin how the new recruit took over instruction in chemical warfare within a week of arriving to train for it, and was being consulted by the commander of his unit within the first fortnight. Balchin apparently pioneered the use of punched cards and counter-sorter machines in personnel selection, discrediting brass-hat opposition in just the sort of economically staged scene that crops up in his novels. Balchin, said McMahon, was 'the most intelligently effective *and* effectively intelligent man I have met.' With due allowances for exaggeration, there can't be any doubt that Balchin was a gifted logistical thinker—a natural critical path analyst with a remarkable capacity for absorbing the detail of new fields. He dealt in realities, the art of the possible. The test was relevance.

During the early part of this period, in 1943, Balchin published his smash-hit novel *The Small Back Room*. Very few thrillers have ever been so praised. His technique of presenting the problems of his characters against the background of working out a scientific puzzle, and then presenting all *that* against the background of the war itself, was commended as the sort of complexity that ordinary, intelligent people could understand and appreciate. The book sold 34,000 in hardback and at least 337,000 in cheap editions over the next fifteen years and of course goes on selling still.

Balchin finished the War as a Brigadier, and in the year of victory brought out the novel which is most often identified with his name, *Mine Own Executioner*. For background material, this novel, although set at the end of the War, reverts to his pre-war experience as a psychologist, and one might think that it had therefore broken free from its author's personal chronology: another novel, *A Sort of Traitors*, was apparently planned that year (it was to be published in 1949) and would have fitted the pattern better. But on second thoughts one can see that *Mine Own Executioner* might have a lot to do with Balchin's crisis of occupation, as the artificial circumstances which alone could plumb his talents came to an end. For the moment, though, success—his biggest ever. The book sold 54,000 in hard-back alone, a sale that was more than just a last flare of the wartime reconciliation between Fiction and the Reading Public. The book went on doing good business, and by 1953 had sold 250,000 copies in paperback.

The three wartime novels were built to an artless-looking, highly
refined formula of naturalistic conflict taking place within a thriller
plot. With Balchin's first post-war book the pattern broke, and his
commercial success broke with it. *Lord, I Was Afraid* is a period book
in a way that the wartime books are not. Written in play form, it
is the kind of art-conscious, *angst*-ridden Forties novel that really
belongs to the Thirties, as if V.E. Day had dumped the author back
into the same set of questions he had left behind in 1939. Probably
this air of atavism has more to do with the Experimental lay-out
than with anything else, in the same way that Philip Toynbee's early
books can't help reminding you of *The Dog Beneath the Skin*. There
is a twenty-year continuity of that kind of writing which goes right
through the war as if it wasn't there. *Lord, I Was Afraid* sold 11,000
in hardback, and the sales in cheap edition were apparently negligible.

Balchin was still leading a multiple life but it was necessarily less
defined than in wartime. His fiction, however, achieved—perhaps in
compensation—a sharp personal focus when he published *The Borgia
Testament* in 1948. Balchin's fascination with Cesare Borgia reveals
as much about his mind as the same fascination revealed about
Machiavelli's, and *The Borgia Testament* is by no means an
unworthy adjunct to *The Prince*. For Balchin, feeling kinship with
Cesare wouldn't necessarily have entailed conceit: Cesare's unsentimental appreciation of what needed to be *done* in given circumstances was exactly the power which Balchin had good reason to
think he possessed to an unusual degree. And again like Machiavelli,
Balchin couldn't help pondering the question of how Cesare's career
was cut short. Machiavelli ascribes it to ill fortune. Balchin talks of
failing purpose. This is the enduring problem of Cesare's life-story
and Balchin didn't really have a solution for it—which, for a man
accustomed to having solutions for everything, is a revealing concession in itself. The book is of interest on several levels. Doubtless
it was on the straight narrative level that it attracted its 40,000
buyers for the hardback edition.

After that, Balchin settled down to a steady 36,000 hardback
sales for novel after novel. Presumably there was a loyal audience
who bought every new Balchin as a matter of course. In that event
A Sort of Traitors, which came out in 1949, must have seemed a
welcome return to the wartime formula. This time it was the Cold
War, but the layer-cake was stacked in the same old reliable way,

conflict on top of puzzle on top of background. It was about here that the big change came in Balchin's life. His marriage broke up.

In real life, the parting was apparently a civilized matter, and those concerned were soon friends: the ex-Mrs. Balchin married the artist Michael Ayrton, and Balchin also married again. Artistically, however, it can only be said that Balchin reacted with a thinly disguised cry of self-assertion. *A Way Through The Wood*, published in 1951, is the key to his conception of himself as a social, sexual human being. It illuminates the personal element of all the books before and after.

Sundry Creditors came next, in 1953. As a novel about industry it is irreproachable: this is the way Lord Snow would write about such matters if he had Balchin's sheer deftness of hand. Most of the good critics were agreed, however, that the book's perfection of surface entailed a certain programmatic sketchiness in the characterization, major as well as minor. A collection of short stories, *Last Recollections of My Uncle Charles*, followed in 1954 and proved, among other things, that collections of short stories don't make it as merchandise. Balchin's by-now standard 30,000-plus sales dropped by two thirds. He climbed back to his usual level with *The Fall of the Sparrow* in 1955. This was another of the psychology novels, and this time it covered a long time-scale, so that the main characters were traced right through the war and out the other side. In some ways it is the old, reliably marketable layer-cake. In others it comes uncomfortably close, like the two previous novels, to the shielded surface of it's author's ego.

If one were reading Balchin's books in sequence, the history of his creative effort would by this time bear a marked resemblance to the plot of one of his own novels—a psychological thriller featuring all his cryptic economy and differing only in an obdurate refusal to clear up the central problem of its plot. The reader would find it difficult to refrain from guessing. The narrator is manifestly trying to tell him something; something about being in some kind of trouble. The books project this trouble into their plots, but whether as a way of facing it, or as a way of not facing it, is a puzzle—the abiding puzzle at the centre of Balchin's creative effort.

In 1962 came *Seen Dimly Before Dawn*, a story of sexual awakening in adolescence. *In the Absence of Mrs. Petersen* followed in 1966, having as protagonist a writer obsessed with a lost wife. The book is weak, and its successor, *Kings of Infinite Space* (1967) is even weaker, dealing with a technological matter—space travel—which has outstripped Balchin's capacity for response. His concentration was obviously gone. There was no time to get it back. He died in 1970, aged 61. He left more than £10,000, showing himself to have been competent and provident to the last.

Balchin said that he was influenced by the Icelandic Sagas, in which you were told only what people said or did, and had to work out what they thought from that. His success in adapting this method for the novel provided the handle for the philistine appreciation of Balchin: the novel of action, streamlined to perfection, made the novel of commentary look tubby. But sooner or later most of the intelligent critics realized that the author, invisible behind his armour, was being less than wholly candid in his portrayal of reality. Contributing to the post-war British Council symposium *Since 1939*, Henry Reed was given the job of summarizing activities in the Novel. Balchin got a commendation, but it was at the tail end of the piece, a long way behind the artists. The usual points were made about his skill of craft and solidity of material, but Reed was confident in diagnosing a case of Hemingwayesque sentimentality, of wish-fulfilment masquerading as taciturnity.

Considering that Balchin nowhere sounded very much like Hemingway, it's interesting that several contemporary critics should have concurred in deciding that he did. The reason, I think, is that Balchin makes the same kind of artistic claim, and embodies the same kind of partial failure in backing it up. All is supposed to be revealed in action—the pretension to objectivity is absolute. Any first-person narrator modelled on the author is supposedly as liable as all the other characters to a revelation of his own failings. But when you get right down to it, everything still seems manipulated, by an authorial ego bent on protecting itself. Pamela Hansford Johnson once said that the trouble with most Balchin novels is that everything in them is relevant. And this defence of selfhood is what everything is relevant to.

Balchin's pride in his own real-life competence is easily detected as a projection in his novels. There is always a character, usually a major one and often enough the holder of the main viewpoint, who knows how things ought to be done. But whereas in life Balchin's satisfaction with this ability, if one judges by the tenor of his interviews, seems to have been all of a piece, in the novels the ability comes continually into question, as if the man who possesses it were somehow excluded from the full possibilities of emotion. And the interesting thing—the fundamentally interesting thing in Balchin's creative psychology—is that he can't put this question in an way that will oblige him to try answering it. Stopping the enquiry from reaching that point is one of the duties his technique fulfils. Instead of being fully exploratory, his novels are therapeutic. And the therapy leads to no cure—all it does is continue.

The man of competence in *Darkness Falls From the Air* is the narrator, Bill Sarratt. A volunteer Civil Servant, Sarratt is trying to clear bureaucratic obstructions and get his Ministry working on sound business lines. It's clear to him, and he makes it clear to us, that ordinary muddling-through will lose the War. Without asking the narrator to praise himself, but just by revealing him in action against the inertia of petty office-holders, Balchin manages to convince us of his hero's fitness: we don't question it. But what we can't help questioning is the verisimilitude of the conflict between private characters taking place against the background of this public squabble. Sarratt's wife, Marcia, is infatuated with Stephen, a posturing dreamer. Reading on through Balchin, we learn that this is the standard triangle of his novels. The lady admires the competent man but loses her head over a charmer. The competent man looks on with resignation as the two irrational creatures waste each other's time. For some reason Balchin can't get free of this formula: even when he switches the sexes, it still looms as an obvious plot-element in a narrative technique which otherwise successfully dedicates itself to being the reverse of obvious.

Stephen is outrageous but Marcia feels that he needs her, and can't fight free even when Sarratt threatens to walk out. When Marcia finally tries to achieve seriousness by helping the wounded in the blitzed East End, she is literally immolated. Her death in a raid is presented as some kind of purification, but to the reader it can't help but seem excessive—the couple are reconciled in the wife's ritual punishment. The most that the husband can admit to (and there is no indication that the author's view is any different) is that he might be disqualified from Love. Being so capable, he perhaps offers nothing with which these poor incapable creatures can identify. The bereaved hero is left silent and grim, all set to have his taciturn grief misinterpreted as callousness by the indefatigable Stephen. Stephen is not too bad to be true, but he is bad enough to be unwarrantably convenient to the neatness of the plot. In a subtle, highly sophisticated way, the reader's wishes are being catered to. Everybody is Sarratt, and everybody knows Stephen. But nobody is Stephen. And why else does Marcia ever leave us, except through her lack of strength to cope with our perfections?

In *The Small Back Room* the competent man is the narrator, Sammy, a problem-solver up against a lethal new type of booby-trap being air-dropped by the Luftwaffe. The booby-trap is designed to kill disposal experts, through flattering them into inattention by offering them a decoy solution to its fuse. Sammy has only one foot, and the pain of his stump drives him to drink. But he's the best scientific brain in his department. One of the book's themes is that he partly wastes his ability by not assuming power when it is offered—his reluctance to be promoted beyond the level of ordinary practical problems limits everyone's effectiveness, including his own, since the duffers who inherit the vacant posts direct policy in the wrong direction. His girl-friend, Susan, sees that in being content to just get on with what he knows he's good at he is indulging a weakness. This theme in the book is convincing; there can be few readers who have not been forced to take a long look at their own lives because of it, even if (or perhaps especially when) they don't themselves suffer from Sammy's superabundance of practical ability.

But Sammy's ability is also questioned in another way, a way over which Balchin hasn't, one begins to suspect, quite got control. In the famous scene at the end of the book, where Sammy at last deduces how the booby-trap must work, his courage and mental strength hold up but his physical strength gives out, and he needs assistance to complete the job. This failure he interprets as a catastrophic revelation of weakness. Despite the fact that the novel spends a good deal of its time rubbing in Sammy's sense of physical inadequacy, this conclusion again seems excessive, and sets the reader to wondering if *The Small Back Room* might not be just as programmatic as its predecessor. Susan is strong rather than weak—in fact she's a paragon—and there is no element in her of the author taking revenge on the irrational feminine. She supports Sammy through thick and thin, and her criticism of his character is the sort of news he obviously needs to hear. Nevertheless Sammy's unease about Susan can't be fully accounted for by reference to a missing foot.

As often in Balchin, a ritual maiming tends to distract the reader's eye from a psychological problem that the author is having difficulty either suppressing or facing. Sammy is really a second version of the capable hero threatened by a charming usurper of his woman's affections. The triangle is worked out in compressed form in the chapter where Susan quells her reluctance and dances with the odious, but light-footed, Maurice. Maurice can offer what Sammy can't. Similarly, the department smoothie, one Waring, doesn't let his incompetence in science deter him from charming and finagling his way to the top, and we see that Marcia is attracted to him even while disapproving of him completely. What comes over strongly, and more directly than Balchin seems to intend, is his hero's deadening quality, his lack of lightness. He would suffer from this, you suspect, whether he was maimed or not: his lack is a deficiency of the soul, and the physical inadequacies are simply convenient metaphors. The hero is missing out on something. Perhaps it is something irrational. The true tension in the book comes from Balchin's self-defeating urge to define what that something is, to pull himself up by his own boot-straps and see beyond the limit of rational understanding. But if rational understanding includes everything, there is no beyond. (It's interesting to note, at this point, that when Powell and Pressburger, in the film version of The Small Back Room, changed the ending so that Sammy triumphed, the change was apparently made with Balchin's approval. Wisely given: the original ending would have been very hard to make convincing.)

The triangle is once again at work in Mine Own Executioner, only this time with the sexes switched about. Normally one would be obliged to abandon a critical formula at the moment when it became necessary to substitute for any of its terms, but in this case the reversal is so glaring it can't help but reinforce the idea one has already had. Felix Milne is a capable psychologist with a wonderful wife nicknamed Rhino. Their marriage has everything, but he finds himself irrationally attracted to a girlish femme fatale, Barbara—a female edition of Stephen, with maximum irresponsibility potential. Rhino hangs about with superhuman patience while Felix makes up his mind about Barbara. Switched back the other way, the three-way relationship would simply be the standard one of capable husband (Felix) watching nice wife (Rhino) trying to find some extra, inexplicable fulfilment with an unworthy rival (Barbara). Rhino has been given a disorganizational streak to help the disguise, but the mechanism of the relationship is extremely obtrusive. Meanwhile, Felix's patient, a neurotic ex-pilot (with a bad leg) called Adam Lucian, is periodically seized with the urge to kill his wife, and finally does so.

In *Mine Own Executioner* the true psychological tension has all to do with the author inadvertently supplying hints that the roles have been switched. Felix tells a friend that husbands are always sending him their wives to find out what's gone wrong with the marriage, instead of sending themselves. Felix takes the blame—he has a ritual bout of self-detestation after Lucian dies—and returns to duty in Rhino's arms. Rhino, all-comprehending, forgives. Rhino's dialogue, while humanely waiting for Felix to sort himself out, sounds exactly like Sarratt's. In so far as Felix is a male figure at all, his main point of interest lies in Balchin's attempt to graft onto him the capacity to submit, to give in to a passion. Not surprisingly, it comes out in rather girlish terms: Felix buys things to surprise his wife, and gets petulant when the surprise is spoiled.

The overriding sense given by *Mine Own Executioner* is one of fatalistic resignation: the psychologist is stuck with just slogging on at what he is good at, even though it can do little to stop things being how they are. The book faces up to a post-war lack of purpose, with nothing left to do except comb the rubble and pick up the pieces. But the tension in it comes from what is not being faced, its secret signals. Whether or to what extent Balchin knew he was making these signals is part of the puzzle.

Lord, I Was Afraid is full of couples breaking up and purpose breaking down. 'Lord, I was afraid, and went and hid Thy talent in the earth . . .' All the evidence suggests that the immediate post-war years were a time of crisis for Balchin's sense of himself as a capable man. In 1947 he wrote a Ministry of Information pamphlet on *The Aircraft Builders*, an account of British aircraft production from 1939 to 1945. As a summary of a complicated matter it is quite outstanding in its plainness—Balchin had no equals at this kind of analysis. He demonstrates the principle of interchangeability between the Shadow Factories by choosing a single example—the story of how, after an engine was constructed in one factory and copied in another, both engines were stripped, the parts shuffled, and two engines were built out of the pile. The essence of the whole business is given in a single sentence. Compare Balchin's economical expository style with the prose-poetic rhetoric of the Grierson school of documentary, and you can see how thoroughly Balchin exemplifies the new, terse realism which had come up with the war. But the war was over, and in other bye-writings of the period Balchin showed that he was well aware of the lost dynamism. For the magazine *Occupational*

Psychology he wrote an article on incentives, saying that now Hitler had been defeated and the old sweat-or-starve incentive was being eliminated by the welfare state, the one remaining reason to work— i.e., to gain a higher standard of living—would be of only limited efficacy. And the State was too abstract a concept for people to strive on behalf of. The best one could hope for would be the disappearance of work as an activity separate from private life.

Most of this was prescient, but being right didn't help Balchin out of his fix—the fix being that his range of practical talent had become obsolete. Walter Benjamin said that all aesthetic politics lead to one end: war. The corollary holds: only a war generates aesthetic politics. With peace, and the disintegration of national purpose, Balchin lost the opportunity of contributing to the nation as if the nation were a work of art. He had been demobilized more thoroughly than any front-line soldier. He was being asked to hide his own talent. The other cry of *Lord, I Was Afraid* is not Biblical but Shakespearian: Othello's occupation's gone.

The Borgia Testament is an equally intense, and much more clear, complaint of failing purpose. Machiavelli, in the seventh chapter of *The Prince*, ascribes Cesare Borgia's eventual failure as a conqueror to sheer bad luck. Balchin doesn't take the story quite to the point of Cesare's illness, preferring to concentrate on the possibility of a collapse of will. 'It felt', he makes Cesare write, 'rather as though reality, in some way, was the great illusion . . . I don't understand this. I merely say that it was so . . .' The concluding sentences are especially revealing. 'But above everything . . . I have expected too much reason from the men of my day . . . I could never believe that these barbaric, superstitious, shadowy legends have a real meaning and value for them.' It is not just permissible but obligatory, I think, to assume that in such passages Balchin is looking into himself, and half-perceiving that his own rationality might be a limitation.

A Sort of Traitors, a reversion to the formula of the wartime novels, is something of a caricature. The girl this time is called Lucy and is a decent chap rather along the lines of Susan in *The Small Back Room*. Lucy looks after her one-time lover, Ivor, who has been so comprehensively shot-up in the war that he strikes the irreverent reader as a combination of Jake in *The Sun Also Rises* and John Cleese playing an armless subaltern in a *Monty Python* sketch. The appropriately up-dated version of Stephen is a wet-behind-the-ears young scientist called Marriott, good at stinks but a duffer in matters of real-life emotion. Caving in under the pressure of spoon-feeding Ivor, Lucy can't resist a night out with the intact Marriott, even though she despises him. Petulance is distributed evenly between Ivor and Marriott, but there is no doubt which one of them is supposed to have the real intelligence—Ivor. Maimed, sick of being a burden, be obligingly bumps himself off in the twelfth chapter, leaving his loved one free to enjoy the experiences he cannot provide.

It shouldn't be thought, though, that Ivor is easy to laugh at when the book is actually being read. He is so obviously Too Much that the reader worries for the author's safety—what could be the pain, if only inventing a grotesque like Ivor can lessen it?

Whatever the pain was, it reached flash-point with A *Way Through the Wood*, generally thought of as Balchin's response to the collapse of his marriage. The triangle is at work again, but the atmosphere is vengeful: the tolerance has gone. The quiet capable man does the narrating. His wife, Jill, does the betraying. Bill Bule is the charmer with the boyish grin. Jill has an affair with Bule, and while they are driving in his Lagonda they knock down and kill somebody, thereby setting the district on its ear. The capable man solves the crime, but picks the wrong killer. It wasn't Bule driving, it was his wife. On her own admission, Jill is 'no good'. Having said this, she is free to go and join her lover. Her men have covered up for her.

Manning admits Bule's qualities—Bule is no Stephen—but the wife's flightiness is this time positively evil, and Manning's forgivingness at the end of the book is scarcely a matter of self-abasement. 'I seem to have expected Jill to wear trousers and to have been to a good public school', he narrates understandingly, 'and to have my sort of honour, and my sort of principles, instead of wearing a skirt and having her own.' It is said that intelligent women dislike Balchin's books, and reading stuff like that you can see why. Balchin is at full stretch in A *Way Through the Wood*: he has come as close as he dares to submission. But finally, and seemingly in spite of himself, he asserts: the real reason why Jill loves someone else besides Manning is because she is no good.

A *Way Through the Wood* had some success as a play, called *Waiting for Gillian*. Olivier produced it, with Googie Withers and John MacCallum. It isn't hard to imagine the commuting businessmen in the stalls grunting in sympathy with Manning as he faces his martyrdom with a clear, realistic brain. Even more indicatively, the book was serialized in *Woman's Own*, where the illustrator had no trouble at all in fitting appropriate faces to the characters. How the tongues of knitting ladies must have clucked at the shenanigans of naughty Jill.

With *Sundry Creditors* Balchin is much more in control of his effects. As a novel about business decisions this book is right out on its own. Its multiple-plotted dexterity was widely admired at the time, just as the flatness of its characters was widely complained of. The factory has no competition in establishing itself as the hero. One of the reasons for the thinness of the characters, I think, is that Balchin's obsessions are this time fragmented and scattered, so that the different aspects of his usual situations show up all over the book, without the concentrated impact which previously made them memorable. For a Balchin book, *Sundry Creditors* is overpopulated. It's notable, however, that Walter Lang, the dynamic business brain, loses first his wife, then his daughter, and ends by losing the factory too. There is a purgatorial, leaden-footed run through sand-dunes as he searches for the girl, and finally the collapse of his judgement. Critics at the time said it was hard to care about Lang. In the context of the other novels, however, it is much easier to care about him—or rather, worry about the author. The book is vitally interesting in its practical detail, but would have little tension above the *Planemakers* level if one were not convinced that the author is once again—whether deliberately or inadvertently it is hard to say—revealing a weakness in his own view of life. Limiting the revelation of Walter's character, however, is the presence of a back-up man. There is a character called Lawrence who demonstrates how cool competence—a sense of the possible—is still the answer. Such an unimpeachable objectivist as Lawrence crops up in nearly every book, to show the man racked by spiritual crisis that the antidote to being merely a practical brain is to be an even better practical brain.

In *The Fall of the Sparrow* the charmer is given full value: more so even than in *A Way Through the Wood*. The first person narrator, Henry Payne, is the capable man. Jason Pellew is the charmer, and is traced through a lifetime of going to the dogs. He is about to be jailed when the novel opens. Payne reminisces, and for once we find that the imaginative man is conjured up not as an impractical posturer but as a man of adventurous impulse and genuine sensitivity. An old love of both of them, Leah, addresses Henry:

'It seems an awfully long time since that night when I tried to seduce you at the May Ball.'

'Did you try to seduce me?'

'You know I did. You were very shocked because you had thought I was fond of Jason. Never mind, you repelled me like a gentleman and a true friend.'

For this once only, the capable man's practicality is shown to entail incomprehension. Jason is the man who can join with Leah instinctively. Jason's life is a mess and Henry's is a model of order, but there are intensities of experience from which Henry is debarred. Pamela Hansford Johnson relaxed her strictures about relevance over this one novel. She said that it had *strangeness*, and indeed it has. Balchin has allowed his imaginative charmer an independent personality, one that can't be fully reproduced on a punched card.

In *Seen Dimly before Dawn* the triangle was taken back to the narrator's childhood. A sixteen-year-old boy is staying in the country with his uncle and aunt. The aunt is attractive, and he idolizes her. Together they plan fantasy revenges against the local squire, a dog-kicking heavy. What the boy does not realize, until the traumatic final scene, is that his beloved aunt, who has led him on but not to satisfaction, has for all this time been the squire's mistress. Lennie is not presented as either evil or stupid, and that Balchin can show her falling in love for reasons incomprehensible to the narrator can be counted as a gain. In connection with a sixteen-year-old boy, the shock of recognition rings truer than it does with Balchin's adults.

With *In the Absence of Mrs. Petersen* there is a clear decline, and all one can do is note glumly that Balchin is drawing upon his not especially exalted experience as a Hollywood script-writer (he wrote the *ur*-text of the *Cleopatra* script, among other projects) to write a novel about a Hollywood script-writer going on an obsessive search for a lost (in fact dead) wife. His companion on the quest is his wife's double. As a plot it is no great shakes. As a possible indication of Balchin's lingering preoccupation with loss, it is of some interest. *Kings of Infinite Space* is just a novel of not very adventurous adventure, memorable for a single line of dialogue that bears on the whole of Balchin's productive literary career. One of the female characters says that in sexual affairs there's nothing to touch a properly organized fool's paradise.

That there are undeclared and probably unintended tensions working in Nigel Balchin's novels doesn't invalidate them, but it does help explain why they have always been received as something less than completely serious. They seem less than completely serious because they reinforce the author's deepest wishes more than they clarify them, and some of their popularity can be put down to the fact that they do the same job for the reader. The completely serious artist, even if he can boast only a quarter of Balchin's talent, will go further in breaking down his own psychology than Balchin did. Balchin is remembered by his contemporaries as the kindest of men. He is also remembered (especially, among his acquaintances I've spoken to, by women) as a man whose confidence in pronouncing on other people's motives was unshakeable and finally tedious: the counter-sorter was always ticking over. It appears that Balchin's ego counted on being able to sum everything up. Mysteries did not exist—until they surprised him. The economy of his books rings like falsity, since it has been won at the cost of imposing logic on life. His orderly mind forced him to settle for perfection.

And yet with all that said, Balchin wrote books that were better than the superlative adjectives used in their praise implied. Broadcasting on Irish radio in 1947, Conor Cruise O'Brien said Balchin was 'so intelligent that the most damning adjective a critic can find for him is "clever" '. The intelligence still comes through, and the wartime books, especially, are still contemporary novels. Mobilization for war changed everything in Britain, and Balchin was the first properly equipped novelist of the new meritocracy. The ministerial bumblers in the wartime books are too easily knocked over to be much more than tin targets, but the way the brighter men talk about them is the very tone of the new life to come. Balchin was realistic about power: he knew that the old illusions of greatness were at last over. Kingsley Amis would vehemently deny any direct influence from Balchin, but it remains true that Balchin helped create the audience which read Amis in the Fifties. There are scenes all through *Darkness Falls from the Air* and *The Small Back Room* that are teeming with Professor Welches, Bertrands and Goldsmiths. What's missing is humour. Satire is there in plenty, but true humour was not among Balchin's gifts. He was too certain of himself to let his imagination do its own thinking.

Intensifying what he did was the way he did it. As Arthur Calder-Marshall said when reviewing *Sundry Creditors* in 1953, Balchin's Forties books were 'some of the few books that were writ-

ten.' Balchin's professional skill gives a meaning to brilliance which the word doesn't usually possess. Accomplishment of that order is its own morality—an artistic dedication all on its own. Balchin's best novels (*Darkness Falls From the Air, The Small Back Room, Mine Own Executioner, A Sort of Traitors, Sundry Creditors* and *The Fall of the Sparrow*) are popular novels whose seriousness, as far as it goes, is beyond question. If their neatness depends in part on Balchin's limitations, that is the price we have to pay. Aesthetics are dialectical, not monolithic. A writer as good as Balchin won't go away just because you've established that there are departments of his own psyche he was unable fully to explore.

(*The New Review*, April 1974)

FOOTNOTE ON BALCHIN'S REPUDIATED BOOKS

Balchin's pre-war writings had small success, only the novel *Light-body on Liberty* managing to sell in four figures. He was content to let the market's judgment stand, repudiating all his early work simply by never seeking to have it reprinted. The books—especially the novels—are hard to find. The London Library, for example, has none of them. The British Museum catalogues all three of the novels (*No Sky, Simple Life* and *Lighbody on Liberty*) but seems able to supply only the last two: weeks of waiting failed to lure *No Sky* (1934) out of the Woolwich fastness where all the fiction that never makes it goes to be embalmed. At that rate, the chances of Balchin's early work blazing into present-day fame are pretty slim. Which is almost certainly the way he would have wanted it—compared with *Darkness Falls from the Air* any previous starts are bound to look false.

And yet, as one might expect, the apprentice books can't help being illustrative of his preoccupations. *Simple Life* (1935) tells the story of Rufus, a clever young ad-man who gets himself fired, walks out on his icy girl-friend and goes bush in an Orwellian act of self-discovery. He is taken care of by Mendel, a philosophizing drop-out, and Mendel's girl-friend Ruth. Ruth is a clear forecast of Leah in *The Fall of the Sparrow*. A prototype Balchin triangle quickly forms. Ruth lets Rufus sleep with her but goes on loving Mendel, who Rufus gradually realizes is a complete phoney. The shock comes when Ruth confesses that *she* realizes it, too—Mendel's bogusness is part of what binds her to him. Rufus, the rational man, is power-less to analyse or terminate the irrationality of the lovers: it's a story which the later novels go on and on refining. Particularly in-teresting is the fact that Balchin has projected some of his own qual-ities into Mendel, especially his detachment. 'If you beat him,' says Ruth of Mendel, 'he'd just be coldly interested in what it felt like to be beaten.' But Mendel spends more time as the author's opposite than his like, ending the book as a druid-like mystic, before whom the hero, Rufus, stands uncomprehending—and with no hint that the narrator comprehends any better. Most of Balchin's future themes are already present in this novel, and so is a good deal of his pecu-liar skill. The opening chapters in the advertising agency suffer badly from employing naturalistic technique on the kind of farce which Evelyn Waugh had already proved needed to be treated elliptically or else not at all. But as soon as the hero breaks out into open country the story comes alive. With the front shorn off and the rest trimmed of some of its commentary, *Simple Life* could still be an interesting novel.

Lightbody on Liberty, which came out in 1936, sold marginally better than the others but is a hard read now. It is all a farcical extravaganza, which even the accuracy of Balchin's later manner would not have been able to make attractive—tripping the light fantastic was not something his mind could manage, although *How To Run a Bassoon Factory* (published in 1934 under his *nom de plume* Mark Spade) is a sprightly enough harbinger of the Northcote Parkinson tradition in which organizations are semi-solemnly anat-omized.

But on the whole the example of Waugh's early novels over-whelms what Balchin is trying to do. Nevertheless, the attempt is respectable, reminding us once again that Balchin was by nature a political realist: no mean thing to be in the Thirties. Lightbody is a small-time shopkeeper lured by a police Q-car into breaking the speed limit. Intensely law-abiding until then, he suddenly realizes that he is not free. His case is taken up by Sir Joseph Steers, a Nabarro-*cum*-Maxwell super-patriot in a red, white and blue Rolls Royce. A whole social movement forms around him. He is carried away with excitement, but finds in the end that he has been a dupe. The plot forecasts the disillusionment comedies of the Ealing period (*The Man in the White Suit*) and the even later, wholly cynical films of the Boulting Brothers (especially *I'm All Right Jack*). If the fun had been funnier—had borrowed some of Waugh's technique as well as his tone—the book might have stood out. Certainly it is hard to think of many other contemporary novels which showed an equivalent hard-headedness. Lightbody's son—a Communist under the lunatic impression that his father is a capitalist—constitutes an admirable piece of political observation. Unfortunately the book is at least three times too long. An excellent screen-play could have been boiled out of it, but no British films of a comparable political sophistication were being made at that time. They ordered such things better in France: Renoir and Prévert made *Le Crime de Monsieur Lange*—thematically quite similar—the previous year.

Part Four
POLITICAL CONSIDERATIONS

14. Bitter Seeds: Solzhenitsyn

I wonder if, despite the critical success of *The Gulag Archipelago*, Solzhenitsyn's reputation is quite as high as it was when *August 1914* had not yet seen the light, when its author was still in Russia and when the K.G.B. were obviously looking for some plausible means of stopping his mouth. Even at that arcadian stage, however, I can well remember arousing the scorn of some of my brighter contemporaries by calling Solzhenitsyn a great imaginative writer. This was put down to my customary hyperbole, to my romanticism, to my bad taste, or to all three. Yet it seemed to me a sober judgment, and still seems so. I think Solzhenitsyn is a creative artist of the very first order.

What tends to disguise this is an historical accident—the accident that most of his imaginative energy has had to be expended on the business of reconstructing reality. He has been trying to remember what a whole country has been conspiring, for various reasons, to forget. In such a case it is a creative act simply to find a way of telling some of the truth, as many people realized instinctively when they greeted Nadezhda Mandelstam's first volume of memoirs as the poetic work it is. But to tell as much of the truth as Solzhenitsyn has already told—and all of this truth must be *recovered*, from sources whose interests commonly lie in yielding none of it up— is a creative act of such magnitude that it is hard to recognize as a work of the imagination at all. On the whole, it seems, we would rather think of Solzhenitsyn as an impersonal instrument, a camera photographing the surface of another, airless planet. Hence the common complaint that he is a bit short on human warmth, the general agreement that there is something eerily mechanical about him. Even before *August 1914* (whose characters tended to be described by reviewers as having keys sticking out of their backs) there was talk of how *Cancer Ward* and *The First Circle* proved that Solzhenitsyn was not Tolstoy.

I can recall this last point being made in an argument I had with one of the more gifted members of what I must, I suppose, with chagrin, get used to thinking of as the next generation. He hadn't yet got round to reading *War and Peace* or *Anna Karenina* or *Resurrection*, but in the intervals of urging upon me the merits of Northrop Frye he nevertheless conveyed that he thought he had a pretty fair idea of what Tolstoy had been all about, and that Solzhenitsyn's novels weren't in the same league.

Not only did I concede the truth of such a judgment, I insisted on it. Solzhenitsyn's novels are not Tolstoy's, and never could have been. Tolstoy's novels are about the planet Earth and Solzhenitsyn's are about Pluto. Tolstoy is writing about a society and Solzhenitsyn is writing about the lack of one. My argument might have a touch of sophistry (perhaps one is merely rationalizing Solzhenitsyn's limitations), but surely there is something wilfully unhistorical about being disappointed that Pierre Bezhukov or Andrey Bolkonsky or Natasha Rostov find no equivalents in *Cancer Ward*. Characterization in such wealthy detail has become, in Solzhenitsyn's Russia, a thing of the past, and to expect it is like expecting the fur-lined brocades and gold-threaded silks of the Florentine Renaissance to crop up in Goya's visions of the horrors of war. Solzhenitsyn's contemporary novels—I mean the novels set in the Soviet Union—are not really concerned with society. They are concerned with what happens after society has been destroyed. And *August 1914*, an historical novel in the usual sense, looks to be the beginning of a long work which will show the transition from one state to the other. It is already fairly clear that Solzhenitsyn plans to carry the novel forward until he ends up telling the story of the 1917 Revolution itself, as well as, if he is granted time enough, of the Civil War afterwards. Here one should remember his talks with Susi in the 'eagle's perch' of the Lubyanka, in *Gulag Archipelago*, Part I, Chapter 5. While recollecting them he writes: 'From childhood on, I had somehow known that my objective was the history of the Russian Revolution and that nothing else concerned me.'

Solzhenitsyn is explicit about his belief that he is linked to Tolstoy in some sort of historical mission. His detractors have made much of the meeting between Tanya and Tolstoy in Chapter 2 of *August 1914*. But Solzhenitsyn, even though he is a proud man (and it is a wonder that his pride isn't positively messianic, considering what he has been through and the size of the task which circumstances have posed him), isn't, it seems to me, an especially conceited one. He doesn't see his connection with Tolstoy as one of rivalry. What he sees is an apostolic succession. He knows all about

Tolstoy's superiority. But when Tanya fails to get Tolstoy to admit that love might not be the cure for everything, Solzhenitsyn is showing us (by a trick of retroactive prophecy, or clairvoyance through hindsight) that Tolstoy's superiority will be a limitation in the age to come. What will count above everything else for the writer in the Russian future is *memory*. In the prison state, you should own only what you can carry with you and let your memory be your travel-bag. 'It is those bitter seeds alone which might sprout and grow someday.' (*Gulag Archipelago*, Part II, Chapter 1). The lesson is Tolstoyan, but the context is not. Solzhenitsyn's argument has nothing to do with the perfecting of one's soul. All he is saying —in a tone unifying realism and irony—is that if you try to keep anything tangible the prison-camp thieves will break what is left of your heart when they take it. (An instructive exercise here is to read some of, say, *Resurrection* just after having absorbed a chapter or two of *Gulag Archipelago*. The unthinkable has occurred: Tolstoy seems to have become irrelevant to Russia.)

There can't be much doubt that *August 1914* did damage to Solzhenitsyn's stature in the short run. But in the long run it will probably be the better for him to be liberated from the burden of fashionable approval, and anyway it is far too early to judge *August 1914* as a novel. Most of the reviewers who found it wanting in comparison with *War and Peace* had probably not read *War and Peace* recently or at all: certainly those who talked of its shape or construction had never read it, since *War and Peace* is a deliberately sprawling affair which takes ages to get started. *August 1914* reads like a piece of scene-setting, a slow introduction to something prodigious. I would like to see a lot more of the project before deciding that Solzhenitsyn has failed as a novelist. But it is possible to concede already that he might have failed as a 19th century novelist.

It can be argued that because the setting of *August 1914* is pre-Revolutionary the characters and situations ought therefore to be more earthily lifelike than they are—more Tolstoyan, in a word. I suppose there is something to this. Tolstoy was a transfigurative genius and probably Solzhenitsyn is not; probably he just doesn't possess Tolstoy's charm of evocative utterance. But the loss in afflatus is surely a small thing compared to what we gain from Solzhenitsyn's panoramic realism. In clarifying the history of the Soviet Union (and Solzhenitsyn is already, by force of circumstance, the pre-eminent modern Russian historian) he is making a large stretch

F

of recent time his personal province. He has been writing a Bible, and consequently must find it hard to avoid the occasional God-like attribute accruing to him: omniscience, for example. It must be a constant temptation to suggest more than he knows. Yet when dealing with events taking place in the course of his own lifetime he never seems to, and I would be surprised if he ever did much to break that rule when writing about the pre-Revolutionary period. The use of documents in *August 1914* has been called a weakness. The inspiration for this technique is supposed to come from John Dos Passos, and the purported result is that *August 1914* is as flawed as *U.S.A.* Well, for any novel to rank with *U.S.A.* would not be all that bad a fate, and anyway critics who take this line are underestimating the importance to Solzhenitsyn of documentation of all kinds. He goes in for this sort of thing not because he lacks imagination but because that *is* imagination—to suppose that the facts of the Russian past can be recovered, to suppose that evidence can still *matter*, is an imaginative act. But to assess the boldness of that act, we must first begin to understand what has happened to the truth in the Soviet Union. And it's Solzhenitsyn who more than anyone else has been helping us to understand.

In writing about World War I, Solzhenitsyn can't help having the benefit of his peculiar hindsight. Everything in *August 1914* and its succeeding volumes is bound to be illuminated by what we know of his writings about the Soviet Union. There is no way he can escape this condition and it is childish, I think, to wish that he could. It could well be that the war novel will be artistically less than fully successful because we will have to keep thinking of its author as the author of *Gulag Archipelago* or else miss out on its full force. But we had better accept such a possibility and learn to be grateful that at least the novel is being written. Because nobody else—certainly not Sholokhov—could have written it: Solzhenitsyn's war novel is based on the idea that the truth is indivisible.

At a guess, I would say that Solzhenitsyn's lack of the Tolstoyan virtues will turn out to be an artistic strength as well as a philosophical one. Until recently the key Russian novel about World War I, the Revolution and the Civil War was *Dr. Zhivago*. The book was overrated on publication and is underrated now, but it will always be an instructive text for the attentive reader. One defends Pasternak's right, argued through the leading character, to live and create without taking sides. One can see the importance of the principle which Pasternak is eager to incarnate in Zhivago and Lara. Lara is, if you like, the Natasha that Solzhenitsyn seems doomed never to create. Lara and Yuri are Natasha and Andrey, lovers surrounded by chaos, a private love in the middle of public breakdown. But Pasternak can't seem to avoid an effect of Tolstoy-and-water. Really the time for all this is past, and the rest of his book helps to tell us so. The point about the Civil War lies with the millions who are *not* surviving it—Pasternak, in focussing on these blessed two, is luxuriating despite himself.

However reluctantly and fragmentarily, *Dr. Zhivago* affirms that Life Goes On: Pasternak is old-world. Solzhenitsyn, one of the 'twins of October' (his term for Russians who were born in the first years of the Revolution and came of age just in time to witness the 1937–8 purges, fight in World War II and be imprisoned by Stalin), doesn't believe that life went on at all. He thinks that it stopped, and that death started. In his World War I novel we can expect to hear portents of the future strangeness. But the predominant tone—and this we can already hear—will almost certainly be one of scrupulous political realism. Not *realpolitik*, but the truth about politics. This is what Pasternak was in no position to treat and what the great common ancestor, Tolstoy, simply got wrong. Tolstoy's early appearance in *August 1914* is undoubtedly strategic: he is the innocent, dreaming genius who just has no idea whatsoever of the new world to come.

Two representative moments serve to show how the force of *August 1914* is potentiated by acquaintance with Solzhenitsyn's later work, especially with *Gulag Archipelago*. In Chapter 6 we are told that Roman thinks of himself as superior and imagines that his superiority lies in his brutal frankness. But the truly illustrative detail, presented without comment, is Roman's admiration for Maxim Gorky. (Solzhenitsyn's contempt for Gorky is touched on in *The First Circle* and expressed at length in *Gulag Archipelago*.) And in Chapter 61, when the two engineers Obodovsky and Arkhangorodsky meet in amity, their friendly optimism is a mere hint of the intense, regretful passage in *Gulag Archipelago* I, 5 where Solzhenitsyn laments the destruction of the engineers in the 1920s as the blasting of Russia's best hope. In the *August 1914* passage we read:

Although there was no similarity or even contact between the lives, experience and specialised interest of the two men, they shared a common engineering spirit which like some powerful, invisible wing lifted them, bore them onwards and made them kin.

In the *Gulag Archipelago* passage the same emotion is multiplied, in the kind of paragraph which led several critics to comment (approvingly, let it be admitted) on the book's supposed lack of sobriety:

> An engineer? I had grown up among engineers, and I could remember the engineers of the twenties very well indeed: their open, shining intellects, their free and gentle humour, their agility and breadth of thought, the ease with which they shifted from one engineering field to another, and, for that matter, from technology to social concerns and art. Then, too, they personified good manners and delicacy of taste; well-bred speech that flowed evenly and was free of uncultured words; one of them might play a musical instrument, another dabble in painting; and their faces always bore a spiritual imprint.

It is evident that the optimism of the two friends about the new Russia to come is being treated ironically, but unless we know about Solzhenitsyn's feelings concerning what happened subsequently to the engineers (whose show trials in 1928 are treated at length in Robert Conquest's *The Great Terror*, but without, of course, the epigrammatic power Solzhenitsyn unleashes on the subject in *Gulag Archipelago*) we are unlikely to realize just how bitterly ironical he is being. Whether this is a weakness of the novel isn't easily decided. My own view is that Solzhenitsyn has done the right thing in neutralizing his viewpoint. We have to provide a context from our own knowledge—knowledge which Solzhenitsyn is busy supplying us with in other books. The most pressing reason he writes history is to make the truth public. But a subsidiary reason, and one that will perhaps become increasingly important, is to make his own fiction intelligible. He writes history in order that his historical novel might be understood.

Because Solzhenitsyn deals with modern events over which there is not merely dispute as to their interpretation, but doubt as to whether they even happened, he is obliged to expend a great deal of effort in saying what things were like. The task is compounded in difficulty by the consideration that what they were like is almost unimaginable. To recover the feeling of such things is an immense creative achievement. In Coleridge's sense, it takes imagination to see things as they are, and Solzhenitsyn possesses that imagination to such a degree that one can be excused for thinking of him as a freak. He is a witness for the population of 20th century shadows, the anonymous dead: all the riders on what Mandelstam in his poem called the Lilac Sleigh. Solzhenitsyn can imagine what pain is like when it happens to strangers. Even more remarkably, he is not disabled by imagining what pain is like when it happens to a *million* strangers—he can think about individuals even when the subject is the obliteration of masses, which makes his the exact reverse of the ideological mentality, which can think only about masses even when the subject is the obliteration of individuals. Camus said it was a peculiarity of our age that the innocent are called upon to justify themselves. Nowhere has this been more true than in Soviet Russia, where the best the condemned innocent have been able to hope for is rehabilitation. But Solzhenitsyn has already managed, at least in part, to bring them back in their rightful role—as prosecutors.

Of the ideological mentality Solzhenitsyn is the complete enemy, dedicated and implacable. Here, perhaps, lies the chief reason for the growing uneasiness about the general drift of his work. Nobody in the Left intelligentsia, not even the Marxists, much minds him suggesting that in the Soviet Union the Revolution went sour. But almost everybody, and not always covertly, seems to mind his insistence that the Revolution should never have happened, and that Russia was better off under the Romanovs. In *Dr. Zhivago* Pasternak showed himself awed by the magnitude of historical forces: reviewers sympathized, since being awed by historical forces is a way of saying that what happened should have happened, even though the cost was frightful. Nobody wants to think of horror as sheer waste. Solzhenitsyn says that the Soviet horror was, from the very beginning, sheer waste. Politically this attitude is something of a gift to the Right, since it practically aligns Solzhenitsyn with Winston Churchill. It is no great surprise, then, that on the liberal Left admiration is gradually becoming tinctured with the suspicion that so absolute a fellow might be a bit of a crank.

In *The Great Terror* Robert Conquest valuably widened the field of attention from the purges of 1937-38 to include the trials of the late Twenties—a reorientation which meant that the age of destruction overlapped the golden era of the Soviet Union instead of merely succeeding it, and also meant that while Stalin still got the blame for the Terror, Lenin got the blame for Stalin. But in *Gulag Archipelago* Solzhenitsyn does a more thorough job even than Conquest of tracing the Terror back to the revolution itself: he says that the whole court procedure of the typical Soviet show trial was already in existence in 1922, and that the activities of the Cheka from the very beginning provided a comprehensive model for everything the 'organs', under their various acronyms, were to perpetrate in the decades to come. He has no respect for the Revolution even in its most pristine state—in fact he says it never *was* in a pristine state, since pre-Revolutionary Russia was totally unsuited for any form of Socialism whatsoever and no organization which attempted to impose it could escape pollution. It is the overwhelming tendency of Solzhenitsyn's work to suggest that the Russian Revolution should never have happened. He can summon respect for ordinary people who were swept up by their belief in it, but for the revolutionary intelligentsia in all its departments his contempt is absolute. The hopeful young artists of the golden era (see the paragraph beginning 'Oh ye bards of the twenties', *Gulag Archipelago* I, 9) were, in his view, as culpable as the detested Gorky. Solzhenitsyn's critique of the Soviet Union is a radical critique, not a revisionist one. In condemning him as a class enemy, the regime is scarcely obliged to lie.

(Nevertheless it lies anyway—or perhaps the citizens invent the lies all by themselves. Not much is known of these matters inside the Soviet Union and Solzhenitsyn is generally just a name. One sometimes forgets that *One Day in the Life of Ivan Denisovich* is the only book of his which has ever been published there. A friend of mine just back from Russia tells me that he got into an argument with the director of a metalworkers' sanitorium on the Black Sea. This man was in his early fifties and had fought in World War II. He declared that Solzhenitsyn not only *is* a traitor, but *was* a traitor during the war—that he had been a Vlasov man. Now Solzhenitsyn's understanding of Vlasov is an important element of *Gulag Archipelago*. But Solzhenitsyn was a Red Army artillery officer who fought *against* Germany, not with it. In view of how this elementary truth can be turned on its head, it's probably wise of Solzhenitsyn to harbour as he does the doubt that the facts, once rediscovered, will spread, like certain brands of margarine, straight from the fridge. There is nothing automatic about the propagation of the truth. As he often points out, not even experience can teach it. The prison-camps and execution cells were full of people who were convinced that their own innocence didn't stop all these others being guilty.)

Solzhenitsyn finds it no mystery that the Old Bolsheviks condemned themselves. He resolves the apparent conflict between Koestler's famous thesis in *Darkness at Noon* (Koestler said they co-operated because the Party required their deaths and they had no spiritual resources for disobeying the Party) and Khrushchev's much later but equally famous insistence that they were tortured until they gave up ('Beat, beat, beat . . .'). According to Solzhenitsyn, the Old Bolsheviks were devoid of individuality in the first place, and simply had no private convictions to cling to: certainly they weren't made of the same moral stuff as the engineers they had connived at destroying ten years before, many of whom had preferred to be tortured to death rather than implicate the innocent. In the second place, the Old Bolsheviks had never been as marinated in suffering as they liked to pretend. Koestler was wrong in supposing that torture alone could not have cracked them, and Khrushchev was apparently also wrong in supposing that they needed to be tortured all that hard. Czarist imprisonment was the only kind the Old Bolsheviks had ever known and it was a picnic compared to the kind they themselves had become accustomed to dishing out. Solzhenitsyn sees no tragedy in the Old Bolsheviks. He doesn't talk of them with the unbridled hatred he reserves for the prosecutors Krylenko and Vyshinsky, but there is still no trace of sympathy in his regard. Here again is an example of his disturbing absolutism. He shows inexhaustible understanding of how ordinary people could be terrified into compliance. But for the ideologues trapped in their own system his standards are unwavering—they ought to have chosen death rather than dishonour themselves and their country further. He pays tribute to the Old Bolsheviks who suicided before they could be arrested (Skrypnik, Tomsky, Gamarnik) and to the half dozen who died ('silently but at least not shamefully'—*Gulag Archipelago* I, 10) under interrogation. He condemns the rest for having wanted to live. They should have been beyond that.

Solzhenitsyn takes a lot upon himself when he says that it was shameful for men not to die. Yet one doesn't feel that his confidence is presumptuous—although if one could, he would be less frightening. I remember that when I first read *The First Circle* the portrait of Stalin seemed inadequate, a caricature. My dissatisfaction, I have since decided—and Solzhenitsyn's writings have helped me decide—was a hangover from the romantic conviction that large events have large men at the centre of them. Tolstoy really did sell Napoleon short in *War and Peace*: Napoleon was a lot more interesting than that. But Stalin in *The First Circle* must surely be close to the reality. The only thing about Stalin on the grand scale was his pettiness—his mediocrity was infinite. Solzhenitsyn convinces us of the truth of this picture by reporting his own travels through Stalin's mind: the Archipelago is the expression of Stalin's personality, endlessly vindictive, murderously boring. Time and again in his major books, Solzhenitsyn makes a sudden investigative jab at Stalin, seemingly still hopeful of finding a flicker of nobility in that homicidal dullard. It never happens. That it could produce Stalin is apparently sufficient reason in itself for condemning the Revolution.

With Solzhenitsyn judgement is not in abeyance. He doesn't say that all of this happened in aid of some inscrutable purpose. He says it happened to no purpose. There is little solace to be taken and not much uplift to be had in the occasional story of noble defiance. First of all, the defiant usually died in darkness, in the way that Philip II denied Holland its martyrs by drowning them in secret. And when Solzhenitsyn somehow manages to find out who they were, he doesn't expect their example to light any torches. There are no eternal acts of faith or undying loves. (The typical love in Solzhenitsyn is between the Love Girl and the Innocent, or that unsatisfactory non-affair at the end of *Cancer Ward*—just a brushing of dazed minds, two strangers sliding past each other. No parts there for Omar Sharif and Julie Christie.) Everything is changed: there is no connection with the way things were.

It should be an elementary point that Solzhenitsyn is a critic of the Soviet Union, not of Russia. Yet even intelligent people seemed to think that there may have been 'something in' his expulsion—that he had it coming. (It was edifying to notice how the construction 'kicked out' came to be used even by those nominally on his side.) This sentiment has, I think, been intensified by Solzhenitsyn's argument with Sakharov. It has become increasingly common to hint that Solzhenitsyn has perhaps got above himself, that in telling the world's largest country what it ought to do next he is suffering from delusions of grandeur. Yet it seems to me perfectly in order for Solzhenitsyn to feel morally superior to the whole of the Soviet political machine. Its human integrity is not just compromised but fantastic, and he has lived the proof. He has good cause to believe himself Russia personified, and I am more surprised by his humility in this role than by his pride. To the suggestion that he is a mediocre artist with great subject matter, the answer should be: to see that such stuff is your subject matter, and then to go on and prove yourself adequate to its treatment—these are in themselves sufficient qualifications for greatness. Solzhenitsyn's forthcoming books (apparently there are to be at least two more volumes of *Gulag Archipelago*) will, I am convinced, eventually put the matter beyond doubt. But for the present we should be careful not to understand the man too quickly. Above all we need to guard against that belittling tone which wants to call him a reactionary because he has lost faith in dreams.

(*The New Review*, October 1974)

15. It is of a Windiness: Lillian Hellman

Much praised in the United States, *Pentimento* deals mainly with people other than its author, but there is still a good deal of Lillian Hellman in it—possibly more than she intended—and it's hard not to think of the book as finishing off *An Unfinished Woman*, a memoir which was inundated with laurels but left at least one reader doubting its widely proclaimed first rateness. Meaty details about Dorothy Parker, Hemingway, Scott Fitzgerald and Dashiell Hammett were not quite compensation enough for a garrulous pseudo-taciturnity—distinction of style, it seemed to me, was precisely the quality *An Unfinished Woman* had not a particle of. The very first time Hammett's drinking was referred to as 'the drinking' you knew you were in for a solid course of bastardized Hemingwayese. The drinking got at least a score more mentions. There were also pronounced tendencies towards that brand of aggressive humility, or claimed innocence, which finds itself helpless to explain the world at the very moment when the reader is well justified in requiring that a writer should give an apprehensible outline of what he deems to be going on. Miss Hellman was with the Russian forces when Maidaneck was liberated. It struck me, as I read, that her account of her feelings, though graphic, was oddly circumscribed. She had vomited, but in recounting the fact had apparently failed to realize that no physical reaction, however violent, is quite adequate to such a stimulus. What we needed to hear about was what she *thought*, and it appeared that what she thought was, as usual, a sophisticated version, decked out with Hem-Dash dialogue, of 'I don't understand these things'.

On a larger scale, the same applied—and I think still applies—to her reasoning on the subject of Soviet Russia. She comes over in these two books—implicitly, since her political views have mainly to be pieced together from more or less revealing hints—as an unreconstructed and unrepentant Stalinist. There is no gainsaying her consistency and strength in such matters, even if those qualities are founded in some primal injury to the imaginative faculty. She was brave during the McCarthy era and has a right to be proud of never having turned her coat. Nevertheless it is impossible to grant much more than a token admiration to a professional clerical who can go on being 'realistic' about Russia in the sense (by now, surely, utterly discredited) of believing that the Terror was simply an aberration disturbing an otherwise constructive historical movement. The 'I don't understand these things' syndrome came in depressingly handy whenever she wandered on to the scene of an event about which she might have been obliged to say something analytical if she had. She was well-regarded in Russia, was even there during the war, and met a lot of people. Her reporting of character and incident couldn't help but be interesting. Nevertheless, one felt, she missed out on the fundamentals. On the day she was due to meet Stalin, she was told he was busy. Shortly after which, she recorded, Warsaw fell. The implication being that Warsaw was what he was busy with. But for some reason it just doesn't cross her mind to give an opinion on the fundamental question—which remains a contentious issue to this day—of whether Stalin was busy liberating it or not liberating it: whether, that is, his first aim was to liberate the city or else to delay liberation until the insurrectionists of the ideologically unacceptable Uprising had been wiped out by the Germans.

Lillian Hellman was an early and impressive example of the independent woman, but she never completely forsakes feather-headed femininity as a ploy, and her continuing ability not to comprehend what was going on in Russia is a glaring demonstration. In a section of An Unfinished Woman dealing with a later trip to Russia, she finds herself tongue-tied in the presence of a Russian friend. We are asked to believe that her own feelings about the McCarthy period were welling up to block her speech, just as the Russian friend's experience of the recent past had blocked hers. The two communed in silence. That this equation was presented as a profundity seemed to me at the time to prove that Lillian Hellman, whatever her stature in the theatre, possessed, as an essayist, an attitudinizing mind of which her mannered prose was the logically consequent expression. One doesn't underrate the virulence of McCarthyism for a minute, and it may well be that such goonery is as fundamental to America's history as terror is to Russia's. But the two things are so different in nature, and so disparate in scale, that a mind which equates them loses the ability to describe either. For all its Proustian pernicketiness of recollected detail, An Unfinished Woman was a very vague book.

Still, it shimmered with stars. Parker and Hammett, especially, shone brightly in its pages. There are some additional facts about them scattered through *Pentimento* (Hammett's name is omnipresent, as you might expect) and in a section on the theatre and related performing arts we hear about Edmund Wilson, Theodore Roethke, Tyrone Guthrie, Samuel Goldwyn and Tallulah Bankhead. Just as she was good on Parker's decline, she is good on Bankhead's: Hellman's *grandes dames* go down to defeat in a flurry of misapplied talcum. Roethke features as the falling-down drunk he undoubtedly was most of the time. Lowell gets a mention. It's all good gossip, and all helps.

The bulk of the volume, however, is devoted to memoirs of non-famous characters from Miss Hellman's past. The transatlantic reviewers seem to have convinced themselves that this material is pretty quintessential stuff. We learn from Richard Poirier, quoted on the blurb, that it 'provides one of those rare instances when the moral value of a book is wholly inextricable from its immense literary worth, where the excitations, the pacing, and the intensifications offered by the style manage to create in us perceptions about human character that have all but disappeared from contemporary writing'. I certainly agree that the perceptiveness, such as it is, is closely linked to the style. What I can't see for a moment is how trained literati can imagine that the style is anything less than frantically mannered and anything more than painfully derivative.

'The drinking' has not reappeared, but 'the joking' is there to make up for it. We hear of an historical period called 'the time of Hitler'. 'It is of a windiness', says someone in a German train, and although this might just conjecturably sound like half-translated German, what it can't *help* sounding like is Hemingway's half-translated Spanish. Out-takes from *The Old Man and the Sea* abound:

> You are good in boats not alone from knowledge, but because water is a part of you, you are easy on it, fear it and like it in such equal parts that you work well in a boat without thinking about it and may be even safer because you don't need to think too much. That is what we mean by instinct and there is no way to explain an instinct for the theatre, although those who have it recognize each other and a bond is formed between them.

Such passages read like E. B. White's classic parody *Across the Street and into the Grill*, in which White established once and for all that Hemingway's diction could not be copied, not even by Hemingway. Nor are these echoes mere lapses: her whole approach to moral-drawing is Hemingway's—the excitations, the pacing and the intensifications, if I may borrow Richard Poirier's terminology.

That is what I thought about Aunt Lily until I made the turn and the turn was as sharp as only the young can make when they realize their values have been shoddy.

Or try this:

There are many ways of falling in love and one seldom is more interesting or valid than another unless, of course, one of them lasts so long that it becomes something else, like your arm or leg about which you neither judge nor protest.

Her approach to anecdote is Hemingway's as well. Not just in the dialogue, which is American Vernacular to the last degree ('You are fine ladies', I said after a while, 'the best'), but in the withholding of information—the tip-of-the-iceberg effect. On occasions this works. She is good at showing how children get hold of the wrong end of the stick, giving their loyalties passionately to the wrong people. The first chapter, set in her childhood New Orleans and dealing with a girl called Bethe, shows us the young Lillian failing to understand that Bethe is a hoodlum's girlfriend. We are supplied with this information so grudgingly ourselves that it is easy to identify with the young Lillian's confusion. In other chapters, dealing with characters who entered her life much later on, we are already equipped with knowledge of our own about the relevant period and tend to find the by now less young Lillian's slowness to comprehend a bit of a strain, especially when the period in question is the Time of Hitler.

For action, the chapter about a girl called Julia is the best thing in the book. A childhood friend who went back to Europe, Julia was in the Karl Marx Hof in Vienna when the Austrian government troops (abetted by the local Nazis) bombarded it. She lost a leg, but kept on with the fight against Fascism. Apparently Miss Hellman, passing through Germany on her way to Russia, smuggled 50,000 dollars to Julia in her hat. The money was used to spring 500 prisoners. Miss Hellman was in no small danger when engaged on this enterprise and the results unquestionably constituted a more impressive political effectiveness than most of us ever accomplish. She still revels in the nitty-grittiness of it all: she liked thirties radicalism a lot better than twenties 'rebellion'—the twenties were all style and she is properly contemptuous of style in that vitiated sense.

But with all that said, we are still left with key questions unanswered. Miss Hellman says that she has changed Julia's name because she is 'not sure that even now the Germans like their premature anti-Nazis'. Since they like them well enough to have made one of them Chancellor of West Germany, it's permissible to assume that Miss Hellman means something more interesting, and that Julia was a member of the Communist Party. If she was, it's difficult to see why Miss Hellman can't come straight out and say so. If she fears that we might think the less of the young Julia for it, she surely overestimates the long-term impact of McCarthyism on her readership. Or is she just *compelled* to be vague?

For the truth is that the Julia chapter, like all the others, happens in a dream. Despite the meticulously recollected minutiae, the story reads like a spy-sketch by Nichols and May, even down to the bewilderingly complicated instructions ('You have two hours, but we haven't that long together because you have to be followed to the station and the ones who follow you must have time to find the man who will be with you on the train until Warsaw in the morning') Julia breathes to Lillian under the noses of the lurking Gestapo.

To have been there, to have seen it, and yet still be able to write it down so that it rings false—it takes a special kind of talent. But there are stretches of her writing which somehow manage to sound true, even through the blanket of her supposedly transparent prose. She liked Samuel Goldwyn and has the guts to say so. Whether or not it took bravery to like him, it still takes bravery to admit it. She is, of course, perfectly right to admire Goldwyn above Irving Thalberg. Here again her suspicion of Style led her to the truth. Scott Fitzgerald, infinitely more sensitive but over-endowed with reverence, fell for Thalberg full length.

Less prominent this time but still compulsively invoked, the true hero of *Pentimento* is Dashiell Hammett. Theirs, I think, will be remembered as a great love. The only thing that could possibly delay the legend would be Miss Hellman's indefatigable determination to feed its flames. In this volume the Nick-and-Nora-Charles dialogue reads as much like a screenplay as it did in the previous one.

I phoned the Beverly Hills house from the restaurant. I said to Hammett, 'I'm in New Orleans. I'm not coming back to Hollywood for a while and I didn't want you to worry.'

'How are you?" he said.

'O.K. and you?'

'I'm O.K. I miss you.'

'I miss you, too. Is there a lady in my bedroom?'

He laughed. 'I don't think so, but they come and go. Except you. You just go.'

'I had good reason,' I said.

'Yes,' he said, 'you did.'

I like it now and my mother liked it then, when William Powell and Myrna Loy rattled it off to each other in the thirties. The *Thin Man* movies, with their unquestioned assumption that man and wife were equal partners, played a vital part in raising the expectations of women everywhere. Such are the unappraised impulses of modern history—when the fuss dies down it turns out that turns of speech and tones of voice mattered just as much as battles.

On Broadway Lillian Hellman took her chances among the men, a pioneer women's liberationist. Her plays were bold efforts, indicative social documents which are unlikely to be neglected by students, although as pieces for the theatre they will probably date: they are problem plays whose problems are no longer secrets, for which in some measure we have her to thank. She is a tough woman who has almost certainly not been relishing the patronizing critical practice—more common in America than here, and let's keep it that way —of belatedly indicating gratitude for strong early work by shouting unbridled hosannahs for pale, late stuff that has a certain documentary value but not much more. She says at one point in *Pentimento* that in her time on Broadway she was always denied the benefits of the kind of criticism which would take her properly to task.

(*The New Review*, May 1974)

16. The Watcher in Spanish

And I Remember Spain: A Spanish Civil War Anthology edited by Murray Sperber

There were only five thousand English-speaking volunteers in the Spanish Civil War but fifteen hundred books in English came out of it. Murray Sperber, the editor of this exceptionally interesting anthology, seems to have read as many of them as is compatible with mental health. From English and from all the other relevant languages except Spanish—an understandable exclusion, since that would need another anthology on its own—he has chosen writings which fulfil his requirement of capturing the apocalyptic mood without being rendered senseless by it. The propaganda remains in oblivion.

The war in Spain ran from 1936 to 1939, during which years the generation now approaching middle age were busy being born. For them, the whole of life has been lived in the illumination of the lessons taught in Spain. The older generation had a rude awakening. The younger generation grew up taking it all for granted. What strikes me most about this book is its familiarity. Here are men and women at least as intelligent as I am, certainly braver and more independent than I am, agonizedly discovering in the middle of a blood-bath truths which to me seem the very fundamentals of political and artistic reality. But perhaps these things now seem clear only because they were first written in flames.

The primary lesson, of course (and the 'of course' is ours—there was no 'of course' about it then), concerned the nature of ideological war. Orwell emerged as its chief teacher, and fittingly a piece from *Homage to Catalonia* closes the book. It is an up-beat extract ('Curiously enough the whole experience has left me with not less but more belief in the decency of human beings') but Orwell's whole effect was to tell the world that totalitarianism existed on the Left as well as on the Right and that it wasn't enough to be anti-fascist, you had to be anti-totalitarian—the informing political insight governing the interpretation of cultural history from that day to this.

Every famous name in the book can be assessed according to whether or not he submitted his independence to an orthodoxy. And often enough—just often enough to make the anthology encouraging reading—you can see orthodoxy being transformed into independence under the pressure of experience. A good artist is a good thing to be: the proof is here. There were, needless to say (and that 'needless to say' is ours too), some good artists who backed their side through any amount of atrocity. But on the whole the artists (especially the ones on the spot) learned that the truth is objective after all, and that ensuring it is told is a full-time job—*their* job.

There could have been no more pure a young Communist than John Cornford. Yet even his absurdly short life gave him ample opportunity to find out that the party's interests were not always the people's. In a diary-letter written on the Aragon front, he complained:

> It [the party] is still concentrating too much on trying to neutralise the petty bourgeoisie when by far the most urgent task is to win the Anarchist workers, which is a special technique and very different from broad Seventh Congress phrases. But I don't really know. . .

If he had lived longer he would undoubtedly have found out for certain, although judging from his incipient capacity to ask awkward questions he might have had to step lively in order to avoid being neutralized himself.

Nobody except Stalin's executioners was fully aware at the beginning that the independent Left was Stalin's real enemy in Spain. Orwell was pre-eminently the man who, on behalf of us all, found out. (It would have been useful, incidentally, if this book had made clear the debt Orwell owed Borkenau.) Mr. Sperber, however, perhaps falls into the opposite error of crediting Stalin with too much bloodless rationality. There was his bloodless irrationality to be contended with too. In his introduction, Mr. Sperber writes:

> Even the Russians, who were sent by Stalin to prop up, then manipulate the Republic, developed so much political idealism that they were purged upon their return to the Soviet Union.

Stalin would have purged them even if the only thing they developed had been mumps. He purged them for having been abroad. After 1945 he purged his own army for having been in Germany.

The real news which came out of Spain concerned the forces for good working evil. That the forces of evil worked evil was never news. Nevertheless here are the necessary reminders of just how frightfully the Right made war. G. L. Steer's account of the obliteration of Guernica is useful to have. A lot of the damage was done by incendiaries—the kind of interesting detail it is hard to get from formal history. Professional journalists stack up well beside the name writers. Newsmen, as A. J. Liebling once pointed out, are on the whole a disbelieving lot. This gives the best of them a fresh eye. Jay Allen, then a stringer for the *Chicago Tribune*, wrote a horribly clear account of how Franco's troops killed 4,000 people after the fall of Badajoz. It is essential to have such stories readily to hand, in case one should ever be tempted into the folly of supposing that the atrocities on the Left, simply because they were, in the sense I have already definied, more interesting news, were worse than the atrocities on the Right. The fact is, it was all much of a muchness: it took a saint to choose between.

Bernanos was a royalist. There is a good piece extracted from his *Les grands cimetières sous la lune*. Its pity is withheld from no one: Mr. Sperber has wisely included Bernanos under 'The Witnesses' rather than under 'Authors Take Sides'. 'Let us look them in the eyes for the last time, those enemies of humankind,' Bernanos wrote of the executioners, 'before turning from them to the pages of another book.' The Right's revenge disgusted him.

Simone Weil, in a letter to Bernanos, reminded him that the Left's time in power had been no reign of mercy. Orwell inveighed against what he took to be Auden's conception of 'the necessary murder'. Here, in Weil's letter, is an even more telling indictment. There were about fifty killings a night in Barcelona. Weil would not have understood Orwell's belief in human decency:

> People get carried away by a sort of intoxication, which is irresistible without a fortitude of soul which I am bound to consider exceptional, since I have met with it nowhere.

She overstates her case—just. There is always a residuum of decency or we would never get to hear the truth: a book like this is a testament to the amount of kindness involved in seeing things as they are. *And I Remember Spain* is heavily to be recommended. It is, though, painfully short of critical apparatus. Before a paperback edition is even contemplated the book simply must be provided with

brief critical biographies of the authors. One shouldn't have to go
to *Journey to the Frontier* just to check up on how long Cornford
lived. And what is the truth of the revolting but highly talented
Roy Campbell's claim to be a worker? Did he ever fire a shot in
anger? Such things need to be clearly set down before the people
who still remember them are gone.

(New Statesman, 21 June 1974)

17. Dick's Diaries: Richard Crossman

In contrast to the U.S., which so far has been asked to deal with only one volume of the late R. H. S. Crossman's Diaries, Great Britain by now finds itself contending with two, comprising more than 1,500 pages of text. Philosophers are divided on the question of whether the narrative therein unfolded is grippingly boring or boringly gripping. Perhaps the truth lies somewhere in between. There is so much detail crammed into these books that it is an act of bravery to pick them up. Once picked up, they are difficult to put down. The reader despairs: haunted by the prospect of missing something, he is nevertheless aware that life is very short. Most Britons who claim to have read Crossman through have not done so, even when they own the volumes—all they did was read the extracts published in the London *Sunday Times*. Possibly they took the wiser course. But the patient reader will derive more than just self-satisfaction from tackling the whole thing. Part of its gist lies in the apparent irrelevancies. However unsystematically, in these clotted pages the way of life of the British governing class is being laid out before your eyes, even when the diarist thinks he is talking about something else.

But since the Diaries purport to deal with the Labour government which lasted from 1964 to 1970, rather than with anything so unpindownable as the way of life of the British governing class, we owe it to Crossman's irascible ghost to summarize the more obvious facts first. In the first volume, covering the years 1964-1966, Crossman was Minister of Housing and Local Government. In the cabinet of Her Majesty's Government, a specific job like that is called a Department, mainly because there is a permanent department of the civil service ready (and, theoretically, willing and able) to carry out the minister's policy. Much of the drama of the first volume consists of Crossman's struggle with the civil service, personified by Dame Evelyn Sharp, known to Crossman as the Dame. Unlike the American system, in which a cabinet officer, once appointed by the president, fills the two top echelons of his staff with his own appointees, the British system ensures that the incoming minister is pretty well stuck with what he gets. Crossman was stuck with the Dame.

There has been much controversy in Britain about whether the Dame who bestrides volume one of the Diaries is anything like the reality. However that may be, as Minister of Housing our hero had the absorbing task of carrying out, *per media* the Dame, that part of the Labour government's programme which dealt with putting roofs over people's heads. He was also privy to something of what went on in cabinet and in the small personal circle around the prime minister, Harold Wilson. After almost twenty years as a back-bench MP (meaning that he had been elected to Parliament but had never been invited either into the cabinet when the Labour Party was in power or into the shadow cabinet when it was in opposition), Crossman's belated experience of what cabinet government entailed was a revelation to him—and, through the Diaries, to us.

But with a department to run he was still not in a position to get the full story. There were important committees, among them defence, in which he was not included. For most of the second volume, covering the years 1966–1968, Crossman is still in the cabinet but he is no longer in charge of a department. He is Lord President of the Council and leader of the House of Commons. These are grand-sounding titles but Crossman regarded being given them as a demotion, or kick upstairs. Whatever he felt about the change, however, the Diaries benefit from it. He is able to take a much wider view. True, the Lord President of the Council doesn't see much of anything except the Queen, to whom he takes Orders in Council— i.e., the government's legislation after it has passed through both Houses—to get them signed and sealed.

But the Leader of the House is responsible for getting that legislation through the House of Commons. He is like the stage manager of a theatre putting on a different show every day. With the responsibility of timing the debates and directing party discipline through the Chief Whip, the Leader of the House must necessarily stick close to the prime minister and take an overall view of everybody else's job in the cabinet. Crossman apparently found the task frustrating in comparison with his clear-cut role at Housing, where he rarely doubted his own effectiveness. The Minister of Housing makes a tangible impact on the nation. The Leader of the House has only a parliamentary glory. In other words, Crossman was a bit less of a star than he had been before. Volume two is consequently more self-searching than volume one. Less satisfied, it is more satisfying. Since the declared intention of the Diaries had always been to show how government (or, in Harold Wilson's portentous usage, 'governance') actually works, the second volume represents a step up, even though its author personally thought he was taking a step down.

Meanwhile the country was going broke. The second book would be superior to the first if only for the clearer picture it gives of Harold Wilson dealing with the threat of bankruptcy, or failing to deal with it. The portrait of Wilson given in the Diaries is devastating. Wilson's own writings of course give a countervailing assessment of his own prowess but they attain such a high level of unreadability that Crossman's version is the one bound to endure.

As evoked by Crossman, Wilson is a master of tactics with no idea of strategy. Though in his personal dealings he retains an engaging modesty and straightforwardness, in his public dealings he falls increasingly prey to deviousness and posturing. Far from having any clear-cut socialist programme to save the nation, he sacrifices everything to expediency, with the sole object of surviving as prime minister. What might be done at home is left undone because the electorate might find it unpalatable. In the meantime he attempts to cut a statesmanlike figure on the world stage.

It is in his power to devalue the pound, but he does not do so until too late. It is not within his power to intervene effectively in the Vietnam war, but he wastes time, and strains the loyalty of his party, by attempting to do so. Crossman grants him his consummate skill at reconciling opposites within the Labour movement, but concludes that the net effect is a movement which cannot move. Rome burns with a fitful flame, like an ash tip. Nero's fiddle has rubber strings. Governance is just government unmeant—politics to no purpose.

Crossman's Wilson would be a lasting reference point whether it were a true account or not. As it happens, there are good reasons for thinking that Crossman has got Wilson exactly right. But a *caveat* should be entered. The personality doing the personality-assessing needs some careful assessing in its turn. Crossman is avowedly determined to lay himself open in these pages, but a man who shows you his warts might be intent on convincing you that he is Cromwell. Despite frequent admissions of guilt, clumsiness, and failure, Crossman emerges as being pretty nearly always right. To hear him tell it, he had the clear eye, the sound mind, and the firm voice. But sweet reason went unheard. There is a passage toward the end of Saint-Simon's memoirs where all the nobility are rushing around buying shares in the Mississippi venture. Saint-Simon is the only one who can see that the uproar is about nothing but a patch of blue sky. He comes under heavy Royal pressure to join in, but prefers to remain aloof. The level tones of sanity. Crossman's Diaries have just that tone. But is that what Crossman was really like?

There can be no doubt that he was a clever man. From Winchester he went as a Scholar to New College, Oxford; a First in Mods and Greats; Fellow and Tutor at twenty-three—such an academic record is achieved by no dunces and only a few fools. Whether on the back benches or the front, Crossman was always among the most dazzling of the Labour Party intellectuals. But the abiding question is whether he was ever truly serious, in the sense of being able to listen to what anyone else was saying.

He took legitimate pride in his capacity for blunt speech. There has been corroboration from other politicians for the picture he draws of himself as the awkward cuss who made things hot for Harold in cabinet. But when he says things like 'a pretty good row developed and I was fairly offensive', it seems likely that he was understating the case. Crossman believed that he could handle people but it is doubtful if he really could. Instead, he shouted them down. When he confessed, toward the end of his life, that he was an intellectual bully by nature, it was meant to be disarming, but there is plenty of independent evidence to say that he was merely being accurate. The continuing argument about whether he has been fair to the Dame turns on the question of his proudly flaunted abrasiveness. Did it really energize people, or did it just fill the air with their feathers? As it turned out, he was to be remembered in Whitehall as an effective Minister of Housing and in Westminster as a fruitfully busy Leader of the House, but beyond that his estimate of himself as a master politician ought probably not to have been accepted. He could always see the necessity of devaluing the pound and withdrawing from military commitments east of Suez, but then so could most of his colleagues. His undoubted virtue was the ability to say these things to Wilson's face. But the virtue was coupled to a drawback—arrogance. By the end of volume two, all disclaimers notwithstanding, he is obviously dreaming of himself as leader, not just of the House, but of the Party itself.

In 1970, after the fall of the Labour government, Crossman attained a life-long ambition, becoming editor of the *New Statesman*. In a distinguished obituary for Crossman published in *Encounter*, Paul Johnson later revealed that while Crossman's brilliance as a *New Statesman* contributor during his back-bench days had not been in doubt, none the less it had been tacitly agreed among management and staff that his dreams of editorship should not be allowed to come true. According to Johnson, there is a memo on file written by Kingsley Martin, the magazine's editor in the 1950s, listing all the reasons why Crossman should never be placed in charge. Tantalizingly, Johnson could not bring himself to quote this document. But it is safe to suppose that its contents would hardly come as a surprise to those who worked under Crossman during his brief tenure as editor in the early Seventies. He just about ran the paper into the ground. Among the contributors, even his admirers were demoralized by the way he dealt with them. His blue pencil unerringly removed their best paragraphs. Editorial conferences consisted of listening to him talk. His choice to write a weekly column of dynamic opinion was that fiery young rebel J. B. Priestley. Crossman was hell to have around but he wouldn't go away. One of his literary editors still has a recurring nightmare in which he fires bullets at Crossman's stomach, which in its later life apparently featured a metal patch as the result of an ulcer operation. So the bullets bounce off instead of going in.

Crossman complains many times in the Diaries that he had too often been No. 2 instead of No. 1, but to hindsight it looks probable that the overconfident, uncalculating frankness which made him a valuable member of the government would have made him a ruinous leader of it. To say he lacked touch is to put it gently. He made his most famous blunder in 1969, during the twilight of the Labour government, when he had moved on to become Secretary of State at the Department of Health and Social Security—a period which will doubtless occupy the beginning of volume three. Crossman announced the imposition of prescription charges on false teeth and spectacles three days before the municipal elections. A landslide to the Conservatives duly followed. It will be interesting to see what he says about this.

But the two books we already have are richly peppered with examples almost as endearing. On page 38 of volume two he is to be found planning a speech accepting responsibility for 10,000 men being thrown out of work at the British Motor Corporation. 'I assumed that the right way to handle the news,' he confides, 'was to be tough and say, "Yes, we are deliberately creating transitional redundancy in order to prevent mass unemployment".' Someone stopped him in time. That the working population would swallow a concept like 'transitional redundancy' was a very odd assumption for a Labour cabinet minister to be caught holding. Crossman doesn't seem to spot the anomaly—his writing on the point is quite unguarded. Clearly Crossman had too little of Wilson's ability to conciliate.

Yet he is surely justified in arguing that Wilson had too much of it. Less happy as Leader of the House than as Minister of Housing, Crossman found, as most people do, that discontent broadens the mind. In volume two there is more anxiety than grandiloquence and the pretensions to supreme office should charitably be seen as an aberration. But even if he were wholly wrong about his own political gifts, he would still be a trenchant critic of Wilson's. Again and again he condemns Wilson's lack of vision. Wilson would rather smooth things over or put them off than face up to them. Crossman wasn't like that. *He* was a true socialist.

Yet was he? On this evidence, increasingly less so as time went on. In volume one already, and in volume two more than in volume one, he is to be found doubting whether he is still a socialist of the old kind. But really he should have doubted whether he was still a socialist of *any* kind. His relative equanimity on the topic would amount to gross self-deception, if he were not so patently guileless. In the event, this cleverest of men simply comes over as having been a bit obtuse about his own interior workings. At least Wilson *knew* that he didn't know what he wanted.

Crossman's opacity in this matter is once again a drawback born of a virtue—in this case his cultivation. Just because he was domineering didn't make him a Philistine. In a frantically busy working life compounded by the self-imposed task of dictating these Diaries, he still finds time to read the Greek classics to himself and *Treasure Island* to his son, see *Der Rosenkavalier* at Covent Garden and listen to Beethoven's late quartets at home. None of these strikes you as carefully planted tributes to his own humanism—he was too confident of his own mental stature to put on a show in that regard. There will be argument for some time to come about whether Crossman's success in getting close to Wilson's dream of building 500,000 houses a year really constituted a substantial achievement. What kind of houses? In retrospect, slum clearance looks like a catastrophe. Ten years ago it still looked like progress.

But there can be no doubt that he was a force for civilization in such matters as preserving the historic centres of towns. He took a hand in cancelling the besotted schemes to put a road through Christ Church Meadow in Oxford and to extend the British Museum library even further into the already ravaged Bloomsbury. Even more important, he made sure that an area of Georgian houses in Islington, London, was rehabilitated rather than redeveloped—meaning preserved instead of destroyed. In the long run rehabilitation, though expensive initially, has proved to be cheaper in social costs. Such humane decisions are to Crossman's lasting credit. They were socialism of a kind and paradoxically were more genuinely conservative than anything the Conservative Party has been able to offer in recent years. (It was a Conservative Minister of the Environment who offered to drive a six-lane highway through the middle of the City of London.)

Crossman was far too enthusiastic about some of the New Towns. He was uplifted by the brutalist architecture of the new town at Cumbernauld, for example. So are most people who visit the place, but those who have to live there tend to be rather less exalted. On the whole, though, Crossman's taste is sure—certainly much surer than his touch. Unfortunately he is slow in bringing himself to accept that his enjoyment of the good life must necessarily either modify or falsify his political beliefs. In the end they were modified, but he never quite realized how the trick was worked.

Self-deception is too big a name for his ability to kid himself about his standard of living. He just played things down. He lets us know that rather than hit the high spots in the evenings he prefers a simple gathering for dinner at George Weidenfeld's or Pam Berry's. Actually George Weidenfeld, later Lord Weidenfeld, and Pamela Berry, later Lady Hartwell, maintained, then as now, two of the most luminous tables in London. Crossman was a member of both the Athenaeum and the Garrick. If pressed, he probably would have insisted that these clubs are more raffish than such Establishment fortresses as White's.

Crossman thought of himself as some kind of dangerous rebel because he was reluctant to climb into morning dress. He pretended to hate visiting the Queen, but was proud of getting on with her. In his own eyes he was a simple man. When he was editor of the *New Statesman* he once told a young journalist of my acquaintance to get himself togged out in St. James's. 'I,' said Crossman, 'eat in St. James's, get my hair cut in St. James's, and have my suits, shirts and shoes made in various parts of St. James's. St. James's—that's the place for you, my lad.' To one of the *New Statesman's* notoriously underpaid junior staff members this was good but useless advice, since the shops in St. James's are very expensive. No doubt it struck Crossman as a good socialist solution for an impecunious young man to kit himself out with durable clobber. The factor he neglected was the magnitude of the initial outlay.

But not even Crossman could ignore the problem posed by his country residence, Prescote. A manor house surrounded by 500 acres near Oxford, Prescote is Crossman's great solace throughout the Diaries. There he can recuperate from his political labours and indulge fantasies of the simple life. To his credit, he could never entirely ignore the implications. 'Life here at Prescote gets lovelier the longer it goes on,' he writes early in volume one. 'Is it making me more conservative?' he asks later in the same book. No. By volume two he is asking whether his way of life might not be cutting him off from left-wing socialism. The answer is still no, because 'my radical passions have never been based on a moral or egalitarian philosophy.' In that case, what *were* they based on? But it is useless to carp. We should be grateful he has at least questioned himself that far.

Crossman had always fancied himself to be on the left wing of the Labour Party but when he achieved office he moved quickly enough rightward. At the start he saw himself as a left-wing influence in the cabinet but if he was it was only on certain issues. His attitudes on devaluing sterling and cutting back military commitments didn't make him a radical—just realistic. He was anti-Common Market because he was a Little Englander. On state control of industry, the pivotal socialist issue, he had no consistent views. His general tendency was towards the centre. With the Labour

Party intellectuals that is nearly always the general tendency. An occasional well-connected maverick like Tony Benn might move toward radicalism but men like Crossman, Anthony Crosland, and Roy Jenkins move away from it. Becoming too civilized for their own doctrine, they either change the doctrine or go on preaching it hypocritically. They usually change it. The result is Social Democracy.

Crossman was a Social Democrat, who unlike Crosland and Jenkins never quite admitted to himself what had happened to him. He was even less able than most men to follow the dialogue of his own interior drama. Less able to follow it, he was less able to censor it, which is why the Diaries are so revealing in their incidental detail. For example, in volume two (page 700), Crossman talks about the Oxbridge students protesting against the Vietnam war. He grants them their right to be indignant about the Labour Party's equivocations, but not their right to shout him down. The trouble, he argues, lies precisely in their being 'students' and not 'undergraduates.' In other words, they are not gentlemen. The wrong children are being sent to the right places. So much for a lifetime of believing in social reform through education.

Crossman's portrait of Wilson is fair enough in itself but unfair in the sense that as prime minister any other Social Democrat would probably have been forced to the same compromises, devoting most of his energy to restraining his own left. 'Poor Jim Callaghan,' as Crossman calls him, was ready to accept this fact. All Callaghan's talents are for conciliation. Roy Jenkins, who emerges from these volumes as the best prime minister Great Britain never had, was hopelessly overqualified.

If the Labour Party were ever to disintegrate, it might not be just because the left had decided to expel the Social Democrats. The Social Democrats might simply tire of maintaining an increasingly unnatural alliance. *Credo quia impossibile*—Crossman was proud of that. But other people thrive less on paradoxes. If the Conservative Party were ever to disintegrate (and there is a school of thought which believes that it already has), the Social Democrats of the Labour Party, taking the Liberal Party with them, could easily hive off and fill the gap. Such a realignment of forces would merely reflect what is already going on in people's minds.

It was going on in Crossman's mind well before he died in 1974.

Hence the outstanding value of these Diaries. They purport to be about men governing institutions, but they are just as much about institutions governing men. Orwell said we should get our beliefs in line with our desires. Crossman couldn't. Hardly anybody can, quite. Wilson's strength—which Crossman could acknowledge without being able to explain—lay in the simplicity of his wishes. Mediocre, he was not divided. His subsequent hostility to Crossman's writings springs not just from injured *amour propre* but from the traditional contempt of the realist for the dreamer.

(*New York Review of Books*, 31 March, 1977)

18. Unpatriotic Gore: Gore Vidal

Most of the pieces in Gore Vidal's *Collected Essays* we have seen before—mainly in his two earlier collections, 'Rocking the Boat' and 'Reflections Upon a Sinking Ship'—but they gain from being assembled in one volume. Vidal has always had a title to being amongst the most fluently entertaining of American essayists. I think it can now be seen that he has also been among the most substantial. He has had the usual trouble of writers who are not solemn, in that the humourless have been slow to take him seriously. But by now the quality of his intelligence should be obvious to all.

There are twenty years of adventurous essay-writing here. One of the themes of his early pieces was that American society was not uneasy enough to encourage satire. The Eisenhower era was a period of imposed tolerance. Vidal was looking forward to a period of flux, in which prejudices and obsessions would be out in the open. The period promptly arrived, and Vidal spent the next two decades commenting on it, both in fiction and in formal prose. Even early on, he was already a Roman—he was the knowing voice piercing the mist at the baths, ridiculing the hypocrisies of a stifling hegemony. As the hegemony crumbled into an age of transition, he became more recognizably a Roman figure than ever, viewing the anabases of the new Caesars with an unfoolable eye.

In a piece written *circa* 1960 called 'The Twelve Caesars' he said that world events were the work of individuals and that the motives of those individuals were often frivolous, even casual. There is something of Suetonius and Plutarch in Vidal's unblushing readiness to view contemporary history in terms of character. Without discounting ordinary political analysis, Vidal is keen to demonstrate that character is destiny. He is always interesting when discussing a would-be or current President. He is interesting because he is interested—well aware that the interior constitution of the man he is writing about really matters. He is as good a novelist in his political essays as he is in his novels.

Some would say a better one—a glib opinion. Though none of his fictions is the Great American Novel (the writing of which was an ambition he emphatically disclaimed at an early date), each is considerable. His aims in the novel have been, he says, to create worlds rather than to be didactic. I don't think he has succeeded in creating worlds, but paradoxically he has succeeded in being didactic. It would be hard to find a Vidal novel which does not contain a thesis, and hard to find, among those theses, one that was not instructive. Really the novels and the essays go together, as works of the assertive intelligence.

Assertive he always is. He would be a teacher, were his tone more dry. As it is, he is the wit who knows what is going on, and whose ideas, which impress you first as conundrums, tend to linger as food for thought and finally add to your picture of the truth. He saw commendably early that the collapse of the religious systems would leave the absolutist spirit free to fulfil Arnold's prophecy about art becoming a religion: academicism was taken over by theologians. He is against that spirit and never talks about art as holy writ. Nevertheless creativity is his touchstone, to be believed in—the one thing that can be, in a civilization which is becoming, and ought to become, faithless. Vidal endorses Flaubert's admiration for the century before Christ's birth, a time in which the old gods were gone, the new ones had not yet arrived, and man was alone. The great negative is for him a positive. He mocks the God-bothering rhetoric of the Presidents out of a certainty that their fake faith is the key to their bad faith.

Prophecy is not the test of political analysis but it is remarkable how often Vidal has been right. In 1968 he guessed Nixon would be the one. He knew that Kennedy's presidency was an irreversible disaster from the Bay of Pigs on, and his pieces on the Kennedy family ('The Holy Family' and 'The Manchester Book') will remain cogent documents for the study of power in modern America. Here, as elsewhere, Vidal writes with the advantages of being born into the American ruling class. (That he knew a class system existed was another of his originalities.) He saw that Edmund Wilson's 'The Cold War and the Income Tax'—a pamphlet which was a joke in America and a flop here—was an important diagnosis. He knew that the only interesting thing about Howard Hughes was the man's transcendental mediocrity.

Vidal, a declared bi-sexual, is always diverting on sexual matters. He thinks sex doesn't illuminate much of life except itself—a view calculated to enrage everyone, and one with which I concur. On the other hand he has fought long, hard and fearlessly for freedom of sexual expression. (See 'Sex and the Law' of 1965.) If I said that I saw a certain emptiness in his confidence about the liberating effect of bi-sexual promiscuity, he would probably call me repressed. But his was the side of the argument it took bravery to favour. With that conceded, however, I still think his fine essay on Eleanor Roosevelt would be even better if he could see that the nobility of character he praises was connected with the self-denial he regrets. There is often room to disagree with Vidal. But there is no room at all for denying that he is a superlative essayist, whose elegant concision is a gage thrown down to everyone else in the field.

(*Observer*, 28 July 1974)

19. Kennedy's Ideal Biographer: Lord Longford

I have never held with the common belief that Lord Longford is the greatest fool in England. There are professors in Cambridge who have to call the A.A. to help them park their cars. But it is certainly true that Lord Longford has always appeared to possess the combination of qualities indispensable to anyone wishing to be regarded as a great fool—i.e., considerable mental energy allied with a chronic inability to see the world as it is. On top of all that, of course, and lifting him from the ruck of ordinary great fools into the category of those who might be considered for the title of greatest fool in England, has always been his raging thirst for publicity. This ungovernable passion for getting his name and face in the papers and up on the screen would in itself be a good cause for giving him the title. When you add the piquant fact of his reiterated claims to Humility, it is hard to see how anybody else could possibly be considered for the championship: the laurels should be his in perpetuity.

And yet somehow he has never quite made it. Just as Joe Bugner can do everything but punch and David Bedford can do everything but win, Lord Longford somehow lacks that decisive touch—what football journalists call the ability to *finish*—which characterizes the genuinely transcendental fool. However fleeting, there has always been a gleam of sanity in those eyes. There has always been a disturbing hint of normality about his otherwise impeccably absurd behaviour. His new book on Kennedy, for example, is nothing like so ridiculous as one had a right to expect from a man of such distinction. Lapses into common sense disfigure it at every point, while a moment's reflection should have told its author that his major conclusions were far too reasonable for a man of his reputation to be caught arriving at.

Very little of the book properly fulfils the promise of its jacket, which has a toothsome photo of J.F.K. on the front and a rather less aesthetically pleasing, though arguably more awe-inspiring, snap of Lord Longford on the back. Look here, upon this picture, and on this. (The contrast is made no less edifying by the fact that J.F.K. turned out to be the satyr. Which makes you-know-who Hyperion.) 'For John Kennedy, Lord Longford must be the ideal biographer,' the blurb announces, but even though the proposition is self-evident there is a generous willingness to back it up with argument. 'His family and the Kennedys are united both by their Catholic faith and their Irish heritage.' (By the same criterion, Lord Longford must also be the ideal biographer of Sean McStiofain. Doubtless Lord Weidenfeld is already on to this.)

'Moreover,' the rhapsodist continues, as if further proof were needed, 'Lord Longford is at home in the world of power, politics and diplomacy, which the young President entered with so little experience and so much ambition.' The implications here are delightful, but we ought not to revel in them. It is, after all, undoubtedly true that the young President was destined never to attain the long experience of his ideal biographer; and anyway, in the book itself the ideal biographer is less keen to stress his own virtues than you might imagine.

Even more interestingly, he finds it hard to put his whole heart into stressing Kennedy's, either. Here the ideal biographer's legendary naïveté leads him closer to the truth than many sophisticates have been able to go. He quotes with seeming approval Arthur Schlesinger's idea that Kennedy's patronage of writers seemed 'to prefigure a new Augustan age of poetry and power'. That this was always a deeply philistine notion Lord Longford has not critical powers enough to see, but nor is he ready to go along with the still-prevailing myth of the young President's all-devouring intellectual curiosity. Lord Longford is able to see that the young President's wide reading was in fact pretty narrow. He can't quite bring himself to say so, but neither can he bring himself to endorse the contrary opinion. It would have been too much to expect that Lord Longford would follow up these leads and attempt a properly sceptical assessment of the amount of bogusness which went to supporting the Kennedy image. For the moment it is enough, and more than enough, that the ideal biographer's innocent nostrils have detected the odd whiff of hokum.

The nostrils are in remarkable working order, considering the strain they are placed under by his radiant smile. They have also detected at least one red herring. Whatever the chip on Joe Kennedy's shoulder, Lord Longford argues persuasively, there wasn't even a splinter on J.F.K.'s. There was no element of revenge in his rise to the top. Here Lord Longford's social instinct stands him in good stead. The ideal biographer, with his wealth of experience, is well aware that the route to the top has nowadays less to do with birth than with star-quality. There is no need for the stars to get in with the well-born. The well-born are too keen to get in with the stars. Lord Longford has never actually sat down and worked all this out, but he *feels* it, being a star himself. He can respond to the sheer kick J.F.K. got out of being on the make, since he himself is never off it.

But if innocence has pluses on top of its minuses, it has even more minuses on top of its pluses. Sophisticates profess to admire the young President's achievements as a womanizer. The ideal biographer is too uncomplicated to be led into such a trap. 'I am bound to record my opinion that here was a serious defect in his character.' So far, so true; but Lord Longford in his pious reticence is unable to follow the matter up. A pity, because the subject ought to be illuminating. It is not just for moral reasons that a Don Juan is a sad thing to be.

Lord Longford thinks that J.F.K. was growing in the job and would have grown further, all the way to greatness. The proofs he adduces are not as substantial as he thinks they are. Nor is his otherwise salutary naïveté a sufficient instrument to get very far with the job of separating myths from realities. He can see that Kennedy's fine phrases were put in his mouth by Theodore Sorensen but can't see that the fine phrases were poor stuff whoever composed them. Kennedy was perfect casting as president only in the sense that the presidency is an actor's role. It ought not to be. So the ideal biographer leaves all the real issues untouched. But that his book does not confuse them further is a disheartening portent. Lord Longford can no longer be counted on to say the one irrelevant thing. We could be witnessing the start of an irreversible decline into coherence.

(*New Statesman*, 21 January 1977)

Part Five
OUT ON THEIR OWN

20. Mailer's *Marilyn*

'She was a fruitcake,' Tony Curtis once told an interviewer on B.B.C. television, and there can't be much doubt that she was. Apart from conceding that the camera was desperately in love with her, professional judgements of Marilyn Monroe's attributes rarely go much further. It would be strange if they did: there's work to be done, and a girl blessed with equivalent magic might happen along any time—might even not be a fruitcake. Amateur judgements, on the other hand, are free to flourish. Norman Mailer's new book, *Marilyn*, is just such a one.

Even if its narrative were not so blatantly, and self-admittedly, cobbled together from facts already available in other biographies, the Mailer *Marilyn* would still be an amateur piece of work. Its considerable strength lies in that limitation. As far as talent goes, Marilyn Monroe was so minimally gifted as to be almost unemployable, and anyone who holds to the opinion that she was a great natural comic identifies himself immediately as a dunce. For purposes best known to his creative demon, Mailer planes forward on the myth of her enormous talent like a drunken surfer. Not for the first time, he gets further by going with the flow than he ever could have done by cavilling. Thinking of her as a genius, he can call her drawbacks virtues, and so deal—unimpeded by scepticism—with the vital mystery of her presence.

Mailer's adoration is as amateurish as an autograph hunter's. But because of it we are once again, and this time ideally, reminded of his extraordinary receptivity. That the book should be an embarrassing and embarrassed rush-job is somehow suitable. The author being who he is, the book might as well be conceived in the most chaotic possible circumstances. The subject is, after all, one of the best possible focal points for his chaotic view of life. There is nothing detached or calculating about that view. It is hot-eyed, errant, unhinged. Writhing along past a gallery of yummy photographs, the text reads as the loopiest message yet from the Mailer who scared Sonny Liston with thought waves, made the medical breakthrough which identified cancer as the thwarted psyche's revenge, and first

rumbled birth control as the hidden cause of pregnancy. And yet
Marilyn is one of Mailer's most interesting things. Easy to punish,
it is hard to admire—like its subject. But admire it we must—like
its subject. The childishness of the whole project succeeds in emit-
ting a power that temporarily calls adulthood into question: The
Big Book of the Mad Girl. Consuming it at a long gulp, the reader
ponders over and over again Mailer's copiously fruitful aptitude for
submission. Mailer is right to trust his own foolishness, wherever it
leads: even if the resulting analysis of contemporary America impresses us as less diagnostic than symptomatic.

Not solely for the purpose of disarming criticism, Mailer calls
his *Marilyn* a biography in novel form. The parent novel, we quickly
guess, is *The Deer Park*, and we aren't 75 pages into this new book
before we find Charles Francis Eitel and Elena Esposito being referred
to as if they were people living in our minds—which, of course, they
are. The permanent party of *The Deer Park* ('if desires were deeds,
the history of the night would end in history') is still running, and
the atom bomb that lit the desert's rim for Sergius O'Shaugnessy
and Lulu Meyers flames just as bright. But by now Sergius is out
from under cover: he's Norman Mailer. And his beloved film star
has been given a real name too: Marilyn Monroe. Which doesn't
necessarily make her any the less fictional. By claiming the right to
launch vigorous imaginative patrols from a factual base, Mailer gives
himself an easy out from the strictures of verisimilitude, especially
when the facts are discovered to be contradictory. But Mailer's fantasizing goes beyond expediency. Maurice Zolotow, poor pained
scrivener, can sue Mailer all he likes, but neither he nor the quiescent
Fred Lawrence Guiles will ever get his Marilyn back. Mailer's
Marilyn soars above the known data, an apocalyptic love-object no
mundane pen-pusher could dream of reaching. Dante and Petrarch
barely knew Beatrice and Laura. It didn't slow them down. Mailer
never met Marilyn at all. It gives him the inside track.

Critical fashion would have it that since *The Deer Park* reality has
been busy turning itself into a novel. As Philip Roth said it must,
the extremism of real events has ended up by leaving the creative
imagination looking like an also-ran. A heroine in a 50s novel, Lulu
was really a girl of the 40s—she had some measure of control
over her life. Mailer now sees that the young Marilyn was the
true 50s heroine—she had no control over her life whatsoever. In the
declension from Lulu as Mailer then saw her to Marilyn as he sees

her now, we can clearly observe what is involved in dispensing with the classical, shaping imagination and submitting one's talent (well, Mailer's talent) to the erratic forces of events. Marilyn, says Mailer, was every man's love affair with America. He chooses to forget now that Sergius was in love with something altogether sharper, just as he chooses to forget that for many men Marilyn in fact represented most of the things that were to be feared about America. Worshipping a doll was an activity that often came into question at the time. Later on, it became a clever critical point to insist that the doll was gifted: she walks, she talks, she plays Anna Christie at the Actors' Studio. Later still, the doll was canonized. By the time we get to this book, it is as though there had never been any doubt: the sickness of the 50s lay, not in overvaluing Marilyn Monroe, but in undervaluing her.

Marilyn, says Mailer, suggested sex might be as easy as ice cream. He chooses to forget that for many men at the time she suggested sex might have about the same nutritional value. The early photographs by André de Dienes—taken before her teeth were fixed but compensating by showing an invigorating flash of panty above the waistline of her denims—enshrine the essence of her snuggle-pie sexuality, which in the ensuing years was regularized, but never intensified, by successive applications of oomph and class. Adorable, dumb tomato, she was the best of the worst. As the imitators, and imitators of the imitators, were put into the field behind her, she attained the uniqueness of the paradigm, but that was the sum total of her originality as a sex-bomb. Any man in his right mind would have loved to have her. Mailer spends a good deal of the book trying to drum up what mystical significance he can out of that fact, without even once facing the possibility of that fact representing the *limitation* of her sexuality—the criticism of it, and the true centre of her tragedy. Her screen presence, the Factor X she possessed in the same quantity as Garbo, served mainly to potentiate the sweetness. The sweetness of the girl bride, the unwomanly woman, the *femme* absolutely not *fatale*.

In her ambition, so Faustian, and in her ignorance of culture's dimensions, in her liberation and her tyrannical desires, her noble democratic longings intimately contradicted by the widening pool of her narcissism (where every friend and slave must bathe), we

can see the magnified mirror of ourselves, our exaggerated and
now all but defeated generation, yes, she ran a reconnaissance
through the 50's. . . .

Apart from increasing one's suspicions that the English sentence is
being executed in America, such a passage of rhetorical foolery raises
the question of whether the person Mailer is trying to fool with it
might not conceivably be himself. If 'magnified mirror of ourselves'
means anything, it must include Mailer. Is Mailer ignorant of culture's dimensions? The answer, one fears, being not that he is, but
that he would like to be—so that he could write more books like
Marilyn. As Mailer nuzzles up beside the shade of this poor kitten
to whom so much happened but who could cause so little to happen,
you can hear the purr of sheer abandon. He himself would like very
much to be the man without values, expending his interpretative
powers on whatever the world declared to be important. Exceptional people, Mailer says (these words are almost exactly his, only
the grammar having been altered, to unveil the epigram), have a
way off living with opposites in themselves that can be called
schizophrenia only when it fails. The opposite in Mailer is the hick
who actually falls for all that guff about screen queens, voodoo prize
fighters, and wonder-boy Presidents. But his way of living with it
hasn't yet quite failed. And somehow, it must be admitted, he seems
to get further, see deeper, than those writers who haven't got it to
live with.

  In tracing Marilyn's narcissism back to her fatherless childhood,
our author is at his strongest. His propensity for scaling the mystical
ramparts notwithstanding, Mailer in his Aquarius/Prisoner role is
a lay psychologist of formidable prowess. The self-love and the un-
assuageable need to have it confirmed—any fatherless child is bound
to recognize the pattern, and be astonished at how the writing
generates the authentic air of continuous panic. But good as this
analysis is, it still doesn't make Marilyn's narcissism ours. There is
narcissism and there is narcissism, and to a depressing degree Marilyn's was the sadly recognizable version of the actress who could
read a part but could never be bothered reading a complete script.
Mailer knows what it took Marilyn to get to the top: everything
from betraying friends to lying down under geriatric strangers.
Given the system, Marilyn was the kind of monster equipped to
climb through it. What's debilitating is that Mailer seems to have

given up imagining other systems. He is right to involve himself in the dynamics of Hollywood; he does better by enthusiastically replaying its vanished games than by standing aloof; but for a man of his brains he doesn't *despise* the place enough. His early gift for submitting himself to the grotesqueness of reality is softening with the years into a disinclination to argue with it. In politics he still fights on, although with what effect on his allies one hesitates to think. But in questions of culture—including, damagingly, the cultural aspects of politics—he has by now come within an ace of accepting whatever is as right. His determination to place on Marilyn the same valuation conferred by any sentimentalist is a sure token.

On the point of Marilyn's putative talents, Mailer wants it both ways. He wants her to be an important natural screen presence, which she certainly was; and he wants her to be an important natural actress, which she certainly wasn't. So long as he wants it the first way, he gets it: *Marilyn* is an outstandingly sympathetic analysis of what makes somebody look special on screen, and reads all the better for its periodic eruptions into incoherent lyricism. But so long as he wants it the second way, he gets nowhere. He is quite right to talk of *Some Like It Hot* as her best film, but drastically overestimates her strength in it. Mailer knows all about the hundreds of takes and the thousands of fluffs, and faithfully records the paroxysms of anguish she caused Billy Wilder and Tony Curtis. But he seems to assume that once a given scene was in the can it became established as a miracle of assurance. And the plain fact is that her salient weakness—the inability to read a line—was ineradicable. Every phrase came out as if it had just been memorized. *Just* been memorized. And that film was the high point of the short-winded, monotonous attack she had developed for getting lines across. In earlier films, all the way back to the beginning, we are assailed with varying degrees of the irrepressible panic which infected a voice that couldn't tell where to place emphasis. As a natural silent comedian Marilyn might possibly have qualified, with the proviso that she was not to be depended upon to invent anything. But as a natural comedian in sound she had the conclusive disadvantage of not being able to speak. She was limited ineluctably to characters who rented language but could never possess it, and all her best roles fell into that category. She was good at being inarticulately abstracted for the same reason that midgets are good at being short.

To hear Mailer overpraising Marilyn's performance in *Gentlemen Prefer Blondes* is to wonder if he has any sense of humour at all. Leaving out of account an aberration like *Man's Favourite Sport* (in which Paula Prentiss, a comedienne who actually knows something about being funny, was entirely wasted), *Gentlemen Prefer Blondes* is the least entertaining comedy Howard Hawks ever made. With its manic exaggeration of Hawks's already heavy emphasis on male aggressiveness transplanted to the female, the film later became a touchstone for the Hawksian cinéastes (who also lacked a sense of humour, and tended to talk ponderously about the role-reversals in *Bringing Up Baby* before passing with relief to the supposed wonders of *Hatari*), but the awkward truth is that with this project Hawks landed himself with the kind of challenge he was least likely to find liberating—dealing with dumb sex instead of the bright kind. Hawks supplied a robust professional framework for Marilyn's accomplishments, such as they were. Where I lived, at any rate, her performance in the film was generally regarded as mildly winning in spite of her obvious, fundamental inadequacies—the *in spite of* being regarded as the secret of any uniqueness her appeal might have. Mailer tells it differently:

> In the best years with DiMaggio, her physical coordination is never more vigorous and athletically quick; she dances with all the grace she is ever going to need when doing *Gentlemen Prefer Blondes*, all the grace and all the bazazz—she is a musical comedy star with panache! Diamonds Are a Girl's Best Friend! What a surprise! And sings so well Zanuck will first believe her voice was dubbed. . . .

This is the language of critical self-deception, fine judgement suppressed in the name of a broader cause. What does it mean to dance with all the grace you are ever going to need? It doesn't sound the same as being good at dancing. The fact was that she could handle a number like the 'Running Wild' routine in the train corridor in *Some Like It Hot* (Wilder covered it with the marvellous cutaways of Lemmon slapping the back of the bull-fiddle and Curtis making ping-pong-ball eyes while blowing sax), but anything harder than that was pure pack-drill. And if Zanuck really believed that her voice was dubbed, then for once in his life he must have made an intuitive leap, because to say that her singing voice didn't sound as if it belonged to her was to characterize it with perfect accuracy. Like her speaking voice, it was full of panic.

It took more than sympathy for her horrible death and nostalgia for her atavistic cuddlesomeness to blur these judgments, which at one time all intelligent people shared. The thing that tipped the balance towards adulation was Camp—Camp's yen for the vulnerable in women, which is just as inexorable as its hunger for the strident. When Mailer talks about Marilyn's vulnerability, he means the inadequacy of her sense of self. Camp, however, knew that the vulnerability which mattered was centred in the inadequacy of her talent. She just wasn't very good, and was thus eligible for membership in the ever-increasing squad of Camp heroines who make their gender seem less threatening by being so patently unaware of how they're going over. On the strident wing of the team, Judy Garland is a perennial favourite for the same reason. If common sense weren't enough to do it, the Camp enthusiasm for Monroe should have told Mailer—Mailer of all people—that the sexuality he was getting set to rave about was the kind that leaves the viewer uncommitted.

Mailer longs to talk of Monroe as a symbolic figure, node of a death wish and foretaste of the fog. Embroiled in such higher criticism, he doesn't much concern himself with the twin questions of what shape Hollywood took in the 50s and of how resonantly apposite a representative Marilyn turned out to be of the old studio system's last gasp. As the third-string blonde at Fox (behind Betty Grable and June Haver) Marilyn was not—as Mailer would have it —in all that unpromising a spot. She was in luck, like Kim Novak at Columbia, who was groomed by Harry Cohn to follow Rita Hayworth in the characteristic 50s transposition which substituted apprehensiveness for ability. For girls like them, the roles would eventually be there—mainly crummy roles in mainly crummy movies, but they were the movies the studios were banking on. For the real actresses, times were tougher, and didn't ease for more than a decade. Anne Bancroft, for example, also started out at Fox, but couldn't get the ghost of a break. Mailer isn't careful enough about pointing out that Fox's record as a starmaker was hopeless in all departments: Marilyn was by no means a unique case of neglect, and in comparison with Bancroft got a smooth ride. Marilyn was

just another item in the endless catalogue of Zanuck's impervious-
ness to box-office potential. James Robert Parish, in his useful history, *The Fox Girls*, sums up the vicissitudes of Marilyn's career at
Fox with admirable brevity and good sense, and if the reader would
like to make up his own mind about the facts, it's to that book he
should turn.

Right across Hollywood, as the films got worse, the dummies and
the sex-bombs came into their own, while the actresses dropped
deeper into limbo. Considering the magnitude of the luminary he
is celebrating, it might seem funny to Mailer if one were to mention
the names of people like, say, Patricia Neal, or (even more obscure)
Lola Albright. Soon only the most fanatic of students will be aware
that such actresses were available but could not be used. It's not
that history has been rewritten. Just that the studio-handout version
of history has been unexpectedly confirmed—by Norman Mailer, the
very stamp of writer who ought to know better. The studios created
a climate for new talent that went on stifling the best of it until
recent times. How, for example, does Mailer think Marilyn stacks up
against an artist like Tuesday Weld? By the criteria of approval
manifested in *Marilyn*, it would be impossible for Mailer to find
Weld even mildly interesting. To that extent, the senescent dream-
factories succeeded in imposing their view : first of all on the masses,
which was no surprise, but now on the elite, which is.

Mailer is ready to detect all manner of bad vibes in the 50s, but
unaccountably fails to include in his read-out of portents the one
omen pertinent to his immediate subject. The way that Hollywood
divested itself of *intelligence* in that decade frightened the civilized
world. And far into the 60s this potato-blight of the intellect went
on. The screen was crawling with cosmeticized androids. Not content
with gnawing her knuckles through the long days of being married
to a test pilot or the long nights of being married to a band leader,
June Allyson sang and danced. Betty Hutton, the ultimate in projected insecurity, handed over to Doris Day, a yelping freckle. The
last Tracy-Hepburn comedies gurgled nostalgically in the straw like
the lees of a soda. The new Hepburn, Audrey, was a Givenchy
clothes-horse who piped her lines in a style composed entirely of
mannerisms. And *she* was supposed to be class. Comedy of the 30s
and 40s, the chief glory of the American sound cinema, was gone
as if it had never been. For those who had seen and heard the great

Hollywood high-speed talkers (Carole Lombard, Irene Dunne, Rosalind Russell, Katharine Hepburn, Jean Arthur) strut their brainy stuff, the let down was unbelievable. Comic writing was pretty nearly wiped out, and indeed has never fully recovered as a genre. In a context of unprecedented mindlessness, Marilyn Monroe rose indefatigably to success. She just wasn't clever enough to fail.

Marilyn came in on the 50s tide of vulgarity, and stayed to take an exemplary part in the Kennedy era's uproar of cultural pretension. Mailer follows her commitment to the Actors' Studio with a credulousness that is pure New Frontier. The cruelty with which he satirizes Arthur Miller's ponderous aspirations to greatness is transmuted instantly to mush when he deals with Mrs. Miller's efforts to explore the possibilities hitherto dormant within her gift. That such possibilities existed was by no means taken as gospel at the time of her first forays into New York, but with the advent of the Kennedy era the quality of scepticism seemed to drain out of American cultural life. *Marilyn* is a latter-day Kennedy-era text, whose prose, acrid with the tang of free-floating charisma, could have been written a few weeks after Robert Kennedy's death rounded out the period of the family's power. Mailer's facility for confusing the intention with the deed fits that epoch's trust in façades to perfection. He is delicately tender when evoking the pathos of Marilyn's anxious quest for self-fulfilment, but never doubts that the treasure of buried ability was there to be uncovered, if only she could have found the way. The true pathos—that she was simply not fitted for the kind of art she had been led to admire—eludes him. Just as he gets over the problem of Marilyn's intellectual limitations by suggesting that a mind can be occupied with more interesting things than thoughts, so he gets over the problem of her circumscribed accomplishments by suggesting that true talent is founded not on ability but on a state of being. Nobody denies that the snorts of derision which first greeted the glamour queen's strivings towards seriousness were inhuman, visionless. In rebuttal, it was correctly insisted that her self-exploration was the exercise of an undeniable right. But the next, fatal step was to assume that her self-exploration was an artistic activity in itself, and had a right to results.

Scattered throughout the book are hints that Mailer is aware that his loved one had limited abilities. But he doesn't let it matter, preferring to insist that her talent—a different thing—was boundless.

Having overcome so much deprivation in order to see that certain kinds of achievement were desirable, she had an automatic entitlement to them. That, at any rate, seems to be his line of reasoning. A line of reasoning which is really an act of faith. The profundity of his belief in the significance of what went on during those secret sessions at the Actors' Studio is unplumbable. She possessed, he vows, the talent to play Cordelia. One examines this statement from front-on, from both sides, through a mirror, and with rubber-gloves. Is there a hint of a put-on? There is not. Doesn't he really mean something like: she possessed enough nerve and critical awareness to see the point of trying to extend her range by playing a few fragments of a Shakespearean role out of the public eye? He does not. He means what he says, that Marilyn Monroe possessed the talent to play Cordelia. Who, let it be remembered, is required, in the first scene of the play, to deliver a speech like this:

> Good my lord,
> You have begot me, bred me, lov'd me: I
> Return those duties back as are right fit,
> Obey you, love you, and most honour you.
> Why have my sisters husbands, if they say
> They love you all? Haply, when I shall wed,
> That lord whose hand must take my plight shall carry
> Half my love with him, half my care and duty:
> Sure I shall never marry like my sisters,
> To love my father all.

Leave aside the matter of how she would have managed such stuff on stage; it is doubtful she could have handled a single minute of it even on film: not with all the dialogue coaches in the world, not even if they had shot and edited in the way Joshua Logan is reputed to have put together her performance in some of the key scenes of *Bus Stop*—word by word, frame by frame. The capacity to apprehend and reproduce the rhythm of written language just wasn't there. And even if we were to suppose that such an indispensable capacity could be dispensed with, there would still be the further question of whether the much-touted complexity of her character actually contained a material resembling Cordelia's moral steel: it is not just sweetness that raises Cordelia above her sisters. We are bound to conclude (if only to preserve from reactionary scorn the qualities Marilyn really *did* have) that she was debarred from the wider range of classical acting not only by a paucity of ability but by a narrowness of those emotional resources Mailer would have us believe were somehow a substitute for it. Devoid of invention, she could only draw on her stock of feeling. The stock was thin. Claiming for her a fruitful complexity, Mailer has trouble conjuring it up: punctuated by occasional outbreaks of adoration for animals and men, her usual state of mind seems to have been an acute but generalized fear, unreliably counterbalanced by sedation.

Mailer finds it temptingly easy to insinuate that Marilyn's madness knew things sanity wots not of, and he tries to make capital out of the tussle she had with Olivier in *The Prince and the Showgirl*. Olivier, we are asked to believe, was the icy technician working from the outside in, who through lack of sympathy muffed the chance to elicit from his leading lady miracles of warm intuition. It's a virtuoso passage from Mailer, almost convincing us that an actor like Olivier is a prisoner of rationality forever barred from the inner mysteries of his profession. You have to be nuts, whispers Mailer from the depths of his sub-text, to be a *real* actor. The derivation from Laing's psychology is obvious.

The author does a noble, loyal, zealous job of tracing his heroine's career as an artist, but we end by suspecting that he is less interested in her professional achievement than in her fame. The story of Norma Jean becoming Somebody is the true spine of the book, and the book is Mailer's most concise statement to date of what he thinks being Somebody has come to mean in present-day America. On this theme, *Marilyn* goes beyond being merely wrong-headed and becomes quite frightening.

As evidence of the leverage Marilyn's fame could exert, Mailer recounts a story of her impressing some friends by taking them without a reservation to the Copacabana, where Sinatra was packing the joint to the rafters every night. Marilyn being Monroe, Sinatra ordered a special table put in at his feet, and while lesser mortals were presumably being asphyxiated at the back, he sang for his unexpected guest and her friends, personally. Only for the lonely. Mailer tells such stories without adornment, but his excitement in them is ungovernable: it infects the style, giving it the tone we have come to recognize from all his previous excursions into status, charisma, psychic victory, and the whole witchcraft of personal ascendancy. *Marilyn* seems to bring this theme in his work to a crisis.

In many ways *The Naked and the Dead* was the last classic novel to be written in America. The separately-treated levels of the military hierarchy mirrored the American class structure, such as it was, and paralleled the class structure of the classic European novel, such as it had always been. With *The Deer Park* the American classes were already in a state of flux, but the society of Hollywood maintained cohesion by being aware of what conditions dictated the mutability of its hierarchy: Sergius the warrior slept with Lulu the love queen, both of them qualifying, while fortune allowed, as members of the only class, below which was the ruck—the unlovely, the unknown, the out. *The Deer Park* was Mailer's last attempt to embody American society in fictional form: *An American Dream* could find room only for its hero. Increasingly with the years, the broad sweep of Mailer's creativity has gone into the interpretation of reality as it stands, or rather flows, and he has by now become adept at raising fact to the level of fiction. Meanwhile society has become even more fluid, to the extent that the upper class—the class of celebrities—has become as unstable in its composition as the hubbub below. Transformation and displacement now operate endlessly, and the observer (heady prospect) changes the thing observed. Mailer's tendency to enrol himself in even the most exalted action is based on the perception, not entirely crazed, that the relative positions in the star-cluster of status are his to define: reality is a novel that he is writing.

On her way to being divorced from Arthur Miller, Marilyn stopped off in Dallas. In Dallas! Mailer can hardly contain himself. 'The most electric of the nations,' he writes, 'must naturally provide the boldest circuits of coincidence.' Full play is made with the rumours that Marilyn might have had affairs with either or both of the two doomed Kennedy brothers, and there is beetle-browed speculation about the possibility of her death having placed a curse on the family—and hence, of course, on the whole era. Mailer himself calls this last brainwave 'endlessly facile', thereby once again demonstrating his unfaltering dexterity at having his cake and eating it. But this wearying attempt to establish Marilyn as the muse of the artist-politicians is at one with the book's whole tendency to weight her down with a load of meaning she is too frail to bear. Pepys could be floored by Lady Castlemaine's beauty without ascribing to her qualities she did not possess. The Paris intellectuals quickly learned that Pompadour's passion for china flowers and polite theatre was no indication that artistic genius was in favour at Versailles—quite the reverse. Where hierarchies were unquestioned, realism meant the ability to see what was really what. Where the hierarchy is created from day to day in the mind of one man interpreting it, realism is likely to be found a hindrance.

Mailer doesn't want famous people to mean as little as the sceptical tongue says they do. To some extent he is right. There *is* an excitement in someone like Marilyn Monroe coming out of nowhere to find herself conquering America, and there *is* a benediction in the happiness she could sometimes project from the middle of her anguish. Without Mailer's receptivity we would not have been given the full impact of these things; just as if he had listened to the liberal line on the space programme we would not have been given those enthralling moments in *A Fire on the Moon* when the launch vehicle pulls free of its bolts, or when the mission passes from the grip of the earth into the embrace of its target—moments as absorbing our first toys. Mailer's shamelessness says that there are people and events which mean more than we in our dignity are ready to allow. He has nearly always been right. But when he starts saying that in that case they might as well mean what he wants them to mean, the fictionalist has overstepped the mark, since the patterning that strengthens fiction weakens fact.

Mailer's Marilyn is a usurper, a democratic monarch reigning by dint of the allegiance of an intellectual aristocrat, the power of whose regency has gone to his head. Mailer has forgotten that Marilyn was the people's choice before she was his, and that in echoing the people he is sacrificing his individuality on the altar of perversity. Sergius already had the sickness:

> Then I could feel her as something I had conquered, could listen to her wounded breathing, and believe that no matter how she acted other times, these moments were Lulu, as if her flesh murmured words more real than her lips. To the pride of having so beautiful a girl was added the bigger pride of knowing that I took her with the cheers of millions behind me. Poor millions with their low roar!

At the end of *The Deer Park* the dying Eitel tells Sergius by telepathy that the world we may create is more real to us than the mummery of what happens, passes, and is gone. Whichever way

Sergius decided, Mailer seems finally to have concluded that the two are the same thing. More than any of his essays so far, *Marilyn* tries to give the mummery of what happens the majestic gravity of a created world. And as he has so often done before, he makes even the most self-assured of us wonder if we have felt deeply enough, looked long enough, lived hard enough. He comes close to making us doubt our conviction that in a morass of pettiness no great issues are being decided. We benefit from the doubt. But the price he pays for being able to induce it is savage, and Nietzche's admonition is begining to apply. He has gazed too long into the abyss, and now the abyss is gazing into him. Bereft of judgement, detachment, or even a tinge of irony, *Marilyn* is an opulent but slavish expression of an empty consensus. The low roar of the poor millions is in every page.

(Commentary, October 1973)

21. Count Zero Splits the Infinite: Tom Stoppard

Having made public love to Tom Stoppard by writing him a verse letter in the *New Statesman* and assigning him the dedication of my scurrilous epic *The Fate of Felicity Fark*, I feel honour bound to make the nature of my admiration clear, lest gossip columnists—whose appetite for the flesh of star playwrights has been very fierce of late—start swimming to the wrong conclusions. So this is necessarily a personal appraisal, and had better be prefaced by my disqualifications, the chief of which is a profound lack of sympathy with the contemporary theatre.

The distaste is made stronger by ignorance. I go very rarely to the theatre, for what seems to me the sound reason that anything so repellent in occasional doses would most probably be fatal if the doses were frequent: one would be more likely to share the doom of Charles Bravo than to acquire the immunity of Mithridates. Sedulous non-attendance has been my policy for years. Right from the beginning this plan paid dividends, except for an early tendency to pronounce more and more confidently upon the theatrical world the less I saw of it. But after one rare lapse, in which I fecklessly allowed myself to be present at the first night of John Osborne's *West of Suez*, it was brought home to me that the critical position best befitting aesthetic non-involvement is one of silence.

Appearing on the B.B.C.'s *Late Night Line-Up* half an hour after the curtain fell at the Royal Court, I announced that the weaknesses of *West of Suez* did not detract from Osborne's stature as Britain's leading contemporary dramatist.

My fellow panellist Benedict Nightingale, then as now drama critic of the *New Statesman*, looked astonished, but mercifully waited until later—instead of blowing the whistle right there on camera—to point out that since I had not even the vaguest idea of what most of the other contemporary dramatists were up to, my assertion was largely without meaning. Mulling over this reproof at length, I shamefacedly resolved that if I were to continue staying away from the theatre, I should suit the word to the deed by ceasing to be glibly knowing about what went on there. Indifference would from now on be bodied forth as taciturnity.

And so it was until the middle of June 1974, when by a massive dereliction of duty I found myself committed to a four-week stint as a pundit on Radio 4's *Critic's Forum*, which involved seeing one play per week. This could have been a revelation of the wealth I had been missing, but in the event it was a searing exposure to mediocrity. At the I.C.A. there was some load of semi-improvised flapdoodle about speakers at Hyde Park Corner, in which actors shouted from different parts of the room while the audience wandered about from one centre of alleged interest to the other, while I wandered in the opposite direction. At the Old Vic there was a new play by John Hopkins, whose reputation was for unflinching seriousness and rock-like integrity. The piece had not a scintilla of invention in its whole length, its sole point of interest being the programme note by the author, revealing a marvellous conceit about the pain that composing the play had cost him, which could not have been half the pain that seeing it cost me. Harold Pinter was the producer, and it was difficult to say whether he had found yet deeper levels of tedium in the text itself, or had merely added some tedium of his own. The third week's agony I have repressed entirely. Perhaps it was a whodunnit. I think I took refuge in sleep, or in trying to remember the rhyme-scene of the villanelle.

The fourth offering was hailed as a 'blazing masterpiece' by Harold Hobson and taken with protracted seriousness even by those critics who did not find it wholly successful. It was *Life Class*, by David Storey—a tub of metaphysical sludge stirred into the semblance of activity by Lindsay Anderson. As usual with any theatrical venture involving Anderson, Storey and the actor Alan Bates, the arts pages had been full for days about their collective daring and respective spiritual quests. Anderson is the master of the pre-emptive strike: he once even managed to place an article in the *Observer* explaining why the reviews of his forthcoming film were bound to miss its point. For *Life Class* the ground had been so thoroughly prepared that it would have taken unheard-of independence of mind for any of the regular critics to demur. I was regarded as eccentric for contending on *Critic's Forum* that in the matter of *Life Class* the question of which direction Storey's work was taking did not meaningfully arise, since the only direction this particular script should have taken was towards the waste-paper basket. The characters were half unrealized, which is not the same as universality; the dialogue was unspeakable, which is not the same as authenticity; and the theme was fumbled, which is not the same as exploration. Lindsay Anderson's contribution was principally manifest as a not always infallible capacity, when an actor was talking, to move other actors away from in front of him.

And so a month which had passed like a year in hospital came to an end. All my suspicions of the theatrical world having been confirmed in spades, I promised myself faithfully never to go near it again in all my life. But scarcely another week had gone by before this contract was rescinded. My agent rang to say she had a ticket going begging for the first night of Tom Stoppard's new play *Travesties*. My reaction to such generosity would have been an instantaneous and foul-mouthed refusal, if it had not mercifully occurred to me that Stoppard—none of whose plays, not even *Rosencrantz and Guildenstern Are Dead*, I had ever seen—was generally famed for being devoid of the qualities which those authors whose latest triumphs I had just suffered through were supposed to possess in such abundance. People whose seriousness I had good cause to dread had told me that Stoppard's plays were only revue-sketches. That sounded promising. True, Harold Hobson's oft-trumpeted insistence that Stoppard was brilliantly entertaining persuasively suggested that he wasn't, but not even Hobson can be wrong all the time. Like Saint-Exupéry wooing the one last crash that would prove fatal, I fell into a taxi and headed for the Aldwych.

Before John Wood was half-way through his opening speech I already knew that in Stoppard I had encountered a writer of my generation whom I could admire without reserve. It is a common reaction to *Travesties* to say that seeing it is like drinking champagne. But not only did I find that the play tasted like champagne —I found that in drinking it I felt like a jockey. Jockeys drink champagne as an everyday tipple, since it goes to the head without thickening the waist. *Travesties* to me seemed not an exotic indulgence, but the stuff of life. Its high speed was not a challenge but a courtesy; its structural intricacy not a dazzling pattern but a perspicuous design; its fleeting touch not of a feather but of a fine needle. For me *Travesties* was a personal revelation, which is one of the reasons why I have begun with a personal note. But *caveat lector*: my knowledge of the theatrical world is not much wider than it ever was. And the other Stoppard plays, though I will certainly see them when the opportunity arises, I have so far only read, so there are two likely sources of distortion: an estimate of Stoppard's place in the theatre based mainly on Stoppard, and an estimate of Stoppard's drama based mainly on the text. A double-dyed literary approach.

Ronald Hayman's profile of Stoppard in the *New Review* for December 1974 is the best thing on its subject which has thus far appeared. It would be supererogatory, as well as very difficult, to cover the same ground on my own account, and a good deal of what I think about Stoppard I owe in the first instance to Hayman, who in turn owes a good deal to Stoppard, since no author has ever done a better job of explaining himself—he is a dream interviewee, talking in eerily quotable sentences whose English has the faintly extraterratorial perfection of a Conrad or a Nabokov. Extraterritorial and perhaps even extraterrestrial: in this respect as in so many others, Stoppard can sometimes give you the impression that he is from Out There.

Unless you knew that all its stars lie at different distances and are of different intensities, it would be impossible to guess that the constellation called the Plough does not look like a plough. Equally, unless you knew that from a certain point the appropriate picture forms, it would be impossible to guess that the same aggregate of stars *does* look like a plough, and acquires a name. Either kind of knowledge, or else a bewitching combination of them both, is constantly at work in Stoppard's writings.

In *After Magritte* the curtain rises on an inexplicable-looking stage picture which is explained piece by piece, thereby gradually ceasing to be that picture. When the picture reforms, we know what has caused everything in it: more intelligible, it is less coherent, riddled by our awareness and with all its virginity spent. The escalating bravura—the playwright's enthralling ability to keep on casting light on the unlikely until there is nothing left of it—compensates for the declining mystery, until finally the disappointment of having no puzzle left to solve is transmuted into the pleasure of seeing how perfectly it has all come out. So one kind of childish pleasure modulates into another, with Stoppard knowing very well how children like to be teased: twenty-three pages after we first see them, we are told just enough to enable us to deduce for ourselves that Harris's waders are employed for changing lightbulbs—and so we are surprised by our own perceptiveness at the very moment when the extraordinary becomes ordinary.

Similarly in the radio play *Artist Descending a Staircase*, a seemingly random stretch of jumbled talk and noise bit by bit becomes comprehensible, exchanging one kind of vividness for another, since by the time we learn that the smacking sound means Beauchamp is trying to swat a fly, it is time for us to assume that Beauchamp is trying to swat a fly when he is actually thumping a desk. We had the experience but missed the meaning. (Almost any quotation you can think of from Eliot—or from Joyce or Beckett—is relevant to Stoppard, who is soaked in all three.) But then Stoppard takes the device a further stage, into a territory which we ought to recognize, I think, as entirely his. The original smacking sound returns, but this time it means that Donner is hitting Beauchamp.

It isn't so much that the one sound contains multiple meaning, as that it has different meaning in different places. Stoppard is at his weakest when his Joycean ambiguities are just that and no more—leftover puns from *Finnegans Wake*, slipping from one sketchy context to another just for the sake of proving their mobility, as if the *Philosophical Investigations* needed further illustrating. But he is at his strongest when one precise meaning is transformed into another precise meaning with the context full-blown in each case. It is an elementary point to prove that a word can mean anything we choose it to mean. Many of us must have sometimes felt, when reading the later Wittgenstein, that he is not really saying anything about *words* which Lewis Carroll didn't say equally succinctly. The later Wittgenstein is in this regard the obverse of the early one, only instead of saying that a word is attached to something in the world he is saying that it is not. The early position refuted itself, and the later one needs no proof—artistic endorsements of it are doomed to triviality.

But Stoppard is not really concerned to say that words can mean anything. That is what is supposed to be wrong with Beauchamp's *musique concrète*—it tries to mean anything and condemns itself to meaning nothing. It is the plurality of contexts that concerns

Stoppard: ambiguities are just places where contexts join. And although Stoppard's transitions and transformations of context might be thought of, either pejoratively or with approval, as games, the games are, it seems to me, at least as serious as Wittgenstein's language games—although finally, I think, the appropriate analogies to Stoppard's vision lie just as much in modern physics as in modern philosophy.

Even among those who profess to admire his skill, it is often supposed that there is something coldly calculated about Stoppard's technique. By mentioning his work in the same breath with modern physics one risks abetting that opinion. But there is no good reason to concede that modern physics is cold, or even that to be calculating precludes creativity. Guildenstern is not necessarily right when he tells Rosencrantz (in *Rosencrantz and Guildenstern Are Dead*) that all would be lost if their spontaneity turned out to be part of another order—one of the play's themes is that Chance, while looking deterministic if seen from far enough away, is random enough from close to. Both views are real, just as the two different views of the Plough are real. It could even be assumed that each viewpoint is fixed. That would be a Newtonian picture of Stoppard's universe, and like the Newtonian picture of the real universe could go a long way towards explaining everything in it.

But physics, to the small extent that I understand it, ceased being Newtonian and started being modern when Einstein found himself obliged to rule out the possibility of a viewpoint at rest. Nobody could now believe that Einstein did this in order to be less precise— he did it in order to be precise over a greater range of events than Newtonian mechanics could accurately account for. *Mutatis mutandis*, Stoppard abandons fixed viewpoints for something like the same reason. The analogy is worth pursuing because it leads us to consider the possibility that Stoppard's increasingly apparent intention to create a dramatic universe of perpetual transformations might also spring from the impulse to clarify.

It is perhaps because there is little recognizably *mystical* about him—scarcely a hint of the easy claim to impenetrability—that people are inclined to call Stoppard cold. It might have been a comfort to them if Stoppard had rested content with merely saying: listen, what looks odd when you stand over There is perfectly reasonable if you stand over Here, whereupon the place you left

begins looking odd in its turn. That would have been relativity of a
manageable Newtonian kind, which anyone patient enough could
have hoped to follow. But Stoppard added: and now that you're
Here, you ought to know that Here is on its way to somewhere else,
just as There is, and always was. That was Einstein's kind of relativity—a prospect much less easily grasped. In fact grasping doesn't
come into it. There is not much point in the layman trying to grasp
that the relative speed of two objects rushing away from each other
at the speed of light is still the speed of light. What he needs to
realize is that no other explanation fits the facts. Similarly with
Stoppard's dramatic equivalent of the space–time continuum: it
exists to be ungraspable, its creator having discovered that no readily
appreciable conceptual scheme can possibly be adequate to the complexity of experience. The chill which some spectators feel at a
Stoppard play is arriving from infinity.

Critical talk about 'levels of reality' in a play commonly assumes
that one of the posited levels is *really* real. By the same token, it
would be reasonable to assume that although everything in a Stoppard play is moving, the play itself is a system at rest. But in Stoppard's universe no entity, not even a work of art, is exempt from
travel. *The Importance of Being Earnest* is moving through *Travesties* like one stream of particles through another, the points of col-
lision lighting up as pastiche. The same kind of interpenetration was
already at work in *Rosencrantz and Guildenstern Are Dead*, through
which the play *Hamlet* made a stately transit like a planet encoun-
tering a meteor shower, and with the same pyrotechnic conse-
quences.

'Every exit', the Player tells Rosencrantz, 'is an entrance somewhere else.' The idea holds true for both space and time. In *The Real
Inspector Hound* Felicity repeatedly enters at the same moment to
instigate different versions of the action. In *Travesties* Tristan Tzara
enters up-stage to begin a scene and later exits stage-right uttering
the same initial line, so that the exit becomes an entrance in a play
(the *other* play) speeding away from us into the off-prompt wing. It
isn't helpful to call such effects dazzling, since they are not meant
to dazzle nor be effects—they are glimpses into the kaleidoscope of
possibilities, devices by which you see further. They are Stoppard's
own and growing artistic realization of the hero's view from on high
in the radio play *Albert's Bridge*, whose text is perhaps the most

easily approachable example of Stoppard's fascination with the long straight lines—curves of infinite radius—leading up to and away from here and now.

In a body of work which is otherwise conspicuously impersonal, Albert is probably the character who comes closest to representing Stoppard the artist. Albert is at a point detached enough for arbitrariness to look like order. Fraser, Albert's opposing voice, might usefully be held to represent Stoppard the man—Stoppard when he is not detached. Fraser lives down among the chaos, where he sees it to be a sheer fluke that the right number of people who do not want to milk cows do want to fill teeth and vice versa. Finding the perception intolerable, he chooses suicide. But climbing the bridge in order to jump off it, he sees things from Albert's viewpoint, loses the desire to die, and goes back down, where he sees it to be a sheer fluke that the right number . . . and so on, in a reticulation as endless as painting the bridge. Neither Albert nor Fraser can be right alone.

Here and now in Stoppard is a time and place defined by an infinite number of converging vectors each heading towards it at the speed of light and steadily slowing down to nothing before passing through it and speeding up again. Ignoring for the moment that the still point is itself moving, here and now is what things tend towards, with a tantalizing slowness as they swell into proximity. In this resides much of the significance of Stoppard's fascination with Zeno's paradox—the asymptotic frustration by which the hare never quite catches up with the tortoise. In *Jumpers*, George Moore the philosopher (the *other* George Moore the philosopher) concludes that since the arrow could not have quite reached Saint Sebastian he must have died of fright. It is a fabulous joke but there is fear in it—the awe of watching a slow approach down long perspectives.

Guildenstern says that the more witnesses who attest to the remarkable the thinner it gets and the more reasonable it becomes until it is thin as reality. Here and now is Zero—a word which rings like a gnomic tocsin in Beckett's *Endgame* and arrives in Stoppard's plays as a developed vision. (The word itself passes through like a micro-meteorite during the Farjeonesque game of bridge in *The Real Inspector Hound*.) Stoppard has gradually become more and more capable of bodying this vision forth, but the vision was there at the beginning of his drama and indeed before the beginning. In his novel *Lord Malquist and Mr. Moon*, Mr. Moon is sick with his secret knowledge of the long perspectives, just as Rosencrantz feels sick when he looks into the audience (an echo, but more than an echo, of Clov's similarly bleak gaze in *Endgame*), or Gladys the T.I.M. girl feels sick when she looks down the well of time in the radio play *If You're Glad I'll Be Frank*. But not even madness can make a coherent whole of all Moon sees. Moon is appalled by the shift of a glacier that leads to a man straightening his tie. 'But if it's all random', he asks Lady Malquist, 'what's the point?' And when she replies 'What's the point if it's all inevitable?' he can't deal with the answer.

Moon can't take a side for fear of disappearing into it. He takes both parts, 'refuting myself and rebutting the refutation.' Moon is a guarantee that the supposedly passionless intricacies of Stoppard's plays have all unfolded from a preliminary intuition of extreme intensity. Moon is Stoppard before Albert and Fraser separated and met each other on the bridge. 'He held the vapours in his cupped hands but they would not crystallize.' In the plays, they do.

From *Enter A Free Man* to *Travesties* is a long way. Stoppard's habit of cannibalizing old situations to make new ones tends to suggest repetitiveness but really he has been expanding his scope all the time. Take the meticulously extended preparation for the gag about the Rule Britannia clock in *Enter A Free Man*. In that apprentice work such devices are at first sight tangential enough to seem merely cosmetic. But hindsight reveals that they constitute the play's real originality. Otherwise the plot is like one of Ibsen's turned on its head, with the daughter continually telling her father the truth about himself, instead of the saving lie. The eccentric atmosphere suggests Saroyan's *The Time of Your Life*, which in its turn was more solidly in the Broadway tradition than people thought at the time. If Stoppard had never written anything subsequently, we might think of Riley's indoor rain as being a nod to N. F. Simpson, and the concern with Time to be like J. B. Priestley's, or Christopher Fry's, or, at best, T. S. Eliot's. But in retrospect the architecture looks like decoration and the decoration looks like architecture.

In all the subsequent plays the texture is composed entirely of interweaving preparation. By the time of *Jumpers* it takes the whole play for the separate stories of the tortoise and the hare to catch up with each other—Zeno's paradox resolved at the intersection of long lines of coincidence. And in *Travesties* we find the long lines turning into curves, the planes curving into spheres, and the spheres making music.

And if the music of the spheres sounds cold, would it be more convincing if it sounded warm? There is abundant evidence in Stoppard's plays to show that he is as capable of emotion as anybody. In *Enter A Free Man* Linda is a finely tuned moral invention whose equivalents we might well miss in the later plays, if we really thought they should be there. The mainspring of *Rosencrantz and Guildenstern Are Dead* is the perception—surely a compassionate one—that the fact of their deaths mattering so little to Hamlet was something which ought to have mattered to Shakespeare. And in the radio play *Where Are They Now?* there is a flaring moment of generous anger against the school system which turned childhood into a hell of pointless competition. 'Where are they now?' people ask about all those young winners, and Gale, putting things in perspective on behalf of all the losers, bitterly asks 'Where were they then?'

There is plenty to indicate that if Stoppard had done no more than employ the drama as a vehicle for moral messages, he would still have been a force in the theatre. The playwrights who grapple with those issues supposedly too weighty for Stoppard's frivolous talent are likely to have been inspired by a view of their task which is not only less comprehensive than Stoppard's but less penetrating. Stoppard leaves them behind not because he can't do what they can do, but because he can do what they can do so easily. ('What's wrong with bad art', he told Ronald Hayman, 'is that the artist knows exactly what he's doing.')

In fact the weaknesses of *Travesties*, such as they are, seem to me to crop up in those places where Stoppard atavistically makes concessions to the standard theatrical conception of human warmth. This, I think, is the real problem with the Lenin role, which is recognized by everyone—including the author—to be a small but troublesome spanner in the play's glistening works. It is generally supposed that there is not much in the part for an actor to bite on. My own view is the opposite: I think there is too much. As it happened, the part was wrongly cast in both runs of the production. In the first run Lenin was too sympathetic and in the second he was to diffident. (It is a measure of the play's robustness, incidentally, that it could survive weak casting even among the principal roles. In the second run James Joyce could neither sing nor dance and threw away his key speech on the first night.)

But even if Lenin had been played up to the full power inherent in the role he would still have stood revealed as a personality conceived in terms of show-biz meatiness, with a built-in conflict to suggest complexity. In *Travesties* Lenin is polarized rather too easily between ruthlessness and an appreciation of creative achievement, the latter quality having apparently been extrapolated from his well-known contention that the *Apassionata* moved him to tears. But the real-life Lenin was not divided along so elementary a line. Stoppard emphasizes Lenin's self-contradictions at the expense of playing down his monolithic purposefulness—a purposefulness which we can scarcely begin to contemplate without raising the question of Evil. There is less to the *complexity*, and more to the *force*, of Lenin's personality than Stoppard allows. Lenin's historical significance doesn't even begin to be reconciled within a scheme that adduces Tristan Tzara and James Joyce as revolutionary exemplars, and by suggesting that it does, Stoppard starts a hare which really never *can* catch the tortoise.

This is not to say that Stoppard is disqualified from treating tough subjects. Quite the reverse. In my admittedly limited experience it has usually been the playwrights already famous for treating them who are disqualified, and in the long run it is more likely to be Stoppard who says what counts on the subject of, say, the Final Solution—even if he never approaches it more than tangentially. But Stoppard's is an aesthetic which demands an unfalteringly sensitive apprehension of the real world. A moment's coarseness and the game is lost: astrophysics becomes Construct-O-Straws.

At their best, Stoppard's heady dramatic designs impress us not as deliberately sophisticated variations on the reality we know but as simplified models of a greater reality—the inhuman cosmos which contains the human world, the amoral vastness in which morality is a local accident, the totality from whose perimeter we look like— Zero. ('Nothing', Lord Malquist tells Mr. Moon, 'is the history of the world viewed from a suitable distance.') Stoppard's triumph —which he does not share with Priestley, Fry or Eliot any more than he shares it with *Star Trek* or *Dr. Who*—is to have created this impression not through vagueness but through precision.

When Stoppard tells *One Pair of Eyes* that 'Tom Stoppard doesn't *know*' he doesn't mean that he sees virtue in confusion but that he sees the actual as a realized possibility. If his speculative scope recalls modern physics, his linguistic rigour recalls modern philosophy. It is a potent combination whatever its validity.

And if the whole vaultingly clever enterprise turned out to be merely intuitive—well, what is so mere about that? It might be only in Stoppard's enchanted playground that the majestic inevitabilities of General Relativity can be reconciled with the Uncertainty Principle or quantum physics, but Einstein's life-long search for the Unified Field was the same game, and *he* believed in intuition. He also believed in *Einfühlung*—the intellectual love for the objects of experience. Just such a love, it seems to me, is at work in Stoppard's writing, lending it a poetry which is as far beyond sentimentality as his ebullient detachment is beyond the arrogant solipsism which commonly passes for commitment.

(*Encounter*, November 1975)